Melvin Delgado
Edit

D0144162

Alco of Cul-
tura neously
as *A* ers 1/2
1998

Pre- ve, com-
REV searched
CO djectives
EVA e book,
Latinos: ulturally
by Mel-
serve
illing a
com-
g to-
origi-
g the
effort

SW

More pre-publication
REVIEWS, COMMENTARIES, EVALUATIONS . . .

"**T**he problems surrounding alcohol, tobacco and other drug abuse in our society are of considerable magnitude with devastating effects on individuals, families and communities. One subgroup that has been impacted greatly by this problem is the Hispanic/Latino community comprised of over 30 culturally diverse subgroups. Today, more than ever, health and social service providers are faced with the difficult task of addressing the growing problem of alcohol and substance abuse in a culturally diverse national Latino community. In addressing this issue, Melvin Delgado has compiled an impressive collection of readings entitled, *Alcohol Use/Abuse Among Latinos: Issues and Examples of Culturally Competent Services* from leading writers in social work, urban and Chicano studies, education and related disciplines. This book reflects the state-of-the knowledge on alcohol and drug abuse among Latinos, and proposes a framework for culturally competent intervention at the micro and macro level. Each chapter, written by known experts in the field, is replete with theoretical and empirical data on the prevalence and consequences of alcohol and drug abuse in the Latino community, and the multiple factors that contribute to this problem. However, the strength of this book, and indeed each chapter, is its focus on developing a cross-cultural perspective and a competency based service delivery system grounded in cultural knowledge and skills for effective practice. With considerable insight, writers address such topics as culturally competent prevention and treatment approaches, organizational effectiveness and culturally competent evaluations, feminist and Latina lesbian perspectives on alcohol abuse, drug problems in the workplace, and the rising problems of substance abuse in rural settings. Of particular significance is the emphasis given to Latina perspectives on alcohol and substance abuse practices, and the concrete recommendations for research, policy and treatment. Ostensibly, this book will have widespread appeal for practitioners and educators involved in direct service delivery, organizational planning research or policy development. It is current and relevant to the times, and will add considerably to literature on alcohol, tobacco and other drug abuse."

Steven Lozano Applewhite
University of Houston
Graduate School of Social Work
Houston, Texas

Alcohol Use/Abuse Among Latinos: Issues and Examples of Culturally Competent Services

Alcohol Use/Abuse Among Latinos: Issues and Examples of Culturally Competent Services has been co-published simultaneously as *Alcoholism Treatment Quarterly*, Volume 16, Numbers 1/2 1998.

Alcohol Use/Abuse Among Latinos: Issues and Examples of Culturally Competent Services

Melvin Delgado, PhD
Editor

Alcohol Use/Abuse Among Latinos: Issues and Examples of Culturally Competent Services has been co-published simultaneously as *Alcoholism Treatment Quarterly,* Volume 16, Numbers 1/2 1998.

The Haworth Press Inc.
New York • London

Alcohol Use/Abuse Among Latinos: Issues and Examples of Culturally Competent Services has been co-published simultaneously as *Alcoholism Treatment Quarterly*, Volume 16, Numbers 1/2 1998.

The development, preparation, and publication of this work has been undertaken with great care. However, the publisher, employees, editors, and agents of The Haworth Press and all imprints of The Haworth Press, Inc., including The Haworth Medical Press and The Pharmaceutical Products Press, are not responsible for any errors contained herein or for consequences that may ensue from use of materials or information contained in this work. Opinions expressed by the author(s) are not necessarily those of The Haworth Press, Inc.

The Haworth Press, Inc., 10 Alice Street, Binghamton, NY 13904-1580 USA

Cover design by Thomas J. Mayshock Jr.

Library of Congress Cataloging-in-Publication Data

Alcohol use/abuse among Latinos : issues and examples of culturally competent services / Melvin Delgado, editor.
    p. cm.
    Includes bibliographical references and index.
    ISBN 0-7890-0392-9 (alk. paper).–ISBN 0-7890-0500-X (alk. paper)
    1. Hispanic Americans–Alcohol use. 2. Latin Americans–United States–Alcohol use. 3. Alcoholism–Treatment–United States. 4. Alcoholism–United States–Prevention. 5. Hispanic Americans–Services for–United States. I. Delgado, Melvin.
HV5292.A3853 1998
362.292'2'08968673–dc21
                                      97–46407
                                          CIP

INDEXING & ABSTRACTING

Contributions to this publication are selectively indexed or abstracted in print, electronic, online, or CD-ROM version(s) of the reference tools and information services listed below. This list is current as of the copyright date of this publication. See the end of this section for additional notes.

- *Abstracts in Anthropology*, Baywood Publishing Company, 26 Austin Avenue, P.O. Box 337, Amityville, NY 11701

- *Abstracts of Research in Pastoral Care & Counseling*, Loyola College, 7135 Minstrel Way, Suite 101, Columbia, MD 21045

- *Academic Abstracts/CD-ROM,* EBSCO Publishing Editorial Department, P.O. Box 590, Ipswich, MA 01938-0590

- *ADDICTION ABSTRACTS,* National Addiction Centre, 4 Windsor Walk, London SE5 8AF, England

- *ALCONLINE Database*, Centralforbundet for Alkohol-och narkotikaupplysning, Box 70412, 107 25 Stockholm, Sweden

- *Brown University Digest of Addiction Theory and Application, The (DATA Newsletter),* Project Cork Institute, Dartmouth Medical School, 14 South Main Street, Suite 2F, Hanover, NH 03755-2015

- *Cambridge Scientific Abstracts*, Health & Safety Science Abstracts, 7200 Wisconsin Avenue #601, Bethesda, MD 20814

- *CNPIEC Reference Guide: Chinese National Directory of Foreign Periodicals,* P.O. Box 88, Beijing, People's Republic of China

- *Criminal Justice Abstracts*, Willow Tree Press, 15 Washington Street, 4th Floor, Newark, NJ 07102

- *Criminology, Penology and Police Science Abstracts*, Kugler Publications, P.O. Box 11188, 1001 GD Amsterdam, The Netherlands

- *EAP Abstracts Plus,* EAP Information Systems, P.O. Box 1650, Yreka, CA 96097

- *Excerpta Medica/Secondary Publishing Division*, Elsevier Science Inc., Secondary Publishing Division, 655 Avenue of the Americas, New York, NY 10010

- *Family Studies Database (online and CD/ROM),* National Information Services Corporation, 306 East Baltimore Pike, 2nd Floor, Media, PA 19063

(continued)

- *Health Source: Indexing & Abstracting of 160 selected health related journals, updated monthly*, EBSCO Publishing, 83 Pine Street, Peabody, MA 01960
- *Health Source Plus: expanded version of "Health Source" to be released shortly*, EBSCO Publishing, 83 Pine Street, Peabody, MA 01960
- *Index to Periodical Articles Related to Law*, University of Texas, 727 East 26th Street, Austin, TX 78705
- *INTERNET ACCESS (& additional networks) Bulletin Board for Libraries ("BUBL") coverage of information resources on INTERNET, JANET, and other networks.*
  - <URL:http://bubl.ac.uk/>
  - The new locations will be found under <URL:http://bubl.ac.uk/link/>.
  - Any existing BUBL users who have problems finding information on the new service should contact the BUBL help line by sending e-mail to <bubl@bubl.ac.uk>.
  The Andersonian Library, Curran Building, 101 St. James Road, Glasgow G4 0NS, Scotland
- *Medication Use STudies (MUST) DATABASE*, The University of Mississippi, School of Pharmacy, University, MS 38677
- *Mental Health Abstracts (online through DIALOG)*, IFI/Plenum Data Company, 3202 Kirkwood Highway, Wilmington, DE 19808
- *NIAAA Alcohol and Alcohol Problems Science Database (ETOH)*, National Institute on Alcohol Abuse and Alcoholism, 1400 Eye Street NW, Suite 600, Washington, DC 20005
- *Psychological Abstracts (PsycINFO)*, American Psychological Association, P.O. Box 91600, Washington, DC 20090-1600
- *Referativnyi Zhurnal (Abstracts Journal of the Institute of Scientific Information of the Republic of Russia)*, The Institute of Scientific Information, Baltijskaja ul., 14, Moscow A-219, Republic of Russia
- *Social Planning/Policy & Development Abstracts (SOPODA)*, Sociological Abstracts, Inc., P.O. Box 22206, San Diego, CA 92192-0206
- *Social Work Abstracts*, National Association of Social Workers, 750 First Street NW, 8th Floor, Washington, DC 20002
- *Sociological Abstracts (SA)*, Sociological Abstracts, Inc., P.O. Box 22206, San Diego, CA 92192-0206

(continued)

- *SOMED (social medicine) Database*, Landes Institut für Den Offentlichen Gesundheitsdienst NRW, Postfach 20 10 12, D-33548 Bielefeld, Germany
- *Studies on Women Abstracts*, Carfax Publishing Company, P.O. Box 25, Abingdon, Oxfordshire OX14 3UE, United Kingdom
- *Violence and Abuse Abstracts: A Review of Current Literature on Interpersonal Violence (VAA)*, Sage Publications, Inc., 2455 Teller Road, Newbury Park, CA 91320

SPECIAL BIBLIOGRAPHIC NOTES

related to special journal issues (separates) and indexing/abstracting

☐ indexing/abstracting services in this list will also cover material in any "separate" that is co-published simultaneously with Haworth's special thematic journal issue or DocuSerial. Indexing/abstracting usually covers material at the article/chapter level.

☐ monographic co-editions are intended for either non-subscribers or libraries which intend to purchase a second copy for their circulating collections.

☐ monographic co-editions are reported to all jobbers/wholesalers/approval plans. The source journal is listed as the "series" to assist the prevention of duplicate purchasing in the same manner utilized for books-in-series.

☐ to facilitate user/access services all indexing/abstracting services are encouraged to utilize the co-indexing entry note indicated at the bottom of the first page of each article/chapter/contribution.

☐ this is intended to assist a library user of any reference tool (whether print, electronic, online, or CD-ROM) to locate the monographic version if the library has purchased this version but not a subscription to the source journal.

☐ individual articles/chapters in any Haworth publication are also available through the Haworth Document Delivery Service (HDDS).

Alcohol Use/Abuse Among Latinos: Issues and Examples of Culturally Competent Services

CONTENTS

ABOUT THE EDITOR

Melvin Delgado, PhD, is Professor and Chair of Macro-Practice Sequence in the School of Social Work at Boston University. A faculty member there since 1979, he has also served the university as the Acting Coordinator of the Racism-Oppression Sequence and as Chairperson of the Community Organization, Management, and Planning Sequence. He has been principal investigator on many studies funded by organizations such as the Center on Substance Abuse Prevention, the U.S. Department of Education, and the National Institutes of Health, among others. In 1994, he received the award for the Greatest Contribution to Social Work Education from the National Association of Social Work, Massachusetts Chapter, and in 1996, he received the Outstanding Contribution to the Boston University School of Social Work Alumni Award. A member of the editorial boards of the *Journal of Multicultural Social Work, Social Work with Groups* and *Alcoholism Treatment Quarterly,* Professor Delgado is co-editor of the book *Social Work Approaches to Alcohol and Other Drug Problems: Case Studies and Teaching Tools for Educators and Practitioners* and is the author of *Social Work Practice in Non-Traditional Urban Settings* (Oxford University Press). He is also the author or co-author of numerous government reports, book chapters, and articles that have appeared in such journals as *Health and Social Work, Social Work in Education, Drugs & Society,* and *Social Work.*

Introduction

Melvin Delgado, PhD

SUMMARY. The continued increase in representation among Latinos in the United States requires that ATOD and other human services organizations develop services that are culture specific. The development of cultural competence with this population is a goal that every staff member and organization needs to strive for as this country approaches the 21st century. *[Article copies available for a fee from The Haworth Document Delivery Service: 1-800-342-9678. E-mail address: getinfo@haworth.com]*

The topic of this volume is on how the field of alcohol, tobacco and other drug abuse (ATOD) has attempted to operationalize culturally competent services for Latinos in the United States. Cultural competence is achieved when organizations and service providers possess the necessary attitudes, skills, and knowledge, to delivery services within the cultural context of the Latino client, be that context individual, family, or community.

The process for achieving this goal is not without challenges and barriers. The achievement of cultural competence is greatly influenced by the interplay of numerous factors. In addition, there are a variety of culture-specific issues and needs related to this rapidly growing population group.

Melvin Delgado is Professor of Social Work and Chair of Macro-Practice Sequence, Boston University School of Social Work, 264 Bay State Road, Boston, MA 02215.

The author wishes to acknowledge and thank the contributors of the special volume who were most generous with their time and insights.

[Haworth co-indexing entry note]: "Introduction." Delgado, Melvin. Co-published simultaneously in *Alcoholism Treatment Quarterly* (The Haworth Press, Inc.) Vol. 16, No. 1/2, 1998, pp. 1-3; and: *Alcohol Use/Abuse Among Latinos: Issues and Examples of Culturally Competent Services* (ed: Melvin Delgado) The Haworth Press, Inc., 1998, pp. 1-3. Single or multiple copies of this article are available for a fee from The Haworth Document Delivery Service [1-800-342-9678, 9:00 a.m. - 5:00 p.m. (EST). E-mail address: getinfo@haworth.com].

These needs will be identified and analyzed with a special focus on alcohol, and a set of recommendations made to help practitioners and organizations better meet the needs of Latinos. The authors invited to submit manuscripts for this volume have extensive practice experience in the field and have published numerous scholarly papers related to their experience.

The focus of the volume is to start with a conceptual framework and proceed to case studies and examples of culturally competent services. The issue will be divided into four sections. The first section (Setting the Context) will focus on setting the context for why cultural competence with Latinos is essential to the field. The article by Dr. Melvin Delgado will provide a basis from which to examine the complexity of cultural competence, identify various barriers organizations, and present a series of recommendations organizations must address in order to achieve success with Latinos.

Dr. Mario R. De La Rosa provides a demographic picture of Latinos in the United States who abuse alcohol. This article provides a foundation from which to examine the nature and extent of the problem within select Latino groups. Dr. Sylvia Rodriguez-Andrew presents a review of the literature and draws upon her extensive experiences in practice and research.

The second section (A View from the Field) is devoted to theoretical and empirically-based articles from the field, and provides a picture of how cultural competence has been operationalized (formally and informally) across Latino sub-groups. Dr. Melvin Delgado's article on Latina beauty parlors addresses the community from an assets perspective and provides a conceptual foundation on organizations which can identify and engage Latino natural support systems as partners in the field of substance abuse with a special emphasis on intervention and prevention.

Dr. Betty Garcia's article stresses why organizations cannot rely solely on hiring Latino staff to ensure culturally competent services; they must also develop mechanisms such as supervision and consultation to help staff further refine their skills and knowledge on the topic.

Drs. Richard C. Cervantes and Cynthia Peña's article addresses the importance of evaluation in the ATOD field and how cultural competence evaluation gets operationalized. There is an increased demand for organizations to examine their practice. However, there is much to be learned about the process and content of evaluation as it relates to cultural competence and Latinos.

The third section (Group Specific) is devoted to research and case studies focusing on various Latino sub-groups. Dr. Juan Paz focuses on the workplace and needs of rural-based Latinos. This group's needs are generally not considered in the setting of ATOD policy, with urban-based groups receiving the greatest attention and resources.

Dr. Edgar Colon focuses on Latino Males in alcohol treatment and the impact gender has on this form of intervention. Dr. Juana Mora, too, examines the impact of gender as a key factor in treatment and focuses specifically on Latinas. Dr. Migdalia Reyes examines Latina lesbians who abuse alcohol and special challenges they face in receiving culturally competent treatment. This group is rarely addressed in the professional literature. The final section (Summary of Key Practice, Research and Policy Implications) is authored by Dr. Melvin Delgado and summarizes the key practice and policy implications.

SETTING THE CONTEXT

Cultural Competence
and the Field of ATOD:
Latinos as a Case Example

Melvin Delgado, PhD

SUMMARY. The field of alcohol, tobacco and other drugs (ATOD) has made important strides in recognizing the importance of culture in the design and implementation of services. The provision of culturally competent services for Latinos is a goal organizations must strive to achieve. This article will provide a foundation from which to examine cultural competence and how it can be implemented in the development of ATOD services for Latinos. *[Article copies available for a fee from The Haworth Document Delivery Service: 1-800-342-9678. E-mail address: getinfo@haworth.com]*

INTRODUCTION

Communities-of-color in the United States have continued to increase numerically with no geographical region of the country unaffected by this

Melvin Delgado is Professor of Social Work and Chair of Macro-Practice Sequence, Boston University School of Social Work, 264 Bay State Road, Boston, MA 02215.

[Haworth co-indexing entry note]: "Cultural Competence and the Field of ATOD: Latinos as a Case Example." Delgado, Melvin. Co-published simultaneously in *Alcoholism Treatment Quarterly* (The Haworth Press, Inc.) Vol. 16, No. 1/2, 1998, pp. 5-19; and: *Alcohol Use/Abuse Among Latinos: Issues and Examples of Culturally Competent Services* (ed: Melvin Delgado) The Haworth Press, Inc., 1998, pp. 5-19. Single or multiple copies of this article are available for a fee from The Haworth Document Delivery Service [1-800-342-9678, 9:00 a.m. - 5:00 p.m. (EST). E-mail address: getinfo@haworth.com].

5

demographic trend (Barringer, 1991; Treas, 1995). This increase in representation has been particularly pronounced for Latinos (Institute for Puerto Rican Policy, 1995; Rohter, 1994). This group has also increased in diversity and no longer can be considered as exclusively consisting of Cubans, Puerto Ricans or Mexicans (Castex, 1994), or having a uniform family structure (Hurtado, 1995; Oboler, 1995; Ortiz, 1995; Vega, 1995).

The field of substance abuse has made important strides over the past fifteen years to recognize the importance of culture in the design and implementation of services (Dyer, 1994; Gordon, 1994; Orlandi, Weston & Epstein, 1992; Trimble, Bolek & Niemcryk, 1992). The impact of alcohol, tobacco and other drugs (ATOD) has been particularly acute in communities-of-color, necessitating the development of innovative approaches that take into account cultural values (Watts & Wright, Jr., 1989). The field of ATOD has not only had to shift paradigms regarding the best context for intervention, with an increased emphasis on community, but it has also had to translate cultural awareness into concrete strategies and competencies to reach communities in greatest need.

This article will examine how cultural competence has been operationalized in the field of ATOD with a special focus on Latinos in the United States. A review of the literature will be presented, along with a series of key principles and recommendations for achieving cultural competence with Latinos.

REVIEW OF THE LITERATURE

The alcohol, tobacco and other drug abuse literature on culture has witnessed an unprecedented explosion in the past five years (Botvin, Schinke & Orlandi, 1995; Gordon, 1994; Orlandi, Weston & Epstein, 1992; Trimble, Bolek & Niemcryk, 1992); Latino-focused publications have also experienced this increase (Bourgois, 1995; Glick & Moore, 1990; Mayers, Kail & Watts, 1993).

The concept of cultural competence has emerged from this, and other literature, to refer to a set of congruent behaviors, attitudes and policies that come together in a system, agency, or intervention to work effectively in multicultural situations (Cross, 1988). This definition reflects a variety of perspectives on how this concept has been operationalized (Freeman, 1994).

Reflections from the Human Service Field

Mason (1994, p. 1) identified five key elements related to the operationalization of cultural competence in the professional literature: "(a) the increasing cultural and racial diversity of consumer populations . . . (b) the role culture plays in help-seeking behaviors . . . (c) the differential service utilization rates of various cultural and racial groups . . . (d) diverse perspectives on the origins or etiology of behaviors, emotions or thoughts that dominate cultures describes as . . . problems; and (e) culturally relevant services may differ from services that ignore cultural differences . . ." These elements reflect how shifts in population diversity influence the design of services.

The concept of cultural competence, although originally applied to counseling with individuals, has evolved to include other dimensions of service delivery, most notably organizational development and research: (1) clarity concerning the target population of services; (2) importance of developing a value base on why cultural competence is important; (3) flexibility in service design to account for within and between group differences; (4) developing a clear vision for services through involvement of community; and (5) development of evaluation measures and tools that reflect a cultural perspective (Mason, 1994).

Many states have taken initiatives in developing services with cultural competence as a central goal. These initiatives have varied according to states and geographical regions of the country; however, these plans usually consisted of at least seven organizational components (Macey & Hanley, 1994): (1) development of policy with an emphasis on cultural competence (Mason, 1994); (2) creation of administrative procedures and mechanisms reinforcing cultural competence goals; (3) human resource development with an emphasis on recruitment and retention of personnel with diverse backgrounds (Williams, 1994); (4) community relations and participation; (5) public education and in-service training; (6) staff supervision and consultation; and (7) evaluation procedures and techniques (Benjamin, 1994; Orlandi, Weston & Epstein, 1992).

Reflections from the ATOD Field

An ATOD cultural competence construct must have as a foundation the following elements in order to be optimally operationalized: (1) multiculturalism; (2) resilience/assets/strengths; (3) competence (skills and knowledge); (4) community capacity development/empowerment (consumer and community); and (5) community participation. These five areas have a profound impact on how cultural competence has evolved and been implemented in the field of ATOD. Each of these areas, in turn, has a set of principles to guide practitioners and organizations seeking to achieve a high level of cultural competence. In short, these principles serve as mechanisms for translating goals and visions into action plans.

1. *Multiculturalism:* Multiculturalism can be defined as " . . . the most common way in which the ideology or philosophy of cultural pluralism is put into practice . . ." (Cordeiro, Reagan & Martinez, 1994). Culture, which is all the ways a specific group adapts to its environment and is based upon their values, beliefs, and perceptions of the world (Axelson, 1985), is much more than ethnicity or race. In fact, it represents the interplay of numerous factors such as economic class, religion, age, skin pigmentation, gender, sexual orientation, physical/mental abilities, rural/ urban upbringing, geography, nationality, profession, and even political affiliation. A focus on ethnicity and race without consideration to how other factors interplay will result in a disservice to the clients and community. The understanding of culture is further complicated because it is dynamic and changing to meet environmental demands.

Cunningham (1994, p. viii) emphasizes the importance of multiculturalism in setting the tone and agenda for substance abuse services: "Multiculturalism is more than a strategy, a model, or technique. It is a way of life that we must embrace and embody with every fiber of our being. Only then can we begin to reflect the creativity, innovation, and synergy resulting from the unity of diverse cultures woven together to form a marvelous tapestry of a healthy and drug-free community."

Gordon (1994, p. xiv) also makes a connection between multiculturalism and ATOD services: "The shift from a traditional service delivery paradigm to an effective 'continuum of empowerment' in the substance abuse field can occur only within a system that values, respects, and builds on the diversity of racial and ethnic groups." There is little doubt that any future advances in the field must use multiculturally-based practice as a bridge between services and communities.

The following three principles stress the importance of organizations hiring Latino staff in order to minimize the emergence of barriers to recovery that can result from having staff of dissimilar background to that of the client.

Principle 1: ATOD Services must be available in the language preference of the consumer. This principle serves to minimize miscommunication between staff and consumer and to encourage communication between families and staff. There is little dispute than an ability to communicate in a language of choice is critical to any form of intervention. In the case where Spanish is the primary language, every effort must be made to ensure that communication occurs in Spanish. Hurtado (1995, p. 51) comments on the importance of the Spanish language for the community: "The high maintenance of Spanish language within Latino families may be explained by their positive attitudes toward their language and by the desire to preserve it as one of the most important aspects of Latino culture."

Communication in language of choice, however, goes beyond language defined in its most narrow sense, namely Spanish or English. Language also encompasses symbols and nonverbal cues the client utilizes to conveys feelings and thoughts.

Principle 2: Organizations must be staffed with Latinos who represent the composition of consumers and community. McLaughlin (1993, p. 65), although commenting on youth leaders and not specifically on drugs and Latinos, raises the importance of staff representing the socio-demographic and ethnic composition of the neighborhoods they serve: "Having a preponderance of staff with backgrounds similar to those of local youngsters and their families makes a big difference in organizational credibility . . . Obviously, the understanding imparted by similar experience allows youth workers to see youth in context and to emphasize with their self-perception. Having been there enables policies and programs that connect with the living reality of youth, not imagined conditions or circumstances." This action, in turn, serves to minimize cultural value conflicts, and provide important role models of individuals who are in active recovery or have never been addicted to drugs.

Principle 3: Services must respect cultural values and reinforce self-esteem. The role of ethnic pride in the development of high self-esteem is critical for both individual and community. An appreciation and celebration of ethnic pride must have a central role in the provision of any services. McLaughlin (1993, p. 60), although referring to youths, stresses the importance of ethnic pride: "Many adults in these settings stressed the importance of alliance with some well-grounded cultural theory as a component of general self-esteem and social competence. Youth workers understood the importance of cultural awareness and pride and of youth's development of a positive sense of this aspect of their identity. Within the broader community context, there is often little with which to ascribe value or pride to . . . Latino youth."

Felix-Ortiz and Newcomb's (1995) research identified the need for interventions to foster cultural identity among Latino youth, positive role models, and constructive community activism. Nevertheless, encouragement of cultural pride and identity should not be considered a "solution" but an essential component of an overall strategy encompassing development of basic coping skills and enhancement of protective factors in the community.

2. *Resilience/Assets/Strengths:* The field of ATOD has made significant contributions to the development of a construct emphasizing resiliency

(Newcomb, 1992). This term is often interchanged with assets, protective factors, coping, strengths, and natural support systems (Davis, 1994; Eckenrode, 1991; Freeman, 1990; Gfroerer & De La Rosa; Hawkins, Lishner & Catalano, 1985; McKnight & Kretzmann, 1992; Saleeby, 1992). Historically, however, the field has relied on a "scarcity" paradigm towards Latinos and other undervalued groups. A scarcity paradigm is racist, blames the victim, and views certain communities as being incapable of helping themselves.

A cultural competence perspective is predicated on the respect and faith in the capacity of an individual, family or community for self-help. As a result, cultural competence necessitates a resiliency/assets/strengths base from which to assess capacity to meet needs: "But in neighborhoods where there are effective community development efforts, there is also a map of the community's assets, capacities, and abilities. For it is clear that even the poorest city neighborhood is a place where individuals and organizations represent resources upon which to build. The key to neighborhood regeneration is not only to build upon these resources which the community already controls, but to harness those that are not yet available for local development purposes. The process of identifying capacities and assets, both individual and organizational, is the first step on the path toward community regeneration" (McKnight & Kretzman, 1991, p. 3).

As a result, an asset map can be used for a multitude of purposes from helping an organization plan for service delivery to serving as a guide for coordinating planning between several agencies in order not to overload any particular sector of the community, e.g., several agencies concurrently approaching an indigenous institution.

It is much easier to develop culture-specific interventions by first identifying strengths. Dyer (1994, p. 25) notes the critical role strengths play in any initial intervention step: ". . . the worker must be able to see the cultural background of the clients in terms of strengths and competencies that the culture brings to the individual. An attitude of cultural relativism . . . , which approaches the culture of another individual with respect, is a necessary first step in being able to see cultural strengths."

Two key principles serve to guide how a resilience/assets/strengths perspective can be operationalzied with Latinos.

Principle 1: ATOD organizations must develop a map of community assets to use in the planning of services. The development of a community assets map is necessary to guide organizational efforts at developing collaborative relations and capacity development initiatives. This process, however, is not easy: "The process of identifying and mapping Hispanic natural support systems is complex and labor-intensive . . . Natural support systems are rarely listed in . . . directories or noted on agency intake forms, etc. Consequently, the identification and listing of natural support systems entails significant changes in how human service settings gather, list and utilize data" (Delgado, 1994, p. 23).

This map provides organizations with a visual perspective on the types and locations of indigenous resources. However, the development of a map requires organizations and staff to venture out into the community and learn about these resources. In short, this task cannot be accomplished from an office!

Principle 2: Cultural strengths, assets, and resiliency must form the cornerstone of any service provision. An organizational reliance on a "deficit" paradigm will not allow active and meaningful engagement of Latinos. Such an approach will always view the consumer and community as lacking the will and resources of helping themselves. Consequently, assistance is only possible when provided by "outsiders" and "experts," a disempowering stance.

A strengths perspective must be evident throughout all aspects of an organization and the services it provides. This perspective will be reflected in the intake process where questions are asked related to abilities, accomplishments, supports, and coping skills and resources noted. This information, in turn, will then be part of any treatment plan. For example, a client with a strong and supportive family must have them incorporated into any form of intervention (Delgado, 1989).

4. *Competence (Skills and Knowledge):* According to the Oxford English Dictionary (1971 p. 480), competence can be defined as "sufficiency of qualification; capacity to deal adequately with a subject." This very simple definition, nevertheless, has a very complex meaning in the field. Cultural competence must be viewed within a broader framework of social competence.

Lee (1994, a) examines the concept of social competence and the skills that enable staff and organizations to function effectively with consumers of varied racial and ethnic backgrounds, and identifies six major arenas: (1) self-confidence; (2) self-esteem; (3) interpersonal skills; (4) clear and purposeful goals and values; (5) self-control; and (6) the ability to build and maintain healthy peer relations. These six arenas, in turn, must be placed within a cultural context which influences how they get operationalized in ATOD practice with Latinos.

Ziter (1987) notes that consumers must be helped to negotiate between their culture and community, which nourishes ethnic identity and pride, and the larger culture, which generally seeks to undermine ethnic identity and pride. Freeman (1994, p. 74) makes a similar observation: "The process of developing a positive ethnic identity and important cultural competencies should be interrelated, integrative experience . . . Practitioners . . . understand the need to facilitate the process of ethnic identity development . . . "

Cultural competence, in addition, must seek to recognize the uniqueness both within and between groups. The presence of new Latino subgroups in all regions of the United States underscores this important factor. ATOD organizations can achieve a high degree of success and cultural competence through systematic efforts at identifying mechanisms ensuring a continuum of care and upgrading staff skills and knowledge.

Principle 1: Organizations must ensure cultural competence at all levels of a continuum of care. Provision of culturally competent services is only as good as the weakest link in the continuum of care. A weak or missing component will seriously undermine any effort at achieving and maintaining recovery. Delgado (1989, p. 84) addresses this key point: "Consequently, a culturally-sensitive continuum of intervention encompasses all of the services and supports needed to achieve sobriety with the added complement of services being grounded in the client's values, traditions, and language. Anything short of the above will result in limited success with Hispanic clients."

For example, a detoxification program that is not adequately staffed by culturally competent staff will, in all likelihood, be unsuccessful with Latinos who have limited or no English language proficiency. As a result, a critical stage of intervention will result in failure to better understand a client. In addition, the client's social support system can not be engaged to help in the recovery process; thus, an important resource in better understanding and assisting a client will be lost. The same can be said for all other stages of a continuum!

Principle 2: Organizations must develop mechanisms to continually upgrade staff cultural competency. Organizations must place a high priority in developing the cultural competency's of staff through supervision, consultation and training. These methods build upon staff strengths and address gaps in skills and knowledge areas. However, the process of achieving cultural competence must be planned and systematic; no staff are born culturally competent.

The provision of "learning opportunities" through staff development can also serve as a means of utilizing well-qualified Latino staff and maximizing their impact. The field of ATOD, like other fields, is severely understaffed by Latino staff. Consequently, it would be unreasonable to expect that all organizations will be fully staffed by Latinos with the pre-requisite credentials. The use of staff development activities represents an opportunity to maximize current resources to help Latino and non-Latino staff develop their competencies (Delgado, 1981, 1982). A program to systematically upgrade staff cultural competence skills serves to reinforce the importance of "quality" services.

Principle 3: Knowledge of ATOD and its historical role in the community. Cultural competence within the ATOD field cannot be achieved without an understanding of the role alcohol, tobacco and other drugs have played in an historical context. The role of drugs within the political economy of many Latino communities in the United States can often be traced to lack of access to "legitimate" jobs and inferior education trapping Latinos into a world of selling and using drugs: "Substance abuse in the inner city is merely a symptom–and a vivid symbol–of deeper dynamics of social marginalization and alienation . . . with . . . daily struggles for subsistence and dignity at the poverty line . . . Retail drug sales easily outcompete other income-generating opportunities, whether legal or illegal" (Bourgois, 1995, pp. 2-3). This understanding of context must be taken into consideration in the development of any services.

This knowledge of history informs staff, organizations, and funding sources concerning the challenge to rid the community of drugs (Bourgois, 1995). For example, alcoholism among Latinos cannot be divorced from the role of sugar cane and rum in the political economy of many Caribbean and Latin American countries.

4. *Community Capacity Development/Empowerment:* Capacity development can serve as an organizing principle for developing culturally competent-based intervention strategies that build upon and utilize individual, family, and community strengths. These strategies, in turn, stress infra-structure development (social and physical). According to McKnight and Kretzman (1991) there are two significant reasons for utilizing capacity development: (1) significant community development can only transpire when local community people are committed to investing themselves and their resources to change efforts. Communities, as a result, can only be developed from the bottom up (outside assistance can be provided if solicited and validates community identity, etc.); and (2) development must start from within since there is a low prospect that significant resources from government will be forthcoming anytime soon.

Capacity development cannot transpire without the use of empowerment. The concept of empowerment first appeared in the human service literature in the 1970s (Lee, 1994, b; Solomon, 1976). However, in the two decades since it has spread to virtually all helping professions, including ATOD. Empowerment refers to (Solomon, 1976, p. 19): ". . . as a process whereby the . . . worker engages in a set of activities with the client . . . that aim to reduce the powerlessness that has been created by negative valuations based on membership in a stigmatized group. It involves identification of the power blocks that contribute to the problem as well as the development and implementation of specific strategies aimed at either the reduction of the effects from indirect power blocks or the reduction of the operations of direct power blocks."

The following two principles relate to community development and empowerment and significantly increase the likelihood that Latino communities can be better prepared to address their own needs.

Principle 1: Organizations must undertake initiatives that develop a community's capacity to help itself. Community capacity development must play a central role in any culturally competent initiatives and be prominent in an ATOD organization's mission. This approach makes an investment in a community and serves to identify and strengthen indigenous resources through efforts such as workshops upgrading community skills and knowledge about ATOD, hiring community residents and training them to work in the field whenever possible, renting local space, and other forms of providing rumination for services and goods. The use of community resources also serves to convey a message that the organization respects and values a community.

Principle 2: Services must empower consumers and community. Empowerment represents a critical dimension of cultural competence and holds great significance in the human service field: "Empowerment requires new thinking about old problems. Empowerment invites us to see the world differently as it abandons the limits and distortions of the pathology model and focuses on human strengths and abilities as the proper starting point for social work practice" (Holmes, 1992, p. 158).

This concept is premised on consumers and communities being the ultimate and best judge of their needs. This perspective requires staff and organizations to strive to involve and provide clients and communities with opportunities and skills to influence the outcome of services.

In addition, empowerment stresses the importance of consumers maintaining self-respect in the help-seeking process. The maintenance of self-respect is critical in any effort to help clients enter and stay in recovery. This aspect gains importance with Latinos who have been taught that they "lazy," "not to be trusted," "not smart," and "incapable of taking care of themselves."

5. *Community Participation:* Sarri and Sarri (1992) note four key factors that lead individuals, organizations and communities to resist or reject change: (1) lack of active, on-going involvement in innovation and change efforts; (2) a sense of powerlessness, actual or perceived; (3) lack of information and knowledge; and (4) lack of active participation and em-

powerment of the target population. Empowerment, as a result, cannot transpire without meaningful participation. The active involvement of the community in all aspects of intervention serves to hold the organization accountable to the community and as a valuable source of information and resources.

Community participation can be manifested in a multitude of ways: (1) memberships on agency boards, advisory committees, task forces; (2) volunteer opportunities in direct client contact or facilitating the delivery of services through indirect client contact; and (3) sources of information on community resources and needs (key informants, focus groups and community forum participants). Two key community participation principles serve to increase representation on key decision-making bodies and collaboration with formal and informal organizations.

Principle 1: Organizations must have community representation on boards and advisory committees. Latino representation on boards of directors and advisory committees will play a critical role in ensuring an organization's continual commitment to the community. This representation serves to minimize "organizational drift" regarding community strengths and needs.

Boards and advisory committees can provide an organization with community legitimacy, expertise, access to various sectors of the community that would not be possible without community representation, and as a political resource to help an agency broker outside resources for the community.

Principle 2: Organizations must collaborate with community-based organizations and natural support systems. It takes an entire community working together to increase the likelihood that prevention and intervention services are successful. Collaboration serves as a vehicle of maximizing available resources. The involvement of Latino community-based organizations serves to increase the possibility that services meet community needs in terms of type and structure.

However, collaboration, if and when undertaken, has generally focused on formal organizations. Delgado (forthcoming publication) comments on this narrow approach: "The definition of community organization must be broadened from the conventional conceptualization (formal institutions receiving and subject to outside funding) to include indigenous institutions that function as natural support systems. These support systems have historical and symbolic meaning, having been deeply rooted in Latino culture . . . unfortunately, these systems are very often overlooked in any efforts at community-level planning." An expansion of the options for collaboration increases the range of institutions that can be involved and the variety of activities that can be initiated.

Natural support systems represent a cultural-based resource with relatively easy accessibility to the community (geographical, psychological, logistical and linguistic). Consequently, the potential for collaborative projects is endless depending upon the capacity of the organization to identify and enlist these systems (Delgado, 1994, 1995 a, b).

CONCLUSION

The demographic trends projected for the twenty-first century reflect both a graying and coloring of the United States. Latinos will continue to represent a significant portion of this country; urban areas in particular will continue to attract this group. The impact of alcohol, tobacco and other drugs has disproportionately impacted on Latinos and all indications are that this will continue for the foreseeable future.

The concept of cultural competence can serve an instrumental role in guiding organizations, funding sources, and institutions of higher learning in the development of a vision concerning the nature of ATOD services needed to meet the needs of Latinos and other undervalued populations. The concept of cultural competence is everchanging, reflecting a dynamic environment. The field of ATOD is in a propitious position to significantly impact other human service fields in how this concept can be operationalized.

According to Yee and Weaver (1994, p. 39) achievement of cultural competence is a never ending process: "Cultural competence is a never completed transformation; it is an ever evolving process, because cultures are not static and sociocultural contexts change." ATOD organizations, too, must be prepared to engage in continual transformation to meet the needs of Latinos and other communities-of-color.

REFERENCES

Axelson, J.A. (1985). *Counseling and development in a multicultural society.* Belmont, CA: Brooks/Cole Publishing Co.

Barringer, F. (March 11, 1991). Census shows profound change in racial makeup of the nation. *The New York Times*, 1, B.8.

Benjamin, M.P. (1994). Research frontiers in building a culturally competent organization. *Focal Point*, 8, 17-19.

Botvin, G.J., Schinke, S. & Orlandi, M.A. (1995). *Drug abuse prevention with multiethnic youth.* Thousand Oaks, CA: Sage Publications.

Bourgois, P. (1995). *In search of respect: Selling crack in El Barrio New York.* New York: Cambridge University Press.

Castex, G.M. (1994). Providing services to Hispanic/Latino populations. *Social Work*, 39, 288-296.

Cordeiro, P.A., Reagan, T.G. & Martinez, L.P. (1994). *Multiculturalism and TQE.* Thousand Oaks, CA: Corwin Press, Inc.

Cross, T.L. (1988). Services to minority populations: Cultural competence continuum. *Focal Point*, 3, 1-4.

Cunningham, M.S. (1994). Foreword. In J.U. Gordon (Ed.). *Managing multiculturalism in substance abuse services* (pp vii-ix). Thousand Oaks, CA: Sage Publications.

Davis, L.V. (Ed.). (1994). *Building on women's strengths.* New York: The Haworth Press, Inc.

Delgado, M. (forthcoming publication). HIV/AIDS and Latinos: Botanical shops as community resources. *Journal of Health and Social Policy.*

Delgado, M. (1995a). Natural support systems and AOD services to communities of color: A California case example. *Alcoholism Treatment Quarterly,* XIII.

Delgado, M. (1995b). Hispanic natural support systems and alcohol and other drug services: Challenges and rewards for practice. *Alcoholism Treatment Quarterly,* 12, 17-31.

Delgado, M. (1994). Hispanic natural support systems and the AODA field: A developmental framework for collaboration. *Journal of Multicultural Social Work.* 3, 11-37.

Delgado, M. (1989). Treatment and prevention of Hispanic alcoholism. In T.D. Watts & R. Wright, Jr. (Eds.). *Alcoholism in minority populations* (pp. 77-92). Springfield, IL: Charles C. Thomas Publisher.

Delgado, M. (1982). Cultural consultation: Implications for Hispanic mental health services in the United States. *International Journal of Intercultural Relations*, 6, 227-250.

Delgado, M. (1981). Consulting to Hispanic staff: Implications for community mental health programs. *The Journal of Urban Psychiatry*, 1, 6-10.

Dyer, L. (1994). Problems of definitions. In J.U. Gordon (Ed.). *Managing multiculturalism in substance abuse services* (pp. 22-41). Thousand Oaks, CA: Sage Publications.

Eckenrode, J. (Ed.). (1991). *The social context of coping.* New York: Plenum Press.

Felix-Ortiz, M. & Newcomb, M.D. (1995). Cultural identity and drug abuse among Latino and Latina adolescents. In G.J. Botvin, S. Schinke & M.A. Orlandi (Eds.). *Drug abuse prevention with multiethnic youth* (pp. 147-165). Thousand Oaks, CA: Sage Publications.

Freeman, E.M. (1994). African-American women and the concept of cultural competence. *Journal of Multicultural Social Work*, 3, 61-76.

Freeman, E.M. (1990). Social competence as a framework for addressing ethnicity and teenage alcohol problems. In A.R. Stiffman & L.E. Davis (Eds.). *Ethnic*

18   ALCOHOL USE/ABUSE AMONG LATINOS

issues in adolescent mental health (pp. 247-266). Newbury Park, CA: Sage Publications.

Gfroerer, J. & De La Rosa, M. (1993). Protective and risk factors associated with drug use among Hispanic youth. *Journal of Addictive Diseases*, 12, 87-107.

Glick, R. & Moore, J. (Eds.). (1990). *Drugs in Hispanic communities*. New Brunswick, NJ: Rutgers University Press.

Gordon, J.U. (Ed.). (1994). *Managing multiculturalism in substance abuse services*. Thousand Oaks, CA: Sage Publications.

Hawkins, J.D., Lishner, D.M. & Catalano, Jr., F. (1985). Childhood predictors and the prevention of adolescent substance abuse. In C.L. Jones & R.J. Battles (Eds.). *Etiology of drug abuse: Implications for prevention* (pp. 75-126). National Institute on Drug Abuse Research Monograph 56. Washington, D.C.: U.S. Government Printing Office.

Holmes, G.E. (1992). Social work research and the empowerment paradigm. In D.S. Saleebey (Ed.). *The strengths perspective in social work practice* (pp. 158-168). New York: Longman Publishers.

Hurtado, A. (1995). Variations, combinations, and evaluations: Latino families in the United States. In R.E. Zambrana (Ed.). *Understanding Latino families: Scholarship, policy, and practice* (pp. 40-61). Thousand Oaks, CA: Sage Publications.

Institute for Puerto Rican Policy. (1995). Puerto Ricans and other Latinos in the United States: March 1994. *IPR Datanote*, No. 17.

Lee, J.M. (1994). Historical and theoretical considerations: Implications for multiculturalism in substance abuse services. In J.U. Gordon (Ed.). *Managing multiculturalism in substance abuse services* (pp. 3-21). Thousand Oaks, CA: Sage.

Lee, J.A.B. (1994, b). *The empowerment approach to social work practice*. New York: Columbia University Press Publications.

Macey, D.V.R. & Hanley, J. (1994). South Carolina department of mental health cultural competence plan. *Focal Point*, 8, 13-15.

Mason, J.L. (1994). Developing culturally competent organizations. *Focal Point*, 8, 1-8.

Mayers, R.S., Kail, B.L. & Watts, T.D. (Eds.). (1993). *Hispanic substance abuse*. Springfield, IL: Charles C. Thomas Publisher.

McKnight, J.L. & Kretzman, J. (1991). *Mapping community capacity*. Evanston, IL: Center for Urban Affairs Policy and Research, Northwestern University.

McLaughlin, M.W. (1993). Embedded identities: Enabling balance in urban contexts. In S.B. Heath & M.W. McLaughlin (Eds.). *Identity & inner-city youth: Beyond ethnicity and gender* (pp. 36-68). New York: Teachers College Press.

Newcomb, M.D. (1992). Understanding the multi-dimensional nature of drug use and abuse: The role of consumption, risk factors, and protective factors. In M. Glantz & R. Pickens (Eds.). *Vulnerability to drug use* (pp. 255-298). Washington, D.C.: American Psychological Association.

Oboler, S. (1995). *Ethnic labels, Latino lives*. Minneapolis, MN: University of Minnesota Press.

Orlani, M., Weston, R. & Epstein, L. (1992). *Cultural competence for evaluators. A guide for alcohol and other drug abuse prevention practitioners working with ethnic/racial communities.* Rockville, MD: Office of Substance Abuse Prevention.

Ortiz, V. (1995). The diversity of Latino families. In R.E. Zambrana (Ed.). *Understanding Latino families: Scholarship, policy, and practice* (pp. 18-39). Thousand Oaks, CA: Sage Publications.

Rohter, L. (January 31, 1994). A Puerto Rican boom in Florida, *The New York Times*, A10.

Saleebey, D.S. (1992). *The strengths perspective in social work practice.* New York: Longman Publishers.

Sarri, R.C. & Sarri, C.M. (1992). Organizational and community change through participatory research. *Administration in Social Work*, 16, 99-110.

Solomon, B.B. (1976). *Black empowerment: Social work in oppressed communities.* New York: Columbia University Press.

The Compact Edition of the Oxford English Dictionary. (1971). New York: Oxford University Press.

Treas, J. (1995). Older Americans in the 1990s and beyond. *Population Bulletin*, 50.

Trimble, J.E., Bolek, C.S. & Niemcryk, S.J. (Eds.). (1992). *Ethnic and multicultural drug abuse: Perspectives on current research.* New York: The Haworth Press, Inc.

Vega, B. (1995). The study of Latino families: A point of departure. In R.E. Zambrana (Ed.). *Understanding Latino families: Scholarship, policy, and practice* (pp. 3-17). Thousand Oaks, CA: Sage Publications.

Watts, T.D. & Wright, Jr., R. (1989). *Alcoholism in minority populations.* Springfield, IL: Charles C. Thomas Publisher.

Williams, D. (1994). Cultural competence: Building a state level system of change in Pennsylvania. *Focal Point*, 8, 15-17.

Yee, B.W.K. & Weaver, G.D. (1994). Ethnic minorities and health promotion: Developing a 'culturally competent' agenda. *Generations*, XVIII, 39-44.

Ziter, M. (1987). Culturally sensitive treatment of Black alcoholic families. *Social Work*, 32, 130-135.

Prevalence and Consequences
of Alcohol, Cigarette,
and Drug Use Among Hispanics

Mario R. De La Rosa, PhD

SUMMARY. This paper presents an overview of the prevalence of alcohol, heavy alcohol, cigarette, cocaine, and marijuana use in the Hispanic population living in the mainland United States and their attitudes and perceptions regarding the availability in alcohol and other drugs in their neighborhood. In addition, this paper will describe the major consequences of drug use and make recommendations for future research. *[Article copies available for a fee from The Haworth Document Delivery Service: 1-800-342-9678. E-mail address: getinfo@haworth.com]*

INTRODUCTION

This paper seeks to: (1) present an overview on the prevalence of alcohol, heavy alcohol,[1] cigarette, cocaine, and marijuana use in the Hispanic[2] population living in the mainland United States and their attitudes and perceptions regarding the availability of alcohol and other drugs in

Mario R. De La Rosa is Health Science Administrator, National Institute on Drug Abuse, 5600 Fishers Lane, Room 9A-42, Rockville, MD 20857.

Opinions expressed in this manuscript are those of the author and do not necessarily reflect the opinions or official policy of the National Institute on Drug Abuse or any part of the U.S. Department of Health and Human Services.

[Haworth co-indexing entry note]: "Prevalence and Consequences of Alcohol, Cigarette, and Drug Use Among Hispanics." De La Rosa, Mario R. Co-published simultaneously in *Alcoholism Treatment Quarterly* (The Haworth Press, Inc.) Vol. 16, No. 1/2, 1998, pp. 21-54; and: *Alcohol Use/Abuse Among Latinos: Issues and Examples of Culturally Competent Services* (ed: Melvin Delgado) The Haworth Press, Inc., 1998, pp. 21-54. Single or multiple copies of this article are available for a fee from The Haworth Document Delivery Service [1-800-342-9678, 9:00 a.m. - 5:00 p.m. (EST). E-mail address: getinfo@haworth.com].

their neighborhoods; (2) provide information on the prevalence of alcohol, heavy alcohol, cocaine, marijuana, and cigarette use among Hispanic youth[3] and risk behaviors associated with their drug use;[4] (3) describe the consequences associated with alcohol, marijuana, cocaine, heroin, and other drug use experience by Hispanics, including the relationships between drug use and AIDS and drug use and criminal behavior; and (4) make recommendations on future research on the drug using behavior of Hispanics living in the mainland United States.

PREVALENCE OF ALCOHOL AND OTHER DRUG USE AMONG HISPANICS

Prevalence of past-month marijuana, cocaine, alcohol, heavy alcohol, and cigarette use in the United States by age, sex, and race/ethnicity from the 1993 National Household Survey on Drug Abuse (NHSDA-1993),[5] as presented in Table 1, indicates that Blacks and Hispanics had a higher prevalence of past-month[6] marijuana and cocaine use than either White, non-Hispanics or Asian/Pacific Islanders (Substance Abuse and Mental Health Administration, 1994a). Particularly striking were the differences in the prevalence of past-month cocaine use; the rates for Blacks and Hispanics were more than twice the rate of Whites, non-Hispanics and Asian/Pacific Islanders. Among persons aged 12-17, as presented in Table 1, the differences in the prevalence of past-month cocaine use were even more striking; rates for cocaine use among Hispanics aged 12-17 were more than three times those of Black and White, (non-Hispanic) youth aged 12-17.

On the other hand, data from the 1993 NHSDA, as presented in Table 1, indicate that the prevalence of past-month alcohol, heavy alcohol, and cigarette use were higher for White non-Hispanics than for Blacks, Hispanics, or Asian/Pacific Islanders. Overall, the 1993 NHSDA indicates that alcohol, followed by cigarettes and then by marijuana, continues to be the drug most frequently used by people in the mainland United States regardless of age, sex, and racial/ethnic background.[7] In addition, these data indicate that, with the exception of heavy alcohol use, Hispanics between the ages of 18-25 had higher prevalence of past-month drug use in each of the surveyed categories, including marijuana, alcohol, cocaine, and cigarette use, than Hispanics in all other age categories (Substance Abuse and Mental Health Administration, 1994a). The results from the 1993 NHSDA also suggest that past-month alcohol, marijuana, cocaine, and cigarette use drops off dramatically among Hispanics as well as other ethnic/racial groups when members of these groups are age 35 and older.

TABLE 1. Prevalence of past-month marijuana, cocaine, alcohol, heavy alcohol, and cigarette use in the United States, by age, sex, and race/ethnicity: 1991-93 (in percentages).

Type of drug	12-17	18-25	26-34	35+	Male	Female	Total
Marijuana							
White[1]	4.5	12.5	6.8	1.7	5.9	2.7	4.2
Black[1]	5.8	9.2	9.9	2.7	8.2	3.4	5.6
Hispanic[1]	6.7	7.8	4.1	2.9	5.9	3.4	4.7
Asian/Pacific Islander	1.6	3.1	3.2	0.3	2.2	0.9	1.5
Cocaine							
White[1]	0.3	1.6	0.9	0.2	0.7	0.3	0.5
Black[1]	0.3	1.3	1.8	1.4	2.0	0.7	1.3
Hispanic[1]	1.0	2.1	1.1	0.7	1.5	0.7	1.1
Asian/Pacific Islander	0.1	1.2	0.2	*	0.6	0.1	0.3
Alcohol							
White[1]	19.2	65.3	66.3	51.5	59.7	46.2	52.7
Black[1]	13.1	45.0	54.5	35.5	46.6	30.4	37.6
Hispanic[1]	17.5	49.9	56.0	47.1	58.2	32.9	45.6
Asian/Pacific Islander	10.5	38.4	36.9	34.6	39.3	27.8	33.3
Heavy alcohol							
White[1]	4.0	23.8	25.2	25.4	33.1	13.9	23.2
Black[1]	3.8	15.5	28.3	17.9	26.8	10.1	17.6
Hispanic[1]	4.9	19.0	20.1	18.7	26.8	7.5	17.2
Asian/Pacific Islander	0.5	2.1	1.7	0.7	2.1	0.2	1.1
Cigarettes							
White[1]	11.0	32.7	31.1	23.4	26.9	22.8	24.7
Black[1]	4.0	16.3	30.5	28.0	22.7	23.9	23.4
Hispanic[1]	8.4	25.5	24.8	21.5	25.0	17.3	21.2
Asian/Pacific Islander	4.8	20.7	21.1	16.7	23.7	10.6	16.9

*Low precision, no estimate reported.
SOURCE: National Household Survey on Drug Abuse, Substance Abuse and Mental Health Services Administration, 1993.

These decreases in the prevalence rates of alcohol and other drug use among Hispanics age 35 years and older does not mean that problems[8] associated with such usage do not persist after discontinuing alcohol and other drug use. Further, Table 1 indicates that Hispanic males have much higher prevalence rates of past-month alcohol, cocaine, marijuana, heavy alcohol, and cigarette use than do Hispanic females.

Past-year prevalence rates for alcohol, heavy alcohol, marijuana, cocaine, and cigarette use among Hispanics as well as White non-Hispanic and Black persons are similar to those reported for past-month use for each of these drugs. For example, data from the 1993 NHSDA indicate that past-year marijuana use among Hispanics was 9.6 percent, compared to 8.8 percent for White non-Hispanics, 10.4 percent for blacks (Substance Abuse and Mental Health Administration, 1994a).[9]

Analysis of data from the 1993 NHSDA on the prevalence of past-month alcohol, heavy alcohol, marijuana, cocaine, and cigarette use among Hispanics by age, sex, and specific Hispanic sub-groups, as presented in Table 2, indicates that persons of Central American ancestry had the lowest prevalence of past-month use for these drugs across age and sex groupings. Among persons belonging to the other Hispanic sub-groups, as also presented in Table 2, Puerto Ricans had the highest prevalence of past-month cocaine use (1.5 percent, compared with 1.3 for all Hispanic) and cigarettes use (28.8 percent compared with 22.4 percent for all Hispanic) and both Puerto Ricans and persons of South American ancestry had the highest prevalence of past-month marijuana use (5.3 percent, compared to 4.3 for all Hispanic). For past-month alcohol use, persons of South American ancestry had the highest prevalence rates (57.3 percent, compared with 46.0 percent for all Hispanics), and persons of Mexican ancestry reported the highest prevalence of past-month heavy alcohol use (6.9 percent, compared with 5.5 percent for all Hispanics).

It should be noted, as presented in Table 2, that the trends for past-month alcohol, heavy alcohol, marijuana, cocaine, and cigarette use by age for persons of Hispanic ancestry are similar to those of other racial/ethnic groups. The use of alcohol, marijuana, and cocaine diminishes significantly by age 35 and older among all the Hispanic sub-groups, with the most dramatic decline reported in the use of marijuana among persons of South American ancestry. The data from the 1993 NHSDA indicate that the prevalence of past-month marijuana use among persons of South American ancestry aged 12-17 was 7.4 percent and among such persons aged 35 and older, 1.3 percent. Data from the 1993 NHSDA also indicate that Hispanic women, like women from other ethnic/racial groups, reported lower prevalence of past-month alcohol, heavy alcohol, marijuana, co-

TABLE 2. Prevalence of past-month drug use among Hispanics in the United States, by age and sex: 1991-93 (in percentages).

Type of drug	12-17	18-26	26-34	35+	Male	Female	Total
Marijuana							
Hispanic	5.4	8.3	4.6	2.0	5.6	2.9	4.3
Puerto Rican	7.0	10.7	7.5	2.1	6.8	4.0	5.3
Mexican	5.1	7.7	3.8	2.5	5.7	2.7	4.3
Cuban	5.5	9.5	*	0.6	6.3	1.4	3.7
Central American	3.2	3.6	0.9	*	2.2	0.8	1.4
South American	7.4	6.2	2.5	1.3	4.7	1.7	3.2
Other	5.6	16.5	7.3	2.1	5.5	5.2	5.3
Cocaine							
Hispanic	1.2	2.2	1.8	0.7	1.7	0.9	1.3
Puerto Rican	1.5	1.6	3.2	0.7	2.4	0.8	1.5
Mexican	1.3	2.5	1.7	1.0	1.9	1.1	1.5
Cuban	0.2	0.9	2.1	0.4	1.3	0.3	0.8
Central American	0.5	1.6	*	*	0.9	*	0.4
South American	0.7	*	1.7	*	0.9	0.2	0.5
Other	0.6	3.0	2.4	*	1.1	0.9	1.0
Alcohol							
Hispanic	18.7	51.7	56.4	46.6	58.1	33.9	46.0
Puerto Rican	19.0	42.5	57.5	45.0	54.0	34.6	43.5
Mexican	18.5	54.7	56.4	48.1	59.0	33.7	47.0
Cuban	13.2	54.3	65.3	43.9	59.1	35.8	46.6
Central American	11.7	31.9	40.7	38.5	48.8	23.5	34.6
South American	29.7	64.6	67.2	56.5	67.5	47.1	57.3
Other	20.4	51.8	59.5	44.4	58.9	34.0	45.6
Heavy alcohol							
Hispanic	1.9	7.5	6.9	5.0	9.5	1.5	5.5
Puerto Rican	0.7	7.0	6.7	3.0	7.3	1.2	4.0
Mexican	2.3	7.9	8.2	7.3	11.6	1.7	6.9
Cuban	0.4	6.8	3.4	2.3	5.2	0.8	2.8
Central American	0.5	2.8	2.3	2.2	4.6	0.3	2.2
South American	*	6.6	2.4	2.1	5.4	0.7	3.0
Other	1.5	11.0	6.6	2.7	6.8	2.2	4.4
Cigarettes							
Hispanic	8.2	24.8	25.9	24.0	27.3	17.5	22.4
Puerto Rican	10.3	34.7	33.7	30.3	32.7	25.5	28.8
Mexican	8.3	24.1	25.4	25.0	27.6	16.6	22.4
Cuban	5.2	19.8	23.6	23.2	28.2	16.2	21.8
Central American	2.7	11.7	15.8	11.0	19.0	5.8	11.6
South American	9.7	29.1	25.9	26.1	28.8	20.5	24.6
Other	7.4	29.7	27.8	17.4	21.8	18.1	19.9

*Low precision, no estimate reported.
SOURCE: National Household Survey on Drug Abuse, Substance Abuse and Mental Health Services Administration, 1991-93.

caine, and cigarette use when compared with men. For example, past-month heavy alcohol use, as presented in Table 2, was considerably lower among Hispanic women than among Hispanic men (respectively, 1.5 percent and 9.5 percent for the two groups). On the other hand, there were variations in the prevalence of past-month alcohol use, heavy alcohol, marijuana, cocaine and cigarette use among women belonging to the various Hispanic sub-groups. For instance, data from the 1993 NHSDA, as presented in Table 2, indicate that of past-month marijuana, cocaine, alcohol, heavy alcohol, and cigarette use, past-month cigarette use had the greatest range in prevalence. Prevalence rates among the sub-groups of Hispanic women ranged from 5.8 percent for women of Central American ancestry to 25.5 percent for women of Puerto Rican ancestry.

In summary, the 1993 NHSDA indicates that alcohol use continues to be the drug most often use by Hispanics and persons from the other ethnic/racial groups. This survey also indicates that marijuana and cocaine use appears to be a more serious problem for Hispanics and Blacks than for White, non-Hispanic persons. Cocaine use particularly appears to be a much more serious problem for Hispanics aged 12-17 than for either Black or White, non-Hispanic persons aged 12-17. Moreover, the 1993 NHSDA indicates that persons of Puerto Rican and South American ancestry have a higher prevalence of marijuana use than do persons from the other Hispanic sub-groups, and Puerto Ricans have a higher prevalence of cocaine use than do persons from all the other Hispanic sub-groups. On the other hand, persons of Mexican and South American Ancestry seem to have a higher prevalence of alcohol use than do persons from other Hispanic sub-groups. Finally, data from the 1993 NHSDA continue to indicate that Hispanic males use alcohol, marijuana, cocaine, and cigarettes more frequently than do Hispanic females. However, data from the 1993 NHSDA also indicate that the prevalence rate for the use of the above-mentioned drugs is narrowing among Hispanic males and females age 12-17.

ATTITUDES AND PERCEPTIONS ABOUT ALCOHOL AND OTHER DRUG USE AMONG HISPANICS

A possible explanation for the higher prevalence of marijuana and cocaine use among Hispanics than among White non-Hispanics or Asian/Pacific Islanders is the perceived ease of obtaining drugs in their communities and their perception of the prevalence of drug dealing activities in their communities. Data from the 1991, 1992, and 1993 NHSDA, presented in Table 3, indicate that both Hispanic and Black persons reported a

TABLE 3. Percentage reporting that obtaining drugs is fairly easy or very easy, by age and race/ethnicity: 1991-93.

Drug of use and race/ethnicity	Age (years)												Total		
	12-17			18-25			26-64			36+					
	1991	1992	1993	1991	1992	1993	1991	1992	1993	1991	1992	1993	1991	1992	1993
Marijuana															
White	53.3	50.0	1.5	81.0	79.5	80.1	76.0[1]	72.2	73.1	55.5[1]	52.6	50.3	62.5[2]	59.4	58.2
Black	57.3	58.2	59.6	79.6	79.5	75.4	70.2	69.9	67.4	63.8	58.6	60.0	67.0	64.3	64.0
Hispanic	53.3	49.5[1]	56.0	66.2	67.7	64.8	62.1	60.6	61.2	53.4[2]	45.9	44.5	57.9[1]	53.9	54.0
Other	45.9	44.6	41.1	62.3	60.6	*	54.8[1]	45.4	36.8	32.6	43.0	31.7	44.2	46.5	37.7
Cocaine or crack cocaine															
White	30.9	28.0	29.2	48.5[1]	46.4	43.7	51.9[2]	46.4	45.3	38.0[1]	35.1	33.8	41.3[2]	38.0	36.6
Black	56.4	56.1	52.6	73.2[1]	74.5[2]	66.6	65.8	66.5	64.8	59.0	52.3	55.7	62.5	59.4	58.9
Hispanic	39.1	36.7	35.1	51.3	49.0	47.9	49.3	46.6	48.6	42.5[1]	33.7	35.8	45.3[1]	40.1	41.1
Other	30.7	31.3	20.1	40.2	28.5	30.8	32.8	28.6	28.0	25.5	22.6	*	30.3	25.6	24.4
Heroin															
White	21.1	20.1	19.7	20.7[2]	23.3	22.2	25.6	25.6	23.9	28.8[1]	25.6	25.1	26.4	24.8	24.0
Black	32.2	32.1	29.0	40.0	41.1[2]	32.5	40.2	43.4	39.1	44.2[1]	38.5	37.4	41.0[2]	39.0	35.7
Hispanic	25.3	23.7	24.7	33.4	31.0	30.2	31.3	30.8	34.0	33.9[2]	26.1	26.5	32.0	27.8	28.7
Other	16.5	21.2	11.8	23.6	17.0	18.0	16.6	18.5	22.0	18.8	18.6	*	18.9	18.6	18.2

* Low precision, no estimate reported.
[1] Difference between estimate in this cell and corresponding estimate for 1993 is statistically significant at the .05 level.
[2] Difference between estimate in this cell and corresponding estimate for 1993 is statistically significant at the .01 level.
SOURCE: 1991-93 National Household Survey on Drug Abuse, Substance Abuse and Mental Health Services Administration, preliminary data, June 1994.

greater ease in obtaining cocaine and heroin in their neighborhoods than did White non-Hispanic persons (Substance Abuse and Mental Health Administration, 1994a). These data also indicate that Hispanic and Black youth aged 12-17 reported a greater ease in obtaining marijuana, cocaine, and heroin in their neighborhoods than did White non-Hispanic youth aged 12-17. However, Blacks of all age categories reported greater ease in obtaining marijuana, cocaine, and heroin in their neighborhoods than did either Hispanic or White non-Hispanic persons.

On the other hand, data presented in Table 3 indicate that the rate at which White, non-Hispanic persons perceived the ease of obtaining marijuana in their neighborhoods was greater than the rate at which Hispanics perceived that ease. Overall, data presented in Table 3, indicate that persons of all racial/ethnic groups perceived obtaining drugs to be more difficult in 1993 than in 1991. Among Hispanics, there was a statistically significant decline in the perception of the ease of obtaining marijuana, cocaine, crack-cocaine, and heroin between 1991 and 1992. These declines were most notable among Hispanic persons aged 35 and older.

The frequency of drug dealing activities in Hispanic neighborhoods, as shown by the NHSDA data from 1992 and 1993 presented in Table 4, suggest that Hispanics were three times more likely than White non-Hispanic persons to have seen the illicit sale of drugs in their neighborhoods (Substance Abuse and Mental Health Administration, 1994a). However, as also presented in Table 4, Blacks were more likely than either Hispanics or White non-Hispanics to have seen the sale of illicit drugs in their neighborhoods. Similarly, data presented in Table 5 from the 1992 and 1993 NHSDA on persons reporting the occasional[10] or more frequent observation of people seeing people drunk or high in their neighborhoods indicate that Blacks were more likely than either Hispanics or White non-Hispanics to report such observations. More than half of all Blacks reported seeing someone drunk or high (53.2 percent in 1992 and 51.2 percent in 1993), followed by Hispanics (42.4 percent in 1992 and 43.0 percent in 1993) and White non-Hispanics (30.8 percent in 1992 and 28.4 percent in 1993).

In summary, the data presented in this paper suggest that while the attitudes and perceptions of Hispanics toward the availability of alcohol, marijuana, cocaine, and heroin in their community play a significant role in the drug using behavior of Hispanics of all ages, other factors may contribute to this behavior. Hispanics have a lower rate of perception than do White non-Hispanics of the ease of obtaining marijuana in their neighborhoods; nevertheless, the prevalence of past-month marijuana use is higher among Hispanics than White non-Hispanic persons. These data

TABLE 4. Percentage reporting seeing people selling drugs in the neighborhood occasionally or more often, by age, sex, and race/ethnicity: 1992-93.

| | Age (years) | | | | | | | | Total | |
| | 12-17 | | 18-25 | | 26-34 | | 35+ | | | |
Race/ethnicity and sex	1992	1993	1992	1993	1992	1993	1992	1993	1992	1993
Total	14.6	14.7	19.0	18.6	14.9	14.2	9.7	8.1	12.4	11.3
Race/Ethnicity										
White	7.4	7.8	12.5	12.9	9.9	9.5	6.5[1]	4.4	8.0	6.7
Black	41.2	42.7	48.1	45.6	39.3	35.8	31.2	33.2	37.0	37.0
Hispanic	23.9	22.2	27.7	28.3	23.4	22.7	19.4	17.6	22.5	21.1
Other	10.0	9.4	9.9	*	10.2	*	5.5	4.3	7.6	7.3
Sex										
Male	14.8	14.9	20.0	19.5	16.2	14.5	9.3	8.2	12.7	11.7
Female	14.4	14.4	18.0	17.8	13.7	13.9	10.1	8.0	12.2	10.9

*Low precision, no estimate reported.
[1]Difference between estimate in this cell and corresponding estimate for 1993 is statistically significant at the .05 level.

SOURCE: 1992-93 National Household Survey on Drug Abuse, Substance Abuse and Mental Health Services Administration, preliminary data, June 1994.

TABLE 5. Percentage reporting seeing people who are drunk or high on drugs in the neighborhood occasionally or more often, by age, sex, and race/ethnicity: 1992-93.

	Age (years)									
	12-17		18-26		26-34		35+		Total	
Race/Ethnicity and Sex	1992	1993	1992	1993	1992	1993	1992	1993	1992	1993
Total	38.7	40.9	48.5	47.6	38.2	37.6	28.8[1]	25.2	34.2	32.1
Race/Ethnicity										
White	34.2	36.5	46.0	45.7	35.1	34.9	25.8[1]	21.9	30.8	28.4
Black	55.7	58.4	64.4[1]	58.2	53.6	50.9	46.6	47.0	53.2	51.2
Hispanic	43.5	46.7	48.3	52.2	44.7	42.8	38.4	38.0	42.4	43.0
Other	37.0	37.0	38.1	33.4	30.2	*	25.6	18.8	29.8	26.1
Sex										
Male	36.4	39.1	50.0	49.5	41.9	40.2	29.8	26.2	35.6	33.5
Female	41.1	42.8	47.1	45.7	34.6	35.0	27.9	24.4	32.9	30.8

*Low precision, no estimate reported.
[1]Difference between estimate in this cell and corresponding estimate for 1993 is statistically significant at the .05 level.
SOURCE: 1992-93 National Household Survey on Drug Abuse, Substance Abuse and Mental Health Services Administration, preliminary data, June 1994.

may suggest that greater access to marijuana and other drugs is not as important a factor in determining marijuana use among Hispanics than among White non-Hispanics. Upon further investigation, it is possible that other factors not examined by the NHSDA surveys such as socioeconomic status, familial and social support systems, religious affiliation, accultura- tion related stress, cultural values and factors such as "machismo,"[11] "marianismo,"[12] "respeto,"[13] "confianza"[14] and "dignidad"[15] and gen- eral attitudes toward the use of marijuana and other illicit drugs may prove as significant in influencing drug use behaviors as the perceptions of Hispanics toward the use of marijuana and other illicit drugs in their communities.

PREVALENCE OF ALCOHOL AND OTHER DRUG USE AMONG HISPANIC YOUTH

A general overview of the prevalence of marijuana, crack-cocaine, alcohol, and heavy alcohol use among Hispanic youth from the 1993-94 Monitoring the Future Study (MTF)[16] is presented in Table 6. Data on White non-Hispanic, Black, and Hispanic youth indicate that Hispanic 8th graders had the highest lifetime prevalence rates for alcohol, cocaine, marijuana, cigarette, and daily alcohol use. But with the exception of crack-cocaine use, White non-Hispanic 12th graders had the highest prev- alence rates for drugs surveyed (Johnston et al., 1995). Among 8th grad- ers, 23.3 percent of Hispanic students reported the use of marijuana in their lifetime, compared with 12.9 percent of White non-Hispanic students and 13.2 percent of Black students. For crack-cocaine use, the lifetime prevalence for Hispanic 8th graders was 7.5 percent, which compares to 2.7 percent for White non-Hispanic and 1.4 percent for Black 8th graders. For lifetime cigarette use, the prevalence for Hispanic 8th graders was 54.2 percent, compared with 46.0 percent for White non-Hispanic and 37.1 percent for Black 8th graders. For alcohol use, the lifetime prevalence rate for Hispanic 8th graders was 63.3 percent, compared to 55.1 for Black and 54.7 for White non-Hispanic 8th graders (Johnston et al., 1995).

As also presented in Table 6, data for 30-day drug use, that is, drug use in the past month, indicate that 1.3 percent of Hispanic 8th graders and 0.4 percent of White non-Hispanic 8th graders had used crack-cocaine, which compares with a 0.3 percent rate of use for Black 8th graders (Johnston et al., 1995). For marijuana use, the 30-day prevalence rate for Hispanic 8th graders was 12.1 percent, compared to 5.6 percent for White non-Hispanic and 5.0 percent for Black 8th graders. Similarly, a higher percentage of Hispanic 8th graders had used alcohol during the 30 days prior to their

TABLE 6. Prevalence of lifetime, annual, 30-day, and daily prevalence of use of selected drugs, by race/ethnicity, for 8th, 10th, and 12th graders: 1994 (in percentages).[a]

Grade	Marijuana 8th	10th	12th	Crack-cocaine 8th	10th	12th	Alcohol 8th	10th	12th	5+ drinks[b] 8th	10th	12th	Cigarettes 8th	10th	12th
Lifetime															
White	12.9	27.2	38.3	1.7	1.8	2.8	54.7	72.0	83.1	-	-	-	46.0	58.9	65.6
Black	13.2	22.1	29.4	1.1	1.0	1.2	55.1	68.1	71.4	-	-	-	37.1	39.6	44.4
Hispanic	23.3	33.5	36.6	1.2	3.5	4.1	63.3	72.7	80.4	-	-	-	54.2	56.5	61.7
Annual															
White	10.0	22.6	30.2	1.0	1.1	1.6	46.6	65.4	76.6	-	-	-	-	-	-
Black	8.9	15.3	20.7	0.5	0.8	0.9	40.7	56.2	59.8	-	-	-	-	-	-
Hispanic	18.1	25.1	26.7	2.1	1.9	2.4	54.2	63.2	71.7	-	-	-	-	-	-
30-day															
White	5.6	13.4	18.4	0.4	0.5	0.6	25.3	40.4	54.0	-	-	-	18.9	27.8	35.2
Black	5.0	9.8	13.1	0.3	0.5	0.7	19.4	29.7	33.8	-	-	-	8.7	9.8	10.9
Hispanic	12.1	15.6	14.9	1.3	0.7	1.2	33.0	37.7	45.9	-	-	-	21.3	19.4	23.6
Daily															
White	0.4	1.6	3.2	-	-	-	0.8	1.6	3.1	12.0	24.5	31.5	9.7	16.5	22.9
Black	0.4	0.8	2.0	-	-	-	1.2	1.2	2.6	11.8	14.0	14.4	2.6	3.8	4.9
Hispanic	1.1	1.9	2.0	-	-	-	1.7	1.8	3.8	22.3	24.2	24.3	9.0	8.1	10.6

-Data not available

Note: The following sample sizes are based on the 1993 and 1994 surveys combined:

Sample Sizes	8th Grade	10th Grade	12th Grade
White	20,900	22,000	21,800
Black	5,500	3,300	3,600
Hispanic	4,000	2,800	3100

[a]Data from two years have been combined to increase sub-group sample sizes
[b]This measure refers to use of five or more drinks in a row in the past two weeks.
SOURCE: The Monitoring the Future Study, the University of Michigan.

32

interview (33.5 percent), followed by White non-Hispanic (25.3 percent) and Black 8th graders (19.4 percent).

The 30-day prevalence rate for cigarette use among Hispanic 8th graders was also higher at 21.3 percent than it was for either White non-Hispanic 8th graders at 18.9 percent or Black 8th graders at 8.7 percent. On the other hand, past-month alcohol, marijuana, heavy alcohol, and cigarette use was higher among White non-Hispanic 12th graders than among Hispanic and non-Hispanic 12th graders. For example, past-month marijuana use was higher among White non-Hispanic 12th graders at a rate of 18.4 percent than it was among Hispanic 12th graders at 14.9 percent. Black 8th and 12th graders had the lowest 30-day prevalence in the use of each of these drugs. The MTF studies also indicate that the prevalence of past-month alcohol use approximately doubled from 25.3 to 54.0 percent between 8th grade and 12th grade among White non-Hispanic students, from 19.4 to 33.8 percent for Black students, and 33.5 to 45.9 percent for Hispanic students (Johnston et al., 1995).

Further, the results from the MTF study presented in Table 6 on daily alcohol, heavy alcohol, and marijuana use, indicate that Hispanic 8th graders had higher prevalence rates than White, non-Hispanic 8th graders and Black 8th graders (Johnston et al., 1995). For marijuana use, the daily prevalence rate for Hispanic 8th graders was double that of White non-Hispanic and Black 8th graders (1.1 percent, 0.4 percent, and 0.4 percent, respectively). As also documented in Table 6, daily alcohol use was also higher among Hispanic 8th, 10th, and 12th graders than White non-Hispanic 8th, 10th, and 12th graders, and Black 8th, 10th, and 12th graders. Moreover, data on heavy alcohol use, that is, the consumption on one occasion of five or more drinks during the prior two weeks, indicate that Hispanic 8th graders at a rate of 22.3 percent were more likely to have drunk heavily than were either White non-Hispanic 8th graders at 12.9 percent or Black 8th graders at 11.8 percent. On the other hand, daily cigarette use was higher among White non-Hispanic 8th graders than among either Hispanic or Black 8th graders (respectively, 9.7 percent, 9.0 percent, and 2.6 percent). Data on daily cocaine use was not available.

Similarly, 22.9 percent of White non-Hispanic 12th graders smoked cigarettes daily, compared with 10.6 percent of Hispanic and 4.9 percent of Black 12th graders (Johnston et al., 1995). For daily marijuana, alcohol, and heavy alcohol use, as documented in Table 6, the prevalence was also higher among White non-Hispanic 12th graders than Hispanic and Black 12 graders. For example, 31.5 percent of White non-Hispanic and 24.3 percent of Hispanic 12th graders reported daily heavy alcohol use, compared with only 14.4 percent of Black 12th graders. As with Hispanic adult users the prevalence rates for past-month alcohol, heavy alcohol, marijuana, cigarette and crack cocaine use were consistently lower among Hispanic 8th, 10th, and 12th grade females than Hispanic 8th, 10th, and 12th grade males.[17] Lifetime and daily use of alcohol, heavy alcohol, marijuana, cigarette, and cocaine was also lower among Hispanic females in the 8th, 10th, and 12th grade than among Hispanic males in the same grades (Johnston et al., 1995).

Trend data from the MTF study on drug use among 12th graders, as presented in Figures 1 and 2, indicate that the prevalence for annual marijuana, cocaine, heavy alcohol, and daily cigarette use, generally moved in parallel fashion. This trend data is particularly apparent during the long decline phase for Hispanics, White non-Hispanics, and Black students alike (Johnston et al., in press). As presented in Figure 1, these trend data also indicate that since 1993, there has been a sharp increase in the annual use of marijuana among 12th graders regardless of sex or race/ethnicity; the steepest increase occurred among Black 12th graders. Among 8th and 10th graders,[18] there also has been a sharp increase in the annual use of marijuana among all three racial/ethnic groups. While Hispanic 8th and 10 graders continue to have the highest annual rate of marijuana use, the sharpest upturn since 1993 in the annual rate of marijuana use among 8th and 10th graders has been among Black students (Johnston et al., in press).

Conversely, data presented in Figure 1 indicate that while there was a significant rise in the annual rate of cocaine use among Hispanics 12th graders from 1984-86, there have been in subsequent years a steady decline and stabilization in the use of this drug for Hispanic 12th graders (Johnston et al., in press). For White non-Hispanic 12th graders, the annual rate of cocaine use over the past 18 years has been lower than that of Hispanic 12th graders, but parallel to the same pattern of increase and decline found among Hispanics. For Black 12th graders, the decline in the annual rate of cocaine use was earlier and has remained lower since 1983. Among 8th and 10th graders,[19] the annual rate of cocaine use in the last two years has risen most among Hispanics, whereas over the same period of time, annual cocaine use has risen relatively modestly among White non-Hispanic and least among Black 8th and 10th graders (Johnston et al., in press).

Trend data for heavy alcohol use among 12th graders, as presented in Figure 2, indicate that the prevalence rates for heavy alcohol use have been consistently lower among Hispanics in the last 18 years than the prevalence rates of White non-Hispanics, but higher than the prevalence rates of Black 12th graders. Figure 2 also indicates that during the 1980s,

FIGURE 1

Trends in Annual Prevalence of Marijuana and Cocaine Use
for Twelfth Graders
by Race/Ethnicity
(Two-year moving average*)

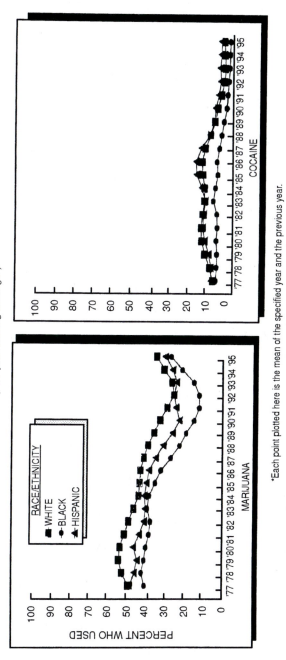

*Each point plotted here is the mean of the specified year and the previous year.

Source: National Survey Results on Drug Abuse from the "Monitoring the Future Study, 1975-1995. (In Press)"

35

FIGURE 2

Trends in Prevalence of 5 or More Drinks in a Row in the Past 2 Weeks and Daily Use of Cigarettes for Twelfth Graders

by Race/Ethnicity

(Two-year moving average*)

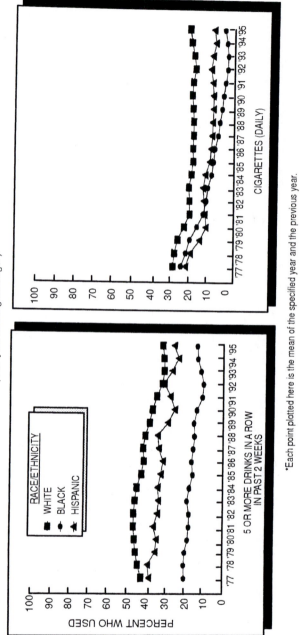

*Each point plotted here is the mean of the specified year and the previous year.

Source: National Survey Results on Drug Abuse from the "Monitoring the Future Study, 1975-1995. (In Press)"

36

there was a gradual decline in heavy alcohol use among Hispanic 12th graders as well White non-Hispanic and Black 12th graders. However, since 1994 there has been a steady increase in the prevalence of heavy alcohol use among Hispanic 12th graders while the rates for White non-Hispanic and Black 12th graders have remained stable during the same time. Among 8th graders,[20] there has been a steady increase of heavy alcohol use among all three racial/ethnic groups, but at the 10th grade level the rate for Blacks has been declining slowly while the rates for Hispanics and White non-Hispanics have been increasing gradually (Johnston et al., in press).

Trend data from the MTF study on daily cigarette smoking among 12th graders, as presented in Figure 2, indicate differential trends for all three racial/ethnic groups. For Hispanics and Black 12th graders, the declines between 1977 and 1981 were sharper than among White non-Hispanic 12th graders. Since then, the daily smoking rates of Hispanic and White non-Hispanic 12th graders have remained quite level while that of Black 12th graders have shown a consistent decline (Johnston et al., in press).

In summary, the findings presented here indicate that the youth at highest risk for using drugs were Hispanic 8th graders, youth who are usually 14 years of age and thus at a point in their lives for the completion of critical developmental tasks that involve major psychological and physical changes. Particularly disturbing were the high prevalence rates of daily heavy alcohol and past-month cocaine use among Hispanic 8th graders; these prevalence rates almost double the rates reported for White non-Hispanic and Black 8th graders. With respect to the higher rates of alcohol and other drug use among White non-Hispanic 12th graders than among Hispanic 12th graders, one may argue that these differences in respective rates may reflect the significantly higher incidence of high school dropouts[21] among Hispanics than among their White non-Hispanic or Black peers. According to U.S. Census Bureau data from 1993, the overall high school dropout rate for Hispanics nationwide was 27.5, compared to 13.6 for Blacks and 7.9 percent for White non-Hispanics (U.S. Census Bureau, unpublished data, October 1993). This higher rate of dropping out of high school may be explained by the possibility that many more Hispanic 8th graders than White non-Hispanic 8th graders who use drugs drop out of high school before reaching the 12th grade. If this circumstance were the case, it would skew the findings on 12th graders reported by the MTF study. One may even be able to argue that the percentage of Hispanic 12th graders who use alcohol and other drugs may be higher than that of White, non-Hispanic 12th graders, if the higher percentage of Hispanic 8th graders who use drugs and drop out from school is factored into the analysis of the MTF study data on the prevalence of alcohol and other drug use among 12th graders.

Other important results reported in this paper indicate that the prevalence of alcohol and other drug use is on the rise for all the three racial/ethnic groups. The dramatic rise in marijuana use since 1993 among Hispanics, White non-Hispanics, and Black high school students is troublesome given the importance that marijuana use has been shown to play as a gateway to other illicit drug use (Kandel et al., 1978). This increase in marijuana use points to the need to redouble the nation's effort to prevent youngsters from using marijuana which, in turn, may influence their use of other illicit drugs, such as cocaine and heroin. The data from the MTF study also indicate that Hispanic male high school students have a higher prevalence of alcohol and other drug use than Hispanic female high school students.

RISKY BEHAVIOR PRACTICES OF HISPANIC YOUTH WHO USE DRUGS

Many researchers have suggested the use of alcohol and other drug poses serious physical and mental health problems for youth which can affect their general well-being. Information obtained from the 1992 Youth Risk Behavior Survey[22] (YRBS) conducted by the Centers from Disease Control and Prevention (CDC) of the U.S. Government indicates that many high school students who use drugs are also involved more often than their peers who do not use alcohol and other drugs in other risk-taking behaviors. Examples of these other risk-taking behaviors include involvement in fights, sex with multiple partners, and riding in a car while the driver is under the influence of alcohol (CDC, 1992). Comparison of data from the YRBS, as presented in Table 7, indicate that youth, regardless of racial/ethnic background, who had used marijuana and cocaine in the 30 days prior to their interview had consistently higher patterns of risk-taking behaviors than youth who had not used marijuana.

As also presented in Table 7, among Hispanics, the highest rate of risk-taking behavior reported was among youth[23] who had used cocaine in the past 30 days and the lowest risk-taking behavior rate was among youth who had not used marijuana in the past 30 days (CDC, 1992). For example, 61.5 percent of Hispanic youth who used cocaine in the prior 30 days carried a concealed weapon compared to only 13.5 percent of Hispanic youth who had not used cocaine in the previous 30 days. Among Hispanics who used cocaine in the prior 30 days, 44.3 percent reported having multiple sex partners during the three months preceding their interview compared to 10.6 percent of the Hispanic youth who had not used cocaine.

TABLE 7. Proportion of youth engaging in risk behaviors, by past 30 days marijuana and cocaine users and nonusers by race and ethnicity: 1992 Youth Risk Behavior Survey (in percentages).

Drug, type of use, and race/ethnicity	Fight in last 12 months	Carried a weapon in last 30 days	Rarely wears seatbelt	Multiple sex partners during last 3 months	Ridden in car while driver is drinking	Used drugs or alcohol before last sexual encounter	Used no condom during last sexual encounter
Marijuana							
Used Last 30 days							
White	54.1	26.4	28.8	29.6	62.5	31.4	57.8
Black	70.0	42.5	45.6	53.7	60.8	36.4	54.9
Hispanic	66.8	42.8	34.3	39.2	61.7	33.2	63.3
Other	64.5	21.9	29.1	30.4[1]	56.8	36.9	59.3
No Use Last 30 Days							
White	34.3	13.3	15.1	6.9	20.3	5.1	55.6
Black	47.1	13.1	19.6	18.3	22.9	4.3	39.1
Hispanic	37.1	11.3	17.9	7.6	20.1	3.9	54.4
Other	32.3	9.9	14.0	9.2	14.9	3.5	46.4
Cocaine							
Used last 30 days							
White	63.6	44.7	48.0	41.8	79.2	4	70.7
Black	84.8	46.1	54.6	55.8	90.9	4.7	52.7
Hispanic	66.2	61.5	34.6*	44.3	88.2	76.6	66.3
Other	-	46.7[1]	*	-	30.5[1]	47.6	*
No use last 30 days							
White	38.3	14.4	16.4	9.7	24.5	7.7	55.8
Black	48.8	15.0	21.5	21.7	25.3	6.2	40.9
Hispanic	39.2	13.5	19.3	10.6	23.3	5.9	55.6
Other	33.2	10.7	14.5	10.3	16.6	5.0	47.0

[1]Based on five or fewer respondents in numerator.
*Low precision, no estimate reported. - No respondents.
SOURCE: National Health Interview Survey, Youth Risk Behavior Survey, Centers for Disease Control and Prevention, 1993.

Table 7 documents similar patterns of risk-taking behavior for White non-Hispanic and Black youth who had used cocaine or marijuana during the previous 30 days.

Nevertheless, the data from the 1992 YRBS, as presented in Table 7, indicate that Hispanic youth who used cocaine and marijuana during the prior 30 days were more likely than White non-Hispanic youth to engage in risk-taking behaviors. Of particular note is the much higher percentage of Hispanic youth than either White non-Hispanic or Black youth who had used cocaine and carried a weapon in the prior 30 days. However, the 1992 YRBS data also shows that Black youth had the highest rate of risk-taking behaviors far surpassing those of White non-Hispanic youth (CDC, 1992).

The findings from the 1992 YRBS are disturbing. The data from this survey indicate that Hispanic as well as non-Hispanic youth who use marijuana or cocaine are involved in significantly more risk-taking behaviors than their peers who do not use marijuana or cocaine. Of particular concern are the findings regarding the availability of weapons among Hispanic youth who use marijuana or cocaine given the documented relationship between the availability of guns and the higher rate of drug-related homicides among Hispanic youth who live in inner-city communities (Rodriguez and Brindis, 1995). The 1992 YRBS data suggest that without a reduction of drug use among Hispanic youth, the use of guns in drug-related homicides will remain high. Given that youth who practice unsafe sex are at much higher risk of becoming infected with HIV and the consequent development of AIDS, the risk-taking sexual practices of Hispanic, Black, and White non-Hispanic youth who use cocaine and marijuana are equally disturbing. Finally, the data from this survey suggest that while Black youth generally have the lowest rate of marijuana and cocaine use, they are more likely than Hispanic or White non-Hispanic youth to be affected negatively by their use of these drugs.

CONSEQUENCES ASSOCIATED WITH DRUG ABUSE AMONG HISPANICS

Alcohol and drug abuse has been associated with many negative health-related consequences, including fatal and non-fatal overdose, HIV infection and AIDS, and other sexually transmitted diseases. In particular, illicit drug use has been found to be closely linked to the drug-related criminal activities of drug-involved offenders (Golub et al., 1995). Research also has found that alcohol and drug use increases the risk of accidents and injuries, complications of pregnancy, adverse birth outcomes such as low birth weight and birth defects, and suicide and other psychiatric problems among those who are habitual users (National Center for Health Statistics, 1994). It should be noted that these results of a linkage between drug use and many of its negative consequences are based primarily on case studies or case reports. Not many methodologically sound, epidemiologic case-control or prospective studies have been conducted in any of the White non-Hispanic, Hispanic, and Black populations (Collins, 1992). Yet evidence exists that Hispanics and Blacks may be overrepresented among those who are negatively affected by the adverse consequences of drug abuse (Arkin and Funkhouser, 1990, National Center for Health Statistics, 1994).

ACQUIRED IMMUNODEFICIENCY SYNDROME

AIDS surveillance data from the CDC[24] indicate that among Hispanic women with AIDS injecting drug use, followed by heterosexual contact, is the exposure category most frequently associated with the disease (CDC, 1994). As presented in Table 8, which provides data on women with AIDS, 46 percent of Hispanic women as of June 1994 had contracted AIDS by injecting drugs, compared to 43 percent of White non-Hispanic women, 51 percent of Black women, and 47 percent of American Indian and Alaska Native women. For Asian/Pacific Islander women, the primary cause of infection with HIV was heterosexual contact (45 percent). As documented in Table 9, among Hispanic men with AIDS, the leading route of exposure as of June 1994 was homosexual contact; however, 38 percent of AIDS cases among Hispanic men and 37 percent of such cases among Black men resulted from injecting drug use; by comparison, only eight percent of White non-Hispanic men contracted HIV through this mechanism.

DRUG-RELATED EMERGENCY ROOM EPISODES AND DRUG-RELATED DEATHS AND CRIMINALITY

Data from the 1994 Drug Abuse Warning Network (DAWN),[25] as presented in Table 10, indicate alcohol-in-combination[26] was the drug most frequently mentioned by Hispanics (27 percent), followed by cocaine (25.6 percent), and heroin/morphine (23.4 percent) responsible for emergency room (ER) episodes (Substance Abuse and Mental Health Administration, 1994b). Among White non-Hispanic persons, alcohol-in-combination was also mentioned as the most frequently drug responsible for ER episodes (29.9 percent), followed by cocaine at a much lower rate than

TABLE 8. Female adult/adolescent AIDS cases, by exposure category and race/ethnicity, cumulative totals through June 1994.

Exposure	White, not Hispanic		Black, not Hispanic		Hispanic	
	No.	(%)	No.	(%)	No.	(%)
Injecting drug use	5,426	(43)	14,160	(51)	4,923	(47)
Hemophilia.coagulation disorder	58	(0)	20	(0)	8	(0)
Heterosexual contact	4,538	(36)	9,014	(33)	4,479	(43)
Receipt of blood transfusion blood components, or tissue	1,489	(12)	725	(3)	389	(4)
Risk not reported or identified	1,047	(8)	3,762	(14)	722	(7)
TOTAL	12,554	(100)	27,681	(100)	10,519	(106)

Exposure	Asian/Pacific Islander		American Indian/Alaska Native		Cumulative Totals[1]	
	No.	(%)	No.	(%)	No.	(%)
Injecting drug use	43	(16)	65	(47)	24,660	(48)
Hemophilia/coagulation disorder	1	(0)	-	-	83	(0)
Heterosexual contact	118	(45)	46	(33)	18,217	(36)
Receipt of blood transfusion, blood components, or tissue	62	(23)	10	(7)	2,676	(5)
Risk not reported or identified	41	(15)	17	(12)	5,599	(11)
TOTAL	265	(100)	138	(100)	51,235	(100)

[1]Includes 78 women whose race/ethnicity is unknown.
SOURCE: Center for Disease Control and Prevention (1994).

42

TABLE 9. Male adult/adolescent AIDS cases, by exposure category and race/ethnicity, cumulative totals through June 1994.

Exposure	White, not Hispanic		Black, not Hispanic		Hispanic	
	No.	(%)	No.	(%)	No.	(%)
Men who have sex with men	142,906	(77)	40,500	(41)	25,645	(45)
Injecting drug use	15,104	(8)	36,428	(37)	21,854	(38)
Men who have sex with men and inject drugs	13,995	(8)	7,434	(7)	3,787	(7)
Hemophilia/coagulation disorder	2,677	(1)	310	(0)	267	(0)
Heterosexual contact	2,080	(1)	4,963	(5)	1,958	(3)
Receipt of blood transfusion, blood components, or tissue	2,623	(1)	732	(1)	420	(1)
Risk not reported or identified	5,111	(3)	9,137	(9)	3,057	(5)
TOTAL	**184,496**	**(100)**	**99,502**	**(100)**	**56,988**	**(100)**

Exposure	Asian/Pacific Islander		American Indian/Alaska Native		Cumulative Totals[1]	
	No.	(%)	No.	(%)	No.	(%)
Men who have sex with men	1,898	(79)	493	(62)	211,779	(61)
Injecting drug use	103	(4)	90	(11)	73,705	(21)
Men who have sex with men and inject drugs	74	(3)	133	(17)	25,447	(7)
Hemophilia/coagulation disorder	38	(2)	22	(3)	3,321	(1)
Heterosexual contact	40	(2)	14	(2)	9,063	(3)
Receipt of blood transfusion, blood components, or tissue	79	(3)	7	(1)	3,872	(1)
Risk not reported or identified	179	(7)	30	(4)	17,589	(5)
TOTAL	**2,411**	**(100)**	**789**	**(100)**	**344,776**	**(100)**

[1]Includes 590 men whose race/ethnicity is unknown.
SOURCE: Centers for Disease Control and Prevention (1994).

TABLE 10. Drugs mentioned most frequently by emerging departments in 1992, by race/ethnicity of patient.

Rank	Drug name	Percent of total episodes	Rank	Drug name	Percent of total episodes
	White patients			*Black patients*	
1	Alcohol-in-combination	29.9	1	Cocaine	54.2
2	Cocaine	13.1	2	Alcohol-in-combination	36.4
3	Acetaminophen	9.2	3	Heroin/morphine	18.3
4	Heroin/morphine	9.2	4	Marijuana/hashish	8.0
5	Alprazolam	5.7	5	Acetaminophen	4.2
6	Marijuana/hashish	5.5	6	Ibuprofen	2.8
7	Aspirin	5.2	7	PCP/PCP combinations	2.2
8	Ibuprofen	4.5	8	Aspirin	1.9
9	Diazepam	3.8	9	Unspecified Benzodiazepine	1.2
10	Lorazepam	3.6	10	Amitriptyline	1.0
	Hispanic patients				
1	Alcohol-in-combination	27.0	6	Aspirin	3.9
2	Cocaine	25.6	7	Ibuprofen	3.6
3	Heroin/morphine	23.4	8	PCP/PCP combinations	3.3
4	Acetaminophen	8.1	9	Methamphetamine/speed	2.8
5	Marijuana/hashish	5.5	10	Alprazolam	2.2

NOTES: These estimates are based on a representative sample of non-federal hospitals with 24-hour emergency rooms in the coterminous United States. Percentages are based on weighted emergency room episode estimates of 235,643 white patients; 122,880 black patients; and 42,174 Hispanic patients.
SOURCE: Drug Abuse Warning Network, Substance Abuse and Mental Health Services Administration, April 1994 provisional data file.

Hispanics (13.1 percent). On the other hand, as documented in Table 10, among Blacks 54.2 percent of all ER episodes involved cocaine compared with 13.1 percent for White non-Hispanics and 25.6 percent for Hispanics.[27]

Regarding drug-related deaths, the 1994 DAWN data, as presented in Table 11, indicate that the drug most frequently reported for Hispanic decedents by medical examiners was heroin/morphine (60 percent, followed by cocaine at 51 percent and alcohol-in-combination at 47.7 percent) (Substance Abuse and Mental Health Administration, 1994b). Not unexpectedly, for Black decedents cocaine was the drug most frequently mentioned by medical examiners (69.9 percent), followed by heroin/morphine (45.1 percent), and alcohol-in-combination (39.7 percent). For White non-Hispanic decedents heroin was the drug most frequently mentioned by medical examiners (41.3 percent), followed by alcohol-in-combination (39.3 percent), and cocaine (32.5 percent).[28]

Other results from the 1994 DAWN indicate differences in the manner that drug-related deaths occurred among persons of Hispanic, Black, and White non-Hispanic ancestry (Substance Abuse and Mental Health Administration 1994b). As presented in Figure 3, Hispanics had the highest percentage of accidental[29] drug-related deaths (80.5 percent), followed by Blacks (62.9 percent) and White non-Hispanics (51.8 percent). On the other hand, the highest percentage of drug-related suicides was among White non-Hispanic persons (26.7 percent), compared with the relatively low percentages of drug-related suicides among Hispanics (11.1 percent) and Blacks (7.8 percent).

The relationship between drug use and crime has been widely studied by many researchers over the years (Chaiken and Chaiken, 1990). This research has concluded that drug use is inextricably linked to criminal behavior. Data from a 1989 national survey of prison inmates serving time in state prisons sponsored by the Bureau of Justice Statistics, U.S. Government[30] provides supporting evidence for the strong relationship between drug use and criminal behavior (U.S. Bureau of Justice Statistics, 1991). As presented in Table 12, Hispanic inmates in state prison were more likely than White non-Hispanic or Black inmates to be under the influence of cocaine/crack or heroin/morphine at the time of the offense, the day, or month before the criminal offense was committed. On the other hand, as Table 12 documents, White non-Hispanic state prison inmates were more likely than Black or Hispanic inmates to be under the influence of marijuana at the time of the offense, the day, or month before the criminal offense was committed.

In summary, the results emerging from the data reported in this manu-

TABLE 11. Drugs mentioned most frequently by medical examiners in 1993, by race/ethnicity of decedent.

Rank	Drug name	Percent of total Episodes
	White decedents	
1	Heroin/morphine[1]	41.3
2	Alcohol-in-combination	39.3
3	Cocaine	32.5
4	Codeine	12.3
5	Diazepam	10.5
6	Methamphetamine/speed	6.3
7	D-Propoxphene	6.2
8	Amitriptyline	6.1
9	Marijuana/hashish	5.9
10	Diphenhydramine	5.4
	Hispanic descendents	
1	Heroin/morphine[1]	60.5
2	Cocaine	51.0
3	Alcohol-in-combination	47.7
4	Codeine	11.4
5	Methadone	7.8

Rank	Drug name	Percent of total episodes
	Black decedents	
1	Cocaine	69.7
2	Heroin/morphine[1]	45.1
3	Alcohol-in-combination	39.7
4	Codeine	10.6
5	Methadone	5.2
6	Quinine	4.4
7	Marijuana/hashish	4.3
8	Amitriptyline	3.5
9	Lidocaine	3.2
10	Diphenhydramine	3.1
6	Marijuana/hashish	5.3
7	PCP/PCP combinations	4.8
8	Methamphetamine	4.1
9	Lidocaine	2.5
10	Amphetamine	2.5

[1]Includes opiates not specified as to type.
NOTES: Percentages are based on raw medical examiner drug abuse case counts of 5,596 male decedents and 1,880 female decedents.
Total raw medical examiner drug abuse case counts included 85 decedents ages 6-17, 732 decedents ages 18-25, 2,170 decedents ages 26-34, and 4,521 decedents age 35 and older.
Drugs with fewer than 10 mentions are excluded.
SOURCE: Drug Abuse Warning Network, Substance Abuse and Mental Health Services Administration, April 1994 provisional data file.

FIGURE 3. Manner of Drug-Related Death, by Race/Ethnicity, DAWN Medical Examiner Data: 1993

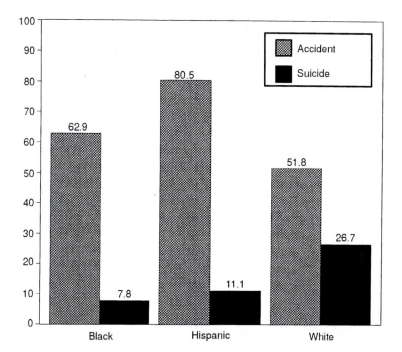

SOURCE. Drug Abuse Warning Network. Substance Abuse and Mental Health Services Administration. April 1994 provisional data file.

script provide strong evidence of the devastating impact that alcohol and drug use has on the lives of those who use drugs regardless of racial/ethnic origin. However, these data also indicate that heroin/morphine use has a more severe negative impact on the physical well-being of Hispanics and is more strongly related to their criminal behavior than it is among persons of Black or White non-Hispanic ancestry. Cocaine/crack use also seems to have a more negative impact on the well-being of Hispanic persons and their criminal behavior than it is among White non-Hispanic persons. On the other hand, the results also suggest that cocaine use has a more severe impact on the physical well-being of Blacks and is more strongly related to their criminal behavior than it was among Hispanics. Finally, the data presented here indicate that injecting drug use continues to have a more significant impact on AIDS prevalence rates for Hispanics and Black drug users than for White non-Hispanic drug users.

TABLE 12. Drug use history of state prison inmates, by type of drug and race/ethnicity: 1991 (in percentages).

Type of drug	Ever used drugs			Used drugs in the month before the offense			Used drugs daily in the month before the offense			Under the influence at time of the offense		
	White[1]	Black[1]	Hispanic	White[1]	Black[1]	Hispanic	White[1]	Black[1]	Hispanic	White[1]	Black[1]	Hispanic
Cocaine/crack cocaine	48.9	48.1	55.3	20.3	28.1	29.1	13.3	17.8	16.8	11.4	17.0	14.9
Cocaine	47.9	41.0	53.1	17.9	20.6	26.0	11.3	12.4	14.1	9.4	10.8	12.3
Crack	16.4	23.5	18.2	6.5	13.8	8.0	4.7	9.2	5.5	2.9	7.3	3.4
Heroin/opiates	27.0	20.0	35.6	7.9	7.5	19.6	6.1	5.2	15.4	4.8	4.1	13.1
Heroin	23.1	19.0	34.7	6.8	7.2	18.8	5.4	5.0	14.9	4.5	4.1	13.1
Other opiates	14.5	4.9	10.3	2.4	0.8	2.6	1.4	0.4	1.6	0.6	0.1	0.2

[1]Includes white, non-Hispanic and black non-Hispanic inmates.
SOURCE: Survey of State Prison Inmates, Bureau of Justice Statistics, 1991.

LIMITATIONS

Although the data presented in this manuscript provides evidence to indicate that alcohol and other drug use is a serious health and social problem confronting Hispanics, it has certain limitations. First, the data are based on self-reports of drug use, and their validity depends on respondents truthfulness and memory recall. Therefore, some underreporting and overreporting of drug use was very likely to occur. Second, the surveys included in this study are crossectional rather than longitudinal in nature. Individuals were interviewed only once and not followed for subsequent interviews. Therefore, these surveys provide an overview of the prevalence of drug use at specific points in times only, rather than how drug use changes over time for groups of individuals and the underlying factors responsible for peoples drug use. Third, the data collected from these surveys only provide a broad measurement of the prevalence of drug use among Hispanics. Therefore, the results from these surveys yield little information on the problem of drug use and drug dealing confronted by many Hispanic communities throughout the country.

RECOMMENDATIONS AND CONCLUSION

Because of these limitations the following types of studies and surveys are suggested:

1. Community based cross-sectional surveys and/or longitudinal studies to determine (a) the extent of the alcohol and other drug use and related social and health problems among and within the various Hispanic sub-groups, including Puerto Ricans living on the island of Puerto Rico, according to type of drug use, age, gender, and socioeconomic status and (b) whether the drug use behavior of Hispanic females is changing and the factors affecting this change.
2. Community based ethnographic and longitudinal studies to investigate (a) the role of individual and family socioeconomic status, (b) the role played by cultural values and factors such as "machismo," "marianismo," "respeto," "dignidad," "confianza," religious affiliation, and general attitudes toward drug use in determining drug use behavior among Hispanic sub-groups; (c) the role of acculturation-related stress in the drug use behavior of Hispanics; and (d) the role of social support systems (family, religious institutions, and such indigenous institutions as the "compadrazco" system) in the drug use behavior of Hispanics by specific sub-group.

3. Investigate via community-based cross-sectional surveys or ethnographic studies: (a) the relationships between injecting drug use and the rate of AIDS among Hispanic drug users and their sexual partners, including whether Hispanic drug users take more risks than White non-Hispanic drug users during the process of injecting themselves (for example, through multiple use of dirty needles or sharing needles with other Hispanic drug users) and (b) the relationship between guns, drug use, and drug-related violence and other criminal behavior among Hispanics and see if differs from that reported in studies conducted on the relationship among Black and White non-Hispanic males and females.

4. Methodological studies which will explore the validity of data collected in household and school-based National Surveys regarding the prevalence of drug use in Hispanic populations.

In summary, the Hispanic population in the United States is rapidly growing. As the population grows, their presence in the social, economic, and political life in the United States will become ever more prominent. Failure by the nation to address the problem of alcohol and other drug use among Hispanics and its various underlying antecedents will prove detrimental for Hispanics and non-Hispanics alike.

NOTES

1. The term "heavy alcohol use" refers to the consumption of five or more drinks on the same occasion on five or more days in the two weeks before the survey interview.

2. The term "Hispanic" includes individuals of Cuban-American, Mexican-American, Puerto Rican, South and Central American ancestry regardless of race living in the mainland United States. Puerto Ricans living on the island of Puerto Rico are not included in this overview because most major national surveys cited in this paper excluded Puerto Ricans living on the island from their samples.

3. The term "youth" refers to individuals between the ages of 12 and 21.

4. The term "drug use" refers to the use of marijuana, cocaine, and heroin. In the case of the use of heroin, the term refers to use of heroin where data is available.

5. The 1993 NHSDA is a survey of a nationally representative sample of the mainland U.S. civilian non-institutionalized population. The sample size for the 1993 NHSDA was 26,489 individuals, with over-sampling for African-Americans, Hispanics, and young people. It excludes Puerto Ricans living on the island of Puerto Rico. Estimates of the prevalence of drug abuse obtained from the NHSDA should be viewed conservatively because potentially high-risk subgroups were not included in the sample (for example, persons with no fixed

residence and prison inmates). Because drug use is an illicit activity and social tolerance for drug use has diminished considerably over time, it also is expected that some respondents under-reported their drug use. The male portion of the NHSDA population was 76.4 percent white, 10.4 percent African-American, 9.3 percent Hispanic, and 3.9 percent other races and ethnicity. The female portion was 75.8 percent white, 11.8 percent African-American, 8.6 percent Hispanic, and 3.8 percent other races and ethnicity. Demographic profile of the sample indicates that 57 percent of the individuals 18 and older were employed full-time, 12 percent were employed part-time, 10 were unemployed, and the remaining 21 percent were other, retired, disabled, homemaker, or student.

6. This paper uses data on past-month drug use because a growing consensus among epidemiologists suggest such drug use is a more accurate indicator of serious drug use than is either past-year use or lifetime drug use.

7. The term "ethnic/racial background" refers to individuals of African-American, Asian/Pacific Islanders, Hispanic and white non-Hispanic background.

8. The term "problems" refers to physical, psychological, and family problems associated with the use of alcohol, marijuana, cocaine, and heroin.

9. Data on lifetime prevalence rates for all racial/ethnic groups were not included in this paper since these rates often denote experimental alcohol or other drug use and are not as indicative of more serious use as are past-year and past-month prevalence rates.

10. The term "occasional" refers to a least seeing once a month someone drunk or selling drugs in the neighborhood.

11. The term "Machismo" refers to the prominence of the male figure as the most important authority in the Hispanic culture. It connotes the power and freedom that males have in the Hispanic culture to be sexually involved at an early age, use alcohol at an early age than Hispanic females, to control their families and women in their lives. It also connotes a sense of responsibility that males have toward protecting their families and been responsible for their well-being.

12. The term "Marianismo" refers to the submissive role of the Hispanic female in the Hispanic culture. It also seeks to view females as pure and suffering virginal figures which must be protected by the family against the ills of society. It also ascribes to females the role of functioning as the emotional and spiritual center of the family which includes the central role of raising children and maintaining social order in the family.

13. The term "respeto" refers to the behaviors that Hispanic persons have toward respecting individuals in positions of authority, the elderly, women, and general behavior when speaking or interacting with family members, friends, and strangers alike.

14. The term "Confianza" refers to the trusting relationship that Hispanics have toward people until they are proven otherwise. This trust affects what Hispanic persons they tell or express to family members and strangers alike.

15. The term "dignidad" refers to behaviors that Hispanics have in conducting themselves with a sense of humbleness and dignity when interacting with others

around them. Hispanics must make efforts in all instances not to embarrass someone on purpose and protect at all cost their dignidad as well as of others around them. This includes talking with others with respect, not behaving arrogantly, deferring to the elderly in any discussion, and showing responsibility toward their families and community.

16. The Monitoring the Future Study is an annualized survey of 8th, 10th, and 12th grade high school students living in the 50 states. The 1993-1994 survey included a combined sample size of 30,400 8th graders, of whom 4,000 were Hispanics, 28,100 10th graders, of whom 2,800 were Hispanics, and 28,500 12th graders, of whom 3,100 were Hispanics. Data exclude Puerto Rican youth living on the island of Puerto Rico. The MTF study does not analyze data by specific Hispanic sub-groups.

17. Data not shown in this paper.

18. Data not shown in this paper.

19. Data not shown in this paper.

20. Data not shown in this paper.

21. The data presented in this paper on high school dropouts is based upon methods used to compute status dropout rate. Several distinct methods aid researchers in computing dropout rates. The methods involve calculation of (1) the event dropout rate, (2) the status dropout rate, and (3) the cohort dropout rate. The event dropout rate measures the number of students dropping out of school during any given year. This rate calculates only the number of students leaving a given school district and may not take into account students who enroll in other school districts or students who leave school, return, and then leave again. The status dropout rate attempts through major surveys to evaluate the proportion of individuals in a given age group who have completed school or are enrolled in school at one time. The status dropout rate always appears higher than the event rate because of its increased sensitivity to the cumulative annual event rate. The cohort dropout rate is obtained by following a single group of students across time and evaluating their school completion rates.

22. The YRBS is a component of the Youth Risk Behavior Surveillance System (YRBSS), maintained by CDC. The 1992 Youth Risk Behavior Supplement was administered to one in-school youth and up to two out-of-school youth in each family selected for the National Health Interview Survey. In 1992, 10,645 youths aged 12-21 were included in the YRBS sample. The purpose of the supplement was to provide information on a broader base of youth, including those not currently attending school, than is usually obtained with surveys. The supplement also sought to obtain accurate information on the demographic characteristics of the household in which the youth reside. It excludes Puerto Rican youth living in Puerto Rico. The data do not include an analysis by either gender or specific Hispanic sub-groups.

23. Because the wide age range of the youth category in the YRBS, the results from this survey on youth risk taking behavior have to be interpreted with caution.

24. AIDS surveillance data are maintained by CDC using information collected by health departments in each state, territory, and the District of Columbia.

Although surveillance activities range from passive to active, most areas employ multi-faceted active surveillance programs, which include four major reporting sources of AIDS information: hospitals and hospital-based physicians, physicians in non-hospital practice, public and private clinics, and medical record systems (for example, death certificates, tumor registries, hospital discharge abstracts, and communicable disease reports). Using a standard confidential case report form, the health departments collect information without personal identifiers that then is coded and computerized either at the CDC or at health departments, from which the information then is transmitted electronically to the CDC.

25. DAWN is a large-scale, on-going drug abuse data collection system which uses information from emergency room (ER) and medical examiner facilities. DAWN collects information about those drug abuse occurrences that have resulted in a medical crisis or death. The major objectives of the DAWN data system include monitoring drug abuse patterns and trends, identifying substances associated with drug abuse episodes, and assessing drug-related consequences and other health hazards. Hospitals eligible for DAWN are non-federal, short-stay general hospitals that have 24-hour ERs. Since 1988, the DAWN ER data have been collected from a representative sample of these hospitals, including 21 over-sampled metropolitan areas. The data from this sample are used to generate estimates of the total number of ER drug use episodes and drug mentions in all such hospitals. The data do not include an analysis by specific Hispanic subgroup. Puerto Ricans living in the Island of Puerto Rico are also excluded from this survey.

26. The term "alcohol-in-combination" refers to alcohol as the primary drug reported as the cause of death but where other drugs were found in the decedent's body during toxicological examinations by the medical examiners.

27. Data for ER admission by gender for alcohol and other drug use for Hispanics or persons from other racial/ethnic groups was not available from the DAWN.

28. Data for drug-related deaths by gender for alcohol and other drug use for Hispanics or persons of other racial/ethnic groups was not available from the DAWN.

29. The term "accidental death" refers to causes of death which involved unintended drug overdoses or any other accidents such as a car accident.

30. The Survey of State Prison Inmates is a periodic survey conducted of persons who are inmates in state correctional facilities. These surveys are conducted by the Census Bureau for the Department of Justice. The survey collects information on the characteristics of inmates in state prisons across the nation. These characteristics include sociodemographic classifications, reason for incarceration, length of sentence, and behavioral attributes including drug use. Inmates in state correctional facilities usually have committed the most serious offenses or have the most extensive criminal records. Consequently these findings represent the reports of one sample of inmates and should not be generalized to the entire offender population. Data on the role of alcohol in criminal behavior was not available in this survey.

REFERENCES

Arkin, E., and Funkhouser, J. (1990). *Communicating About Alcohol and Other Drugs: Strategies for Reaching Populations at Risk* (Monograph 5). Rockville, MD: Alcohol, Drug Abuse, and Mental Health Administration, 1990.

Bureau of Justice Statistics. (August, 1991). *Special Report: Drugs and Jail Inmates, 1989*. U.S Government Printing Office: Washington, D.C.

Centers for Disease Control and Prevention. (June, 1994). *HIV/AIDS Surveillance Report*. Volume 6, Number 1. Washington, D.C.: U.S. Government Printing Office.

Centers for Disease Control and Prevention. (1992). Youth Risk Behavior Survey.

Chaiken, J.and Chaiken, M.R. (1990). Drugs and predatory crime. In: M. Tonry and J.Q. Wilson. *Drugs and Crime*, 203-240. Chicago: University of Chicago Press.

Collins, L.R. (1992). Methodological issues in conducting substance abuse research on ethnic minority populations. *Drugs and Society*, 6(1/2), 59-78.

Golub, A., Johnson, B., and Fagan, J. (1995). Careers in crack use, drug distribution, and non-drug criminality. *Crime and Delinquency*, 41(3): 275-295.

Inciardi, J., Horowitz, R., and Pottieger, A. (1993). *Street Kids, Street Drugs, and Street Crime: An Examination of Drug Use and Serious Delinquency in Miami*. Belmont, CA: Wadsworth Publishing Company.

Johnston, L.D., O'Malley, P.M., and Bachman, J.G. (1995). *National Survey Results on Drug Use From the Monitoring the Future Study, 1975-1993*. NIH Publication. No. 94-3809. Vol. I. Rockville, MD.

Johnston, L.D., O'Malley, P.M., and Bachman, J.G. (In Press). *National Survey Results on Drug Use From the Monitoring the Future Study, 1975-1995*. NIH Publication. No. 96-4139. Vol. I. Rockville, MD.

Kandel, D.B. , Kessler, R.C., Margulies, R.Z. (1978). Antecedents of adolescents' initiation into stages of drug use: A developmental analysis. *Journal of Youth and Adolescence*, 7, 13-40.

National Center for Health Statistics. (1994). *Health, United States, 1993*. Hyattsville, MD: Public Health Service.

Rodriguez, M.A., and Brindis, C.D. (1995). Violence and Latino youth: Prevention and methodological issues. *Public Health Reports*, 110(3), 260-265.

Substance Abuse and Mental Health Services Administration. (1994a). *National Household Survey on Drug Abuse: Population Estimates, October 1994*. DHHS Pub. No. 94-3017. Washington, D.C.: U.S Government Printing Office.

Substance Abuse and Mental Health Services Administration. (1994b). Data from the Drug Abuse Warning Network (DAWN) 1994 Data File. Rockville, MD.

U.S. Bureau of the Census. (Unpublished Data, October 1993). Current Population Survey. 1993. Washington, D.C.

Alcohol Use and Abuse Among Latinos: Issues and Examples of Culturally Competent Services

Sylvia Rodriguez-Andrew, PhD

SUMMARY. This paper will identify some of the key barriers for developing a better understanding of the impact of alcohol use and abuse among Latinos in the United States. Examples of culturally competent approaches to better researching and serving Latinos are presented to facilitate service provision to this population. *[Article copies available for a fee from The Haworth Document Delivery Service: 1-800-342-9678. E-mail address: getinfo@haworth.com]*

In 1990, one of 11 persons in the U.S. identified themselves as Hispanic. Currently, Hispanics number about 22.7 million–9% of the U.S. population. Introduced by federal statisticians in the 1980 Census, the term "Hispanic" was used as a broad category for aggregating persons of Mexican, Puerto Rican, Cuban, or other Hispanic/Spanish origin. The majority of the U.S. Hispanic/Latino population are of Mexican descent (64%), followed by persons from Central/South America (13%), Puerto Rico (11%), other Hispanic (7%) and persons from Cuba (5%). Although widely used, the term "Hispanic" has not been universally accepted or

Sylvia Rodriguez-Andrew is Dean, San Jose State University School of Social Work, 1 Washington Square, San Jose, CA 955192-0124.

[Haworth co-indexing entry note]: "Alcohol Use and Abuse Among Latinos: Issues and Examples of Culturally Competent Services." Rodriguez-Andrew, Sylvia. Co-published simultaneously in *Alcoholism Treatment Quarterly* (The Haworth Press, Inc.) Vol. 16, No. 1/2, 1998, pp. 55-70; and: *Alcohol Use/Abuse Among Latinos: Issues and Examples of Culturally Competent Services* (ed: Melvin Delgado) The Haworth Press, Inc., 1998, pp. 55-70. Single or multiple copies of this article are available for a fee from The Haworth Document Delivery Service [1-800-342-9678, 9:00 a.m. - 5:00 p.m. (EST). E-mail address: getinfo@haworth.com].

acceptable to the more than 30 Hispanic origin subgroups (Hodgkinson and Outtz, 1996). While the practice of collapsing the various Hispanic subgroups into one general category may be easier for reporting findings, it has not been useful in narrowing the gap in our understanding of the disparity that exists within and among the various Hispanic subgroups. For more than a decade, researchers have urged policy makers to focus on the emerging issues, problems, and policies associated with an increasingly youthful and highly diverse Hispanic population.

Consistently, researchers find wide intercultural and intracultural differences between Mexican Americans, Puerto Ricans, Cubans, South and Central Americans on important indices such as educational attainment, socioeconomic status, and labor force participation (Sanchez-Mayers and Kail, 1993). Alcohol use also varies among the various Hispanic subgroups. For example, Puerto Rican men and women report low rates of abstention, but frequent drinking to the point of intoxication (Caetano, 1985). Mexican American men report higher rates of abstention, but when they drink–they drink to intoxication. Among Hispanic youth, some have reported higher levels of alcohol use compared to their white and African American counterparts, and others report no ethnic differences (Sanchez-Mayers and Kail, 1993). As with the general population, Latino drinking patterns appears to mirror the larger population and has been linked to gender, age, socioeconomic status, and acculturation (Alcocer, 1993). Booth, Castro, and Anglin (1990) found that poverty is generally associated with greater substance abuse, regardless of ethnicity. Similarly, De La Rosa et al. (1990) reported that poverty, limited school and employment opportunities and discrimination increase the propensity for drug abuse.

Unfortunately, one of the difficulties in understanding alcohol use and Latinos has been the practice of aggregating various Latino subgroups into a convenient category. This practice is further complicated when generalizations are made based on the data collected from one Latino group to another Latino group, or to Latinos in general. Some researchers rely on the term(s) respondents use to identify themselves, others utilize previously constructed category(ies) such as Hispanic or Latino, some collapse them if the numbers are too small for analysis, and some use these terms interchangeably.

It is highly unlikely that there will ever be a consensus on a term that is acceptable to all of the Hispanic subgroups. There appears to be regional preferences, however, about what term is preferred and/or used. For example, the term "Hispanic" is widely used in the Eastern part of the U.S., while "Latino" or "Chicano" is used in California. Researchers argue that greater specificity in describing the Latino sample is more likely to increase our understanding about intercultural and intracultural alcohol use. More importantly, researchers and policy makers are now beginning to examine whether specificity in describing the Latino population enhances the development of culturally appropriate and effective prevention and treatment services. This increasing emphasis on culturally appropriate services has challenged human service organizations to assess the adequacy of their services for a highly diverse Latino population (Ramos, 1993).

Alcohol abuse is one of our most pressing public health problems that has multiple and cumulative adverse effects on individuals, families and communities (Singer et al., 1987; Delgado and Rodriguez-Andrew, 1990; Office for Substance Abuse Prevention, 1990; Delgado and Humm-Delgado, 1993). Although early reports on the effectiveness of prevention programs were mixed, the prevention of tobacco, alcohol, and other drugs among our nation's youth remains a priority for many communities across the country (Office for Substance Abuse Prevention, 1990).

The lack of data on the effectiveness of alcohol prevention programs is due in large part to the paucity of research on Latinos and alcohol abuse (Gilbert, 1986). Although much progress has been made during this past decade, more research is needed in our understanding of alcohol use among and between the various Latino groups. The literature on alcohol abuse among Latinos points to several limitations such as: (1) lack of specificity in identifying the population(s) and reliance on atypical samples; (2) variation in defining alcohol use, particularly "abstention"; (3) acculturation; (4) poly-substance abuse; (5) age; and (6) gender. These limitations have important implications for alcohol abuse prevention and treatment services (Gilbert and Cervantes, 1986; Delgado and Rodriguez-Andrew, 1990; Alcocer, 1993).

SPECIFICITY IN IDENTIFYING POPULATIONS

While Latinos as a group have much in common, they differ substantively in terms of drinking patterns and alcohol problem incidence (Gilbert and Cervantes, 1986). The limitations of aggregating Latinos for program planning has been extensively documented (Alcocer, 1982; Gilbert and Cervantes, 1986; Caetano, 1986; Delgado and Rodriguez-Andrew, 1990).

Research on alcohol abuse and the effectiveness of alcohol prevention programs has increased. However, more research is needed in identifying important cultural considerations in program planning and in understanding behaviors that place some Latinos at greater risk for alcohol abuse. Gilbert and Cervantes (1986) summarized the existing literature on alcohol abuse and Latinos as "exploratory" and "descriptive in nature." It is also important to consider that much of the research on alcohol abuse among Latinos has only emerged within the past decade. Most of what is known about alcohol abuse among Latinos is based on data collected from urban areas and largely from three states (California, Texas and New York) (Delgado, 1988). This is not surprising since 60% of all Latinos reside in these three States and 9 in 10 Latinos live in urban areas. Humm-Delgado and Delgado (1983) concluded that "it is difficult to find major conclusive findings or themes that hold true throughout the literature, and it is clear that not only the etiology of substance abuse but also the treatment methods for it need studying." Gilbert and Alcocer's (1988) review "failed to disclose a single empirical article that described treatment strategies, clinical trials or outcome evaluations related to alcohol intervention activities directed to youthful Hispanics."

The first national survey on Hispanic drinking patterns was conducted twelve (12) years ago which stands in sharp contrast to studies on drinking patterns that were initiated more than 50 years ago among the general population (Alcocer, 1993). This much anticipated national survey which focused on Hispanics living in the 48 contiguous States was instrumental in identifying drinking patterns as well as important cultural considerations (Caetano, 1985). Unfortunately, it was limited by small sample sizes in some of the various Hispanic categories. Prior to Caetano's (1985) survey, data on Hispanic drinking patterns were based on data collected from the general population (Cahalan, 1969; Rachael et al., 1975) or from specific regions such as California (Alcocer, 1979) and south Texas (Maril and Zavaleta, 1979).

In 1992, the Alcohol Research Group followed up its 1984 national samples. In general, drinking declined and abstention increased from 1984 to 1992 among all ethnic groups. However, Hispanic women who reported abstaining were more likely to have initiated drinking by 1992 (29%) than their black or white counterparts (19%). In addition, drinking was found to have increased among *younger* women and men in all ethnic categories, particularly among more educated black women and more acculturated Hispanic women (Midanik and Clark, 1994).

Gilbert and Alcocer (1988) also cite the fact that most of the existing large scale studies on Latino adolescents have utilized school-based data and given their high school dropout rate, the results may effectively eliminate as many as 45% of Latino youth. Liu's (1994) analysis of Texas secondary students at high risk of dropping out of school (defined as absent 10 or more days during past school year for either skipping classes, illness or other reasons) found that those more likely to be at risk for dropping out of school were more likely to be female (58%) and Hispanic

(37%). Another limitation of existing studies on Latino youth has been the tendency to utilize convenience samples which limits generalization to Latino adolescents in general.

VARIATION IN DEFINING ALCOHOL ABUSE

Alcocer (1993) found comparisons across existing studies on Latinos and alcohol use problematic because researchers have not utilized standard and consistent data collection instruments for measuring drinking. Generally, alcohol use has been measured as a quantity-frequency variable with subsequent categories to describe levels of drinking. Several studies have relied on similar quantity frequency indices (Cahalan et al., 1974 Cahalan, 1975; Alcocer, 1979; Caetano, 1985) in an attempt to strengthen the validity of their findings. Unfortunately, the small numbers in some of the various Latino subgroups limits the generalizations that can be made.

While quantity-frequency indices are useful for studying adult populations, these same indices may not be appropriate for youth or women. Consumption levels such as quantity and frequency of alcohol and other drug use provide researchers and practitioners useful information about alcohol and drug-related problems; however, these same levels which were designed for adults may be lethal in a younger person (Delgado and Rodriguez-Andrew, 1990). Of particular importance for adolescent Latino prevention programs is the variation in defining "abstainer." Gilbert and Cervantes' (1986) review of existing studies found wide variation in the term abstainer. Abstainers have been defined as someone who had not consumed any alcohol in the past "six months," "past year," "30 days," or "never used." Some collapse the "never used" with those who have not used in the "past six months." According to Gilbert and Cervantes (1986), the implications for program planning will be significantly different for youth who have never used alcohol and for youth who have not used within the past six months or past year.

Alcocer has also raised possible problems with the reliability and validity of self-reported alcohol use data. His 1979 study of adult California Hispanic drinking patterns suggested possible underreporting of self-reported frequency and quantity of drinking.

ACCULTURATION

The role of acculturation as either a mediating or contributing factor in alcohol use has received considerable attention in the recent professional literature. Among Cuban Americans, Page (1990) found that substance abuse was linked to disruption resulting from immigration and acculturation. Similarly, Rio et al. (1993) considered acculturation a central issue in their treatment model and focused on the differential rates in which parents and children acculturate and its impact on family dynamics. As with Cuban Americans, Alcocer (1993) suggests that there is a direct relationship between substance abuse and acculturation among Mexican Americans. According to Caetano (1987) acculturation increases the likelihood for alcohol abuse.

Research with various Latino subgroups suggest that level of acculturation may be an important moderating variable in understanding differences among Latino subgroups. Furthermore, acculturation appears to occur differently for Mexican Americans, Cuban Americans, and Puerto Ricans (Booth et al., 1990). Among the Cuban community, researchers have consistently reported that the disruption associated with immigration and acculturation is related to subsequent substance abuse. As a result of these findings, acculturation issues are critical components of the treatment and intervention services at the Spanish Family Guidance Center in Miami (Booth et al., 1990 and Page, 1990). Similar findings have been reported for Mexican Americans (Amaro et al., 1990).

The role of acculturation and alcohol abuse also appears to differ for women. Caetano (1987) found that acculturation was more strongly associated with alcohol use among Mexican American women than Mexican American men.

FAMILY FACTORS

Gilbert and Cervantes (1986) suggest that more data is needed on Hispanic's parental attitudes and the subsequent socialization of their children towards alcohol use. Among youth in the general population, approval or disapproval by parents and friends has been linked to substance abuse. Caetano's (1985) and Alcocer and Gilbert's (1979) studies both concluded that early initiation of alcohol use by adolescents age 16 or younger was perceived as inappropriate by both men and women. The role of parental alcohol abuse in increasing risk for alcohol abuse among Latino youth has been contradictory. Estrada et al.'s (1982) study of Mexican American youth found that sibling and parental drinking provided the greatest amount of explained variation in alcohol consumption. Guinn's (1978) early study of largely Mexican American Texas high school students found that paternal but *not* maternal drinking was associated with higher levels of alcohol use by adolescents. Mennon et al. (1990) found that parental substance abuse was a significant predictor of substance abuse among Mexican American youth. On the other hand, Kail's (1993) secondary analysis of Texas data found parental alcohol abuse to be lowest among Mexican American youth. Family intactness, defined as the presence or absence of 1 or 2 parents, does not appear to be associated with Puerto Rican (Dembo et al., 1979) or Mexican American adolescent drinking (Linskey, 1985).

Szapocznik and his colleagues have examined the extensive literature on high risk behaviors that place youth at risk for substance abuse, particularly family functioning factors. The literature consistently reports high rates of family disruption, conflict, inappropriate and inconsistent behavior control techniques in families of adolescent substance abusers. Based on extensive research and clinical experience, Szapocznik and his colleagues identified four protective family characteristics in Hispanic (mostly Cuban) adolescents. First, parents or parent figures demonstrate good family management. Second, communication between family members is characterized by directness, reciprocity, and specificity. Third family members demonstrate flexibility in handling intra and extra familial stressors in adaptive ways and finally, conflicts are allowed to survey and families are able to reach some level of conflict resolution.

Vega's (1996) five year longitudinal study of the drug using behaviors of 3,639 Hispanic and 2,285 non-Hispanic male 6th-7th graders found that family pride was the most significant protective and risk factor associated with student drug use. Unlike their non-Hispanic white and African American counterparts, Hispanic youth who were *not* proud of their families were found to be most vulnerable to drug use. Family pride was defined as a person's positive or negative views of their family's traditional Hispanic values and lifestyle. Vega's (1996) recent findings support earlier findings reported by Szapozcnik and his colleagues that suggest that drug use is more prevalent among Hispanic male adolescents who do not share their family's traditional Hispanic values.

Drug using peers have been found to be related to alcohol use, however, some peer group affiliations may actually decrease the risk for substance abuse (Barrera and Reese, 1993). For Mexican American youth, peers account for only 16% of the variance in drug use compared to 55% of the variance for white youth. Research on the use of natural support networks, have been identified as having potential for either deterring or decreasing alcohol abuse.

Wallace's (1996) national survey of 3,200 Hispanic eighth graders found that drug use was lowest among youth who reported low levels of peer drug use than among youth who reported high levels of peer drug use.

Among Hispanic eighth graders who reported that *none* of their friends used drugs, 22% smoked cigarettes, 30% used alcohol, 5% smoked marijuana and 2% used cocaine. Of those who reported that *some* of their friends used drugs, 64% smoked cigarettes, 68% had used alcohol, 37% used marijuana, and 24% used cocaine. Among those who reported that *all* of their friends used drugs, 85% used cigarettes, 92% used alcohol, 80% used marijuana and 42% had used cocaine.

According to Barrera and Reese (1993), the literature on the use of social supports for improving psychological distress and physical health has been well documented, but similar evidence that social support systems reduce Hispanics' risk for substance abuse is still largely exploratory.

POLY-SUBSTANCE ABUSE

Substance abuse refers to a wide range of substances whose chemical composition, physiological effects and legal consequences vary significantly. Political, moral, and cultural norms add yet another important dimension to society's perception and understanding of substance abuse (Sanchez-Mayers and Kail, 1993). Consistently, studies on Latinos just as with studies on the general population, find patterns of poly-substance use which means that alcohol use is combined with the use of other drugs either at the same time or over a period of time.

While alcohol use is the first and most frequent drug used, most studies have focused on illicit drug use (Delgado and Rodriguez-Andrew, 1990). Existing surveys have tended to be exhaustive in asking about alcohol and various drug use, but they rarely inquire about simultaneous or alternating use of several substances. The concurrent use of alcohol and other drugs may be increasingly common among younger women in treatment for alcohol problems (Lex, 1993).

GENDER CONSIDERATIONS

There is general consensus that there are significant gender differences in alcohol use among Latino men and women. Gilbert (1993) found that Mexican American men hold more positive expectations about alcohol than women. Caetano (1985) noted striking differences in the drinking patterns of Hispanic men and women. Generally, Hispanic women reported drinking less than men; however, recent studies suggest that this gap may be narrowing (Wilsnack and Wilsnack, 1978; Perez et al., 1980; Edwards et al., 1995). The research on women and alcohol use provides growing evidence that women experience higher alcohol blood levels at the same dose and are at higher risk for alcohol related health problems (McCready, 1988).

AGE

The age in which youth are reporting alcohol use has been declining which suggests the need to target younger children. The fact that youth are using alcohol at a younger age is further exacerbated for Latino communities because of the youthfulness of their population. More than a third (35%) of all Latinos are under the age of 18. As a group, Latino children are the youngest, largest, and fastest growing group of children in America. By the year 2030, one fourth of our nation's youth will be Latino. According to Hayes-Bautista (1988), California's Latino population is expected to increase from 25% to 45% by the year 2030. The effectiveness of prevention programs for Latinos, however, has only recently been explored.

The age of onset for alcohol use among Latino youth ranges from 11-14 depending on the sample and region (Alcocer, 1993). It appears, however, based on the studies reviewed by Alcocer (1993) that Latino youth appear to begin drinking later than their white counterparts. Unfortunately, problems arise when comparing alcohol use patterns to other ethnic groups because most fail to differentiate between males and females. Most studies have consistently reported lower drinking among females and higher rates of abstention than their adolescent male counterparts which may distort age of onset.

While alcohol related problems and heavy drinking peaks in the general population between the ages of 18-29 then decreases, this same pattern is not reflected among Mexican American men (Gilbert and Cervantes, 1986).

CULTURALLY SENSITIVE SERVICES

Since the 1986 Drug Free Schools and Communities Act established the Office for Substance Abuse Prevention (OSAP), service providers have reported that those seeking alcohol prevention services are highly diverse. Some have provided anecdotal evidence to suggest that services historically believed to be relevant for a specific Latino subgroup may no longer be as effective with the same Latino subgroup today. Some of the reasons for this dramatic shift can be attributed to a more mobile Latino population, immigration, or influx of newer Latino subgroups into previously homogeneous Latino neighborhoods. This diversity within Latino communities reflects similar trends throughout the U.S. More and more human service providers are finding that services, if they are to be effective, must be modified or tailored to those seeking services. It is not surprising, then, that "cultural competence" has emerged within the past decade as an integral part of professional competence. Human service organizations, having both private and public funding sources, and professional organizations are requiring services that are "culturally appropriate," "culturally relevant," "ethnic sensitive" or "multicultural" as a condition of funding. Much of the discussion on cultural competence, however, has focused on the skills and knowledge of practitioners. Relatively little attention has been given to the human service infrastructure. Ramos (1993) argues that changing and improving the effectiveness of the service delivery system should be a priority given the increasing diversity of those seeking prevention and treatment services. Institutional change can only occur when accrediting bodies require facilities to meet standards and criteria that incorporate multicultural content (Ramos, 1993). Similarly, the accrediting bodies of professional schools should be increasingly concerned about the impact professionals lacking cultural competence have on diverse populations. Given today's emphasis on managed care and cost effectiveness, failure to provide culturally relevant services by competent providers is both detrimental and costly.

The significant contributions of cultural factors in intervention and treatment outcomes have been reported by several clinical investigators (Sue and Zane, 1987 and Acosta et al., 1982). Culturally sensitive and responsive therapists are generally more credible, trusted, and effective (Sue and Zane, 1987; Gutierrez, 1990). According to Santisteban et al. (1993), those who work with Hispanic clients should have a basic understanding of the culture, history, values, and sociopolitical orientation of the Hispanic subpopulation(s) with which they work; and when working with Spanish monolingual or bilingual Hispanics, the professional should be matched linguistically with the client. Yet, the role of cultural factors in preventing alcohol abuse among youth has only recently been explored.

Delgado and Rodriguez-Andrew (1990) summarized the three perspectives cited in the literature on the use of culture in intervention:

1. Ethnic-sensitive practice. Two important themes shape this approach—ethnicity and social class shape life's problems and influence how solutions are sought, and intervention must simultaneously seek solutions at the microlevel and macrolevel (Devore and Schlesinger, 1981).

2. Ethnic minority practice. This approach consists of three key dimensions–systematic process or stage approach to practice, generic principles of practice universal to people of color, and the use of case material to develop direct practice continuity through single family case study at various stages (Lum, 1986).
3. Green's (1982) crosscultural awareness practice. This model attempts to sensitize non-ethnic minority practitioners to ethnic minority culture, beliefs, and so forth.

Delgado and Humm-Delgado (1993) identified several emerging themes in services that are culturally sensitive to Hispanics: (1) importance of the family; (2) value attached to cooperation vs. competition; (3) getting along well with others; (4) role of respect in dealing with individuals; and (5) action orientation to problem solving.

"Familism" has been consistently cited as a cultural value regardless of national origin or acculturation level even when family contact is minimal (Sabogal et al., 1987). The perception of family as a strong source of support and solver of problems should be considered an integral feature in alcohol prevention education programs and treatment services for youth (Kail, 1993). Familism refers to the strong identification and attachment of individuals with their nuclear and extended families and it involves strong feelings of loyalty, reciprocity and solidarity among family members (Triandis et al., 1982). According to Sabogal et al. (1987) there are three components to familism: (1) familial obligations, (2) perceived support from the family, and (3) family as referents. This reliance on family for social support may well be the only viable option for Latinos given detrimental social and environmental conditions coupled with limited access to resources. At the same time, some have argued that overreliance on the family may also inhibit seeking help with alcohol abuse problems.

EXAMPLES OF CULTURALLY COMPETENT SERVICES

Galan (1988) stresses that professionals need to understand the conflicts Hispanic youth face if they are planning alcohol prevention programs: (1) ethnic identity; (2) biculturality; (3) spanish language fluency; (4) gender specific role expectations; (5) skin color; (6) family history of alcoholism; and (7) overall sense of self. Similarly, Delgado (1988) suggests that professionals explore five critical areas with Hispanic adolescents as part of the routine intake process: patterns/practices of alcohol use; adolescent's ethnic identity; language preference; adolescent's social network; and previous requests for assistance.

Although not specific to alcohol abuse prevention programs, Shartrand's (1996) recent publication on *Supporting Latino Families* identified 11 family support programs that are providing culturally sensitive services to highly diverse Latino families. Among the many commonalities and differences within and across these programs were: recognition of family strengths, infusion and validation of cultural strengths and most important-ly, that services must be provided in the social context of the realities facing families such as poverty, service gaps, institutional bureaucracy, and discrimination.

The Hispanic Family Intervention Program (HFIP) evolved from the existing literature on substance abuse prevention and Hispanic youth in particular (Cervantes, 1993). The program addresses multiple risk factors and endeavors to strengthen ties to family, school, peers, and culture. Participants were referred to HFIP by the local school if they were experi-encing behavioral and emotional problems in the school as well as aca-demic difficulty not related to a learning disorder or lack of English profi-ciency. Using a psychoeducational approach for identifying stressors, the 8-week curricula provides not only substance abuse education but also enhances individual and family coping. Groups are held concurrently for both youth and their parents. Cervantes (1993) reports an 8-10% attrition rate for the eight week program and most attend 6-7 sessions. Although their results are preliminary, they have identified the following as contrib-uting factors to their success in participants' improvement in self esteem, school performance, and overall conduct: (1) collaborative screening of participants, (2) provision of services in spanish, (3) bi-lingual staff re-sponsible for conducting outreach services for retention.

Another innovative prevention program is COSSHMO's "teatro" proj-ect which was implemented in six communities with large concentrations of Hispanics. "Teatro" or theater has been used historically as an effective vehicle for providing information and coping strategies for a number of pressing social issues. For example, during the two Mexican Revolutions, teatro presented critical incidents about oppression. During the sixties, the Teatro Campesino relied on teatro to provide a visual representation about the plight of farmworkers. Based on anecdotal evidence of their effective-ness, COSSHMO similarly relied on the use of teatro for drawing attention to the growing problem of substance abuse in Latino communities. Youth participants received a substance abuse education program and were en-couraged to integrate their personal experiences in the community teatro presentations on substance abuse. Grounded in Bandura's social learning theories, the project's evaluation findings demonstrated that the use of teatro was an effective prevention tool. Participants reported increased levels of self-esteem and lower levels of substance use (Paz, 1993).

SUMMARY AND RECOMMENDATIONS

While much progress has been made during the past decade in increasing our knowledge and understanding of alcohol abuse among Latinos, particularly youth, more research is needed in identifying salient factors in effective prevention and treatment services. The Office for Substance Abuse Prevention (OSAP) now the Center for Substance Abuse Prevention (CSAP) was instrumental in developing the bulk of the knowledge base on Latinos and substance abuse prevention. Most of the grantees that provided demonstration projects collected rich qualitative data that can be the basis for subsequent research and hypothesis testing. Innovative strategies such as the use of teatro, and family-focused programs, were initiated with promising preliminary results. These early attempts at defining, developing, and implementing culturally appropriate services in diverse Latino communities across the country need to be encouraged and sustained. Perhaps the hardest lesson learned from these early demonstration projects was that they could not be sustained beyond the three or five years of funding. Many reported difficulties in accessing and maintaining youth in their programs. However, many of those that reported difficulties in recruitment and program implementation were those who had not been particularly successful with the identified target population. As a result of the projects funded by the CSAP, much has been learned about the importance of culturally relevant services. In fact, CSAP's RFPs (requests for proposals) all stressed that culturally sensitive services were a condition of funding. Eventually program evaluation of these projects were expected to reflect the unique aspects of providing services to highly diverse populations.

Alcohol prevention services need to be tailored to the target population and must consider gender, age, and acculturation factors. Strategies that have been effective with elementary school children in a school setting may not be effective if it is delivered in a community setting or vice-versa. Similarly, gender-specific prevention and treatment services are needed. Much work has been done in articulating the role of acculturation and alcohol abuse; however, most of it has been conducted with adults. It is not clear whether acculturation is or is not as critical a variable for youth. In addition, more research is needed on the role of acculturation among the various Latino subgroups and alcohol abuse. Finally, more research is needed to identify culturally competent service providers. According to Gilbert and Alcocer (1988), "ample opportunity for innovative and theory-oriented approaches awaits researchers interested in this field." Clearly, the existing literature remains limited, but what exists provides us with a rich foundation and an opportunity to undertake research that can make a difference in Latino communities across the country.

REFERENCES

Acosta, F., Yamamoto, J. & Evans, L. (1982). Effective psychotherapy for low-income and minority patients. New York: Plenum.

Alcocer, A. (1979). Quantitative Study. In Technical Systems Institute, Drinking practices and alcohol related problems of Spanish speaking persons in California. Sacramento, CA: California Office of Alcohol and Drug Problems.

Alcocer, A. (1982). Alcohol use and abuse among the Hispanic American population. In NIAAA, Special Population Issues (Alcohol and Health Monograph No. 4) Washington, DC: U.S. Government Printing Office.

Alcocer, A. (1993). Patterns of alcohol use among Hispanics. In R. Sanchez-Mayers, B. Kail, & T. Watts (Eds). Hispanic Substance Abuse. Springfield, Ill: Charles C. Thomas.

Alcocer, A. & Gilbert, M. (1979). Drinking practices and alcohol related problems of Spanish speaking persons in California. Sacramento, California Office of Alcohol and Drug Programs.

Amaro, H., Whitaker, R., Coffman, G. & Heerin, T. (1990). Acculturation and marijuana and cocaine use: Findings from HHANES 1982-84. American Journal of Public Health, 80, 54-60.

Booth, M., Castro, F., & Anglin, M. (1990). What do we know about Hispanic substance abuse? A review of the literature. In R. Glick & J. Moore (Eds). Drugs in Hispanic Communities. New Brunswick, NJ: Rutgers University Press.

Caetano, R. (1986). Alternative definitions of Hispanics: Consequences in an alcohol survey. Hispanic Journal of Behavioral Sciences, 8(4), 331-344.

Caetano, R. (1987). Acculturation and drinking patterns among U.S. Hispanics. British Journal of the Addictions, 82, 789-799.

Caetano, R. (1988). Alcohol use among Hispanic groups in the United States. American Journal of Drug and Alcohol Abuse, 14, 293-308.

Cahalan, D., Cisin, I. & Crossley, H. (1969). American drinking practices. Monograph No. 6. New Brunswick, NJ: Rutgers Center of Alcohol Studies.

Cahalan, D., & Room, R. (1974). Problem drinking among American men. Monograph No. 7, New Brunswick, NJ: Rutgers Center on Alcohol Studies.

Cervantes, R. (1993). The Hispanic family intervention program: An empirical approach to substance abuse prevention. In R. Sanchez-Mayers, B. Kail, & T. Watts (Eds) Hispanic Substance Abuse. Springfield, Ill: Charles C. Thomas.

De La Rosa, Khalsa, J., & Rouse, B. (1990). Hispanics and illicit drug use: A review of recent findings. The International Journal of the Addictions, 26, 665-691.

Delgado, M. (1988). Alcoholism treatment and Hispanic youth. Journal of Drug Issues, 18(1), 59-68.

Delgado, M., Humm-Delgado, D. (1993). Chemical dependence, self-help groups, and the Hispanic community. In R. Sanchez-Mayers, B. Kail, & T. Watts (Eds). Hispanic Substance Abuse. Springfield, Ill: Charles C. Thomas.

Delgado, M. & Rodriguez-Andrew, S. (1990). Alcohol and other drug use among Hispanic youth. OSAP Technical Report 4. Rockville, MD: U.S. Government Printing Office.

Dembo, R., Farrow, D., Schmeidler, J. & Burgos, W. (1979). Testing a causal model of environmental influences on the early drug involvement of inner city junior high school youths. American Journal of Drug and Alcohol Abuse, 6(3), 313-336.

DeVore, W. & Schlesinger, E. (1981). Ethnic sensitive social work practice. St. Louis: ÇV Mosby.

Edwards, R., Thurman, P. & Beauvais, F. (1995). Patterns of alcohol use among ethnic minority adolescent women. In M. Galanter (Ed). Recent Developments in Alcoholism and Women (Vol. 12) New York: Plenum Press.

Estrada, A., Rabow, J. & Watts, R. (1982). Alcohol use among Hispanic adolescents: A preliminary report. Hispanic Journal of Behavioral Sciences, 4(3), 339-351.

Galan, F. (1988). Alcoholism prevention and Hispanic youth. Journal of Drug Issues, 18(1), 49-58.

Gilbert, M. & Alcocer, A. (1988). Alcohol use and Hispanic youth: An overview. Journal of Drug Issues, 18(1), 33-49.

Gilbert, M. & Cervantes, R. (1986). Patterns and practices of alcohol use among Mexican Americans: A comprehensive review. Hispanic Journal of Behavioral Sciences, 8(1), 1-60.

Green, J. (1993). Cultural awareness in the human services. Englewood Cliffs, NJ: Prentice Hall, Inc.

Guinn, C. (1978). Alcohol use among Mexican American youth. Journal of School Health, 48, 90-91.

Gutierrez, L. (1990). Working with women of color: An empowerment perspective. Social Work, 149-153.

Hayes-Bautista, D., Schink, W., & Chapa, J. (1988). The burden of support. Stanford, CA: Stanford University Press.

Hodgkinson, H. & Outtz, J. (1996). Hispanic Americans: A look back, a look ahead. The Institute for Educational Leadership, Inc: Center for Demographic Policy, Washington, DC.

Humm-Delgado, D. & Delgado, M. (1983). Hispanic adolescents and substance abuse: Issues for the 1980's. Child and Youth Services, 6 (1/2), 71-87.

Kail, B. (1993). Patterns and predictors of drug abuse within the Chicano community. In R. Sanchez-Mayers, B. Kail, & T. Watts (Eds) Hispanic Substance Abuse. Springfield, Ill: Charles C. Thomas.

Lex, B. (1993). Women and illicit drugs: Marijuana, heroin and cocaine. In E. Gomberg & T. Nirenberg (Eds). Women and substance abuse. Norwood, NJ: Ablex.

Linksey, A. (1985). A report of the first two stages of research into regular substance use and related psychosocial stressors among younger adolescents along the Tamaulipas-Texas border. Paper presented at the Annual Meeting of the U.S. Mexico Border Health Association. San Antonio, Texas.

Liu, L. (1994). Substance use among youths at high risk of dropping out: Grades 7-12 in Texas, 1992. Austin, TX: TCADA.

Lum, D. (1986). Social work practice and people of color. Monterey, CA: Brooks-Cole.

Maril, J. & Zavaleta, A. (1979). Drinking patterns of low income Mexican American women. Journal of Studies on Alcohol, 40(5), 480-484.

Midanik, L. & Clark, W. (1994). The demographic distribution of U.S. drinking patterns in 1990. Description and trends from 1984. American Journal of Public Health, 84, 1218-1222.

McCready, B. (1988). Alcoholism. In E. Blackman and K. Brownell (Eds). Handbook of Behavioral Medicine for Women. New York: Pergamon.

Office for Substance Abuse Prevention (1990). OSAP Prevention Monograph 3. Prevention Research Findings: 1983. Proceedings of the first National Conference on Prevention Research Findings: Implications for alcohol and other drug abuse program planning. U.S. Department of Health and Human Services. Rockville, MD.

Paz, J. (1993). Alcohol and other substance abuse prevention theater initiative. Unpublished report.

Page, J. (1990). Cuban drug users in Miami. In R. Glick & J. Moore (Eds). Drugs in Hispanic Communities. New Brunswick, NJ: Rutgers University Press.

Perez, R. et al. (1980). Correlates and changes over time in drug and alcohol use within a barrio population. Journal of Community Psychology, 8, 621-638.

Ramos, J. (1993). Forward. In R. Sanchez-Mayers, B. Kail, & T. Watts (Eds). Hispanic Substance Abuse. Springfield, Ill: Charles C. Thomas.

Sabogal, F., Marin, G., Otero-Sabogal, R. et al. (1987). Hispanic familism and acculturation: What changes and what doesn't. Hispanic Journal of Behavioral Sciences, 9(4), 397-412.

Sanchez-Mayers, R. & Kail, B. (1993). Hispanic substance abuse: An overview. In R. Sanchez-Mayers, B. Kail, & T. Watts (Eds). Hispanic Substance Abuse. Springfield, Ill: Charles C. Thomas.

Santisteban, D., Szapocznik, J., & Rio, A. (1993). Family therapy for Hispanic substance abusing youth. In R. Sanchez-Mayers, B. Kail, & T. Watts (Eds). Hispanic Substance Abuse. Springfield, Ill: Charles C. Thomas.

Shartrand, A. (1996). Supporting Latino families. Harvard Family Research Project. Cambridge, MA.

Singer, M., Davison, L. & Yalin, F. (Eds). (1987). Conference proceedings: Alcohol use and abuse among adolescents. Hartford: Hispanic Health Council.

Sue, S. & Zane, N. (1987). The role of culture and cultural techniques in psychotherapy: A critique and reformulation. American Psychologist, 41, 37-45.

Triandis, H. et al. (1982). Dimensions of familism among Hispanic and mainstream Navy recruits. Technical Report No. 14. Department of Psychology, University of Ill.

Wilsnack, R. and Wilsnack, S. (1978). Sex roles and drinking among adolescent girls. Journal of Studies on Alcohol, 39(11), 1855-1874.

A VIEW FROM THE FIELD

Alcoholism Services
and Community Settings:
Latina Beauty Parlors
as Case Examples

Melvin Delgado, PhD

SUMMARY. The field of alcoholism prevention and treatment must strive to develop innovative methods for reaching the Latino community in the United States. One way this goal can be accomplished is through the development of collaborative projects involving Latino community-based institutions. Beauty parlors, as a case in point, are very often overlooked by AODA organizations in the develop-

---

Melvin Delgado is Professor of Social Work and Chair of Macro-Practice Sequence, Boston University School of Social Work, 264 Bay State Road, Boston, MA 02215.

The author wishes to acknowledge the financial support of the Carliele Foundation, Framingham, Massachusetts and the Center on Substance Abuse Prevention (SPO15496) for funding the research this article is based upon.

[Haworth co-indexing entry note]: "Alcoholism Services and Community Settings: Latina Beauty Parlors as Case Examples." Delgado, Melvin. Co-published simultaneously in *Alcoholism Treatment Quarterly* (The Haworth Press, Inc.) Vol. 16, No. 1/2, 1998, pp. 71-83; and: *Alcohol Use/Abuse Among Latinos: Issues and Examples of Culturally Competent Services* (ed: Melvin Delgado) The Haworth Press, Inc., 1998, pp. 71-83. Single or multiple copies of this article are available for a fee from The Haworth Document Delivery Service [1-800-342-9678, 9:00 a.m. - 5:00 p.m. (EST). E-mail address: getinfo@haworth.com].

ment of services. This article will report on the findings of a study of seven Latina (Dominican) beauty parlors in a large New England city. Implications for service delivery will be explored. *[Article copies available for a fee from The Haworth Document Delivery Service: 1-800-342-9678. E-mail address: getinfo@haworth.com]*

INTRODUCTION

The field of alcoholism and other drug abuse has struggled with the development of culturally-competent services for communities of color (Delgado, 1995a; Philleo & Brisbane, 1995; Moran & May, 1995; Rebach, 1992; Watts & Wright, 1989). There are few families and communities of color that have escaped the impact of alcoholism (Alcohol Alert, 1994; Fernandez-Pol, Bluestone, Missouri, Morales & Mizruchi, 1986; Gordon, 1989; Hacker, Collins & Jacobson, 1987; Herd, 1989; Kitano & Chi, 1989; Wright & Watts, 1985).

Communities of color, according to recent estimates, are a lucrative market for the alcohol industry: "No one knows the exact size of the inner-city alcohol market, but everyone agrees that billions of dollars worth of beer, wine and other spirits are sold each year . . . the core of the problem is the big slice of the market occupied by the malt liquors and fortified wines, which are sold predominately in urban centers. Nationally, these products accounted for $2 billion in sales last year, three-quarters of which came from malt liquor" (Sims, 1992, p. 6).

The use and abuse of alcohol within the Latino community is well recognized in the field (Alcocer, 1993; Caetano, 1989; Gilbert, 1989, 1993; Glick & Moore, 1990; Singer, Davision & Yalin, 1987). The Latino community, however, has an abundance of resources, institutional and individual-based, that are often overlooked in the development of culturally-competent services (Delgado, 1995b, 1996). These "assets," in turn, can serve as excellent sources for outreach and provision of culturally competent services focused on alcoholism and other drugs (Delgado, 1994, 1995c, 1995d).

The professional literature, as a result, has generally not identified important community-based resources such as beauty parlors in the fight against alcoholism. These settings are natural places for alcohol and other drug abuse (AODA) oriented agencies to engage in the development of innovative collaborative services targeting Latinos.

This article will examine the role of beauty parlors in the Latino community and the "natural" helping roles they play in helping residents with a wide range of social problems. Results from a community-based study of seven Latina (Dominican-owned) beauty parlors in a large New England

(Lawrence, Massachusetts) city will be reported, with a specific focus on how owners of these establishments have identified problems of alcoholism in their customers. In addition, a series of recommendations will be made to help AODA organizations develop collaborative services with these institutions.

REVIEW OF LITERATURE

Barriers to Service Delivery: The field of alcoholism has struggled in the development of culturally competent services targeting communities of color in the United States (Casement & Roberts, 1989; Anderson & Maypole, 1989). Williams' (1985, p. 14) comments on the failure of the field to reach African-Americans are also applicable to other groups of color: "Compounding the situation is the fact that blacks are proportionately underrepresented in the delivery system, both as clients and as caregivers. Black alcoholics and problem drinkers are unlikely to seek out traditional treatment programs unless there is a crisis or mandatory need, such as lifethreatening illness, threat of job termination, or referral by the court or social service agency, according to those in alcoholism treatment settings." This reluctance on the part of African-Americans and other groups of color highlights the presence of institutional barriers to effective service delivery.

The literature has identified five key barriers as to why the field has failed in this important goal: (1) excessive marketing of alcohol to African-American and Latino communities (Hacker, Collins & Jacobson, 1987; Maxwell & Jacobson, 1989; Sims, 1992); (2) lack of staffing reflecting the background of the community being served (Mayers & Feazell, 1985; Swift & Beverly, 1985); (3) failure of services to take the historical role of alcoholism into consideration (Davila, 1987; Delgado, 1995a); (4) lack of community involvement with services (Aguirre-Molina & Parra, 1995; Delgado, 1996a); and (5) failure to take into account the social-cultural context of the client (Hoffman, 1987).

Services to Latinos and other culturally and linguistically "different" groups have also encountered additional barriers that increase the difficulty of receiving services within a culture-specific context: (1) language (Fernandez-Pol, Bluestone, Morales & Mizruchi, 1985); (2) cultural values (Comas-Diaz, 1986; Inclan & Hernandez, 1992; Marin, 1993; Panitz, McConchie, Sauber & Fonseca, 1983; Triandis, Lisansky, Marin & Betancourt, 1984); (3) immigration/citizenship status (Dorrington, 1995); and (4) failure to differentiate between Latino sub-groups.

Clearly, there is a tremendous need to develop innovative services that actively involve the Latino community. This search for innovation, however, must begin with the recognition that Latino communities have resources and a political will to fight the problem of alcoholism. These resources, or "assets," are readily available and willing to collaborate with AODA and other agencies.

Latino Commercial Establishments: The literature on Latino small businesses is very limited, and usually restricted to their economic role within the community; this occurs at the exclusion of other important roles (Sarason & Koberg, 1994; Segura, 1994). Unfortunately, this literature, with few exceptions, has not focused on the social roles of these institutions (Levitt, 1995). Latino, and other ethnic-oriented businesses, are unlike their mainstream counterparts in the United States (Halter, 1995). These small businesses fulfill important social roles within the community. These roles, in turn, provide the field of alcoholism with opportunities to engage in collaborative activities with these establishments.

According to Delgado (1996b), Latino businesses fulfill six key functions, only one of which is commercial, within the community: (1) selling of products and services (this exchange has significant cultural dimensions); (2) provision of employment opportunities for Latinos; (3) personalization of customers (store owners know their customers by name and their families by name); (4) provision of financial services (cashing checks, credit and loans); (5) provision of social services (assistance with an extensive range of human services); and (6) a leadership role in the community. Latino small businesses, as result, must be viewed from a multidimensional perspective in order to fully appreciate their contributions to the community.

Levitt (1995, p. 130), in her study of Latino businesses in Boston, commented on how these establishments develop a clientele and have a community-wide impact: "Store owners earn a reputation for the quality of their merchandise or the way they treat their customers, which allegedly spreads by word-of-mouth . . . They attract customers based on this reputation and their visibility in the Latino community . . . Store owners are public figures whose face-to-face interactions have repercussions extending far beyond their store wall . . . An implicit set of norms and values govern the economic exchanges that take place between salesperson and customer. This shared world-view changes the nature of salesmanship." Latinos businesses, as a result, are much more than economic enterprises; they must also be considered "social enterprises."

Beauty Parlors: The professional literature, unfortunately, makes no mention of Latina beauty parlors and the significant role they play in the community, particularly with regards to women. In fact, the professional literature in general has not focused on beauty parlors regardless of ethnicity or race, although they can be found in virtually all communities across the United States. These establishments lend themselves for provision of a wide range of social services. Most of their customers are women and so are the beauticians. Customers can spend anywhere from 30 minutes to easily more than one hour in a shop, depending upon their cosmetic needs. Customers, in addition, are often expected to return on a periodic basis, facilitating the development of long-term relationships.

A beauty parlor owner's influence increases when she shares the same ethnic background of the clients and lives in the same neighborhood. Owners, as a result, are in a position to know the social-cultural context of their customers. Having beauty shop owners living in the same neighborhood reduces social barriers, and increases the likelihood of their serving as role models. In addition, beauty parlors are nonstigmatizing settings that allow Latinas to seek and receive assistance with personal problems in an atmosphere that encourages mutual support and self-respect.

DESCRIPTION OF SITE AND METHODS

The city of Lawrence, Massachusetts, is located approximately 25 miles north of Boston. According to the 1990 U.S. Census Bureau, Lawrence had a total population of 70,000, making it the fourth largest city in Massachusetts (Gaston, 1992). The Latino community consisted of 29,200 (almost evenly divided between Dominicans and Puerto Ricans).

All beauty parlors located within a clearly defined geographical area of Lawrence were located and asked to participate in this study. This area was selected because of its high concentration of Latino residents and commercial establishments. A total of seven shops were located and all consented to be interviewed.

Beauty shop owners were administered an in-person questionnaire consisting of four major sections: (1) background information on the shops, themselves, and their customers; (2) owner perceptions of customer social needs; (3) identification of the types of social services provided in the shops; and (4) interviewer impressions/observations of the establishments and the owner's willingness to collaborate with the study. The interviews varied in length from 45 to 60 minutes, depending upon the specificity of the responses to the open-ended questions.

FINDINGS

Although data were obtained on a wide variety of community needs such as HIV/AIDS, family violence, and alcoholism, this section will only focus on the latter. As noted in Table 1, all of the beauty parlors indicated a willingness to collaborate with social service agencies, if asked to do so.

Not all of the respondents indicated having an awareness of alcohol-related problems. Only two beauty parlors "A" and "B" indicated knowing customers who had alcohol problems–either themselves or their relatives. Most beauty parlors, however, indicated not having any knowledge of this or other social problems impacting on their customers.

As noted in Table 2, beauty parlor willingness to collaborate with agencies differed by level and type of involvement. Some beauty parlors were most willing to distribute information, i.e., pamphlets, provide advice (counseling), and facilitate lectures/discussions. Two owners ("E" and "G"), who indicated not having very much knowledge on the topic, were the most willing to provide an extensive range of services.

DISCUSSION OF FINDINGS

Not all beauty parlors are alike, even when owners share the same ethnic background and the shops are located in the same geographical area. Even when there is agreement to collaborate with human service agencies, collaboration is operationalized in a variety of ways. The Law-

TABLE 1. Collaborative Possibilities/Awareness of Alcohol Problems

Beauty Parlor	Willingness to Collaborate	Approached by Human Service Agency	Aware of Alcohol Problems of Customers	Aware of Alcohol Problems of Customer Significant Others
"A"	Yes	No	Yes	Yes
"B"	Yes	No	Yes	Yes
"C"	Yes	No	Yes	No
"D"	Yes	No	Don't Know	Don't Know
"E"	Yes	No	Don't Know	Don't Know
"F"	Yes	No	Don't Know	OK
"G"	Yes	No	OK	OK

TABLE 2. Beauty Parlor Collaborative Possibilities

Beauty Parlor	Pamphlets	Video	Lecture/ Discussion	Counseling/ Advice	Information/ Referral
A	Yes	No	Yes	Yes	No
B	Yes	No	No	No	No
C	Yes	No	Yes	Yes	Yes
D	Yes	No	No	Yes	No
E	Yes	Yes	Yes	Yes	Yes
F	Yes	No	No	No	No
G	Yes	Yes	Yes	Yes	Yes

rence study highlights the need for AODA organizations to undertake community based assessments of these establishments, and not taking cooperation and awareness of alcohol-related problems for granted.

Although all beauty parlors indicated that they had not been approached by human service agencies to engage in collaboration or assist in the delivery of services, and all were willing to collaborate in some fashion, there were still major differences between them. As already noted, willingness to collaborate differed in type and intensity. Owners who indicated not having knowledge of customers with alcohol problems showed the greatest willingness to engage in multiple collaborative activities. This willingness reinforces the need for AODA organizations to reach out to these establishments and offer some form of education on the signs of alcoholism and the options available to customers and their families.

IMPLICATIONS FOR SERVICE DELIVERY

The Lawrence study raised the possibility of a number of collaborative ventures between AODA agencies and beauty parlors. The impact of alcohol on Latinos does not allow the field of alcoholism the luxury of not seeking partners in addressing the problem. Consequently, beauty parlors have tremendous potential in this field.

Beauty parlors can collaborate with AODA agencies in the following ways: (1) outreach (information and referral); (2) community education; (3) research (asset and needs assessments); (4) provision of "advice" (counseling); and (5) co-sponsoring community events. These collaborative activities will vary in terms of resources required, time demands, and level of complexity (Delgado, 1994).

1. *Outreach*: Beauty parlors are located in the Latino community they serve and are generally well respected and trusted by the community. This position in the community makes beauty parlors ideal settings for conducting outreach activities. Beauty parlors are in a position to distribute information concerning alcohol and alcoholism, and make referrals to appropriate agencies. These referrals are facilitated if there is a contact person or liaison at the AODA organization who is responsible for all referrals originating from beauty parlors. This staff member, as a result, can work closely with these establishments and develop the necessary protocol, relationships, and trust to facilitate referrals and maintain the confidentiality of the customer.

2. *Community Education*: The initiation of community-based educational activities not only serves to identify potential clients but can also play a pivotal role in primary prevention. Educational activities can take many forms from workshops on increasing awareness of alcoholism to the co-sponsoring of community conferences and health fairs. These community-wide activities also generate positive publicity for the beauty parlors and agencies co-sponsoring the event. Community education projects generally are low labor intensive and do not require a huge expenditure of funds, yet generate a tremendous amount of publicity and awareness on a topic. The showing of videos on alcohol and alcoholism in beauty parlors is another activity that is capable of having a positive impact. The use of videos does not disrupt the daily activities in a beauty parlor, nor does it require customers to self-disclose if they do not wish to do so. The videos, however, must be in Spanish and reflect the socio-cultural background of the customers.

3. *Research*: Access to the Latino community in order to undertake research can prove very difficult for most human service organizations (Becerra & Zambrana, 1985). Consequently, AODA organizations must devise innovative ways of reaching this community. Beauty parlors and the people who work in them are in excellent positions to provide information on community strengths and needs, particularly those regarding women. Beauty parlor participation in asset and needs assessments provide AODA organizations with valuable community input. Beauty parlor personnel can participate in focus groups, as key informants, and on advisory committees. In short, they should be an integral part of any community-based research effort on alcohol. Their involvement in research, in addition, serves as a mechanism to get them involved in program and service delivery.

4. *Provision of Advice (Counseling)*: There is no question that beauticians advise on a multitude of problems facing their customers; this is particularly true with women who have been long-term customers and have

earned their respect and trust. Unfortunately, most beauticians have not been "trained" in providing counseling, or provided with support and consultation to help them carry out this activity. It is not to say, however, that they may not possess a "talent" or "gift" for this type of work. Consequently, any effort made by an AODA organization to "upgrade" beautician counseling skills would have profound impact on a community, particularly in situations where a customer refuses to seek professional help.

5. *Co-Sponsoring Community Events*: The development of partnerships between formal organizations and indigenous institutions offers much potential in creation of community-wide events. AODA organizations, beauty parlors, and other indigenous institutions can co-sponsor community festivals, fairs, and other activities. These events, however, do not have to focus on alcohol or other social problems. Most Latino communities in the United States hold annual Latino festivals of various types that serve to bring the community together and showcase leaders, youth, accomplishments, etc. Beauty parlors can be called upon to help publicize and fund these events.

Several Lawrence beauty parlors noted that they often provide services free of charge for those in need. One beauty parlor owner indicated that they had provided free hair cuts to individuals who were on public assistance and were going for job interviews. Another owner indicated that she welcomed class trips from local elementary schools and as a way of showing children what a career as a beautician was like. AODA organizations and beauty parlors, in essence, can work together on matters that go well beyond alcohol; these activities provide an opportunity for AODA organizations to become a part of the life of a community and not just its problems.

CONCLUSION

Communities of color have a wealth of indigenous resources that are available to address a multitude of social needs. These resources very often represent the first, and maybe only, effort at seeking assistance. Formal agencies, for a variety of reasons, may not be considered in the help-seeking process. Thus, indigenous resources can play a variety of roles in addressing community needs.

Latina beauty parlors are one source for involving women who are reluctant to seek formal help with their problem with alcohol or those of close relatives. The role these establishments can play, however, will vary according to level and type of involvement. In fact, it can be expected that not all beauty parlors will even want to get involved with an AODA organization. However, these establishments must make that decision rather than an agency deciding this.

Relationship building will play a crucial role in the development of collaborative activities, as it does in any form of interagency collaboration. This relationship building requires the investment of time, effort, and the engendering of trust on the part of both parties. Nevertheless, as found in Lawrence, many beauty parlors stand willing and able to join in the fight to prevent and treat alcoholism in the community!

REFERENCES

Aguirre-Molina, M. & Parra, P.A. (1995). Latino youth and families as active participants in planning change: A community-university partnership. In R.E. Zambrana (Ed.). *Understanding Latino families: Scholarship, policy, and practice* (pp. 130-153). Thousand Oaks, CA: Sage Publications.

Alcocer, A. (1993). Patterns of alcohol use among Hispanics. In R.S. Mayers, B.L. Kail & T.D. Watts (Eds.). *Hispanic substance abuse* (pp. 37-49). Springfield, IL: Charles C. Thomas Publisher.

Alcohol Alert (1994). *Alcohol and minorities.* No. 23, Ph. 347. Rockville, MD: National Institute on Alcohol Abuse and Alcoholism.

Anderson, R.B. & Maypole, D.E. (1989). Policy making and administration in minority alcoholism programs. In T.D. Watts & R. Wright (Eds.). *Alcoholism in minority populations* (pp. 177-189). Springfield, IL: Charles C. Thomas Publisher.

Becerra, R.M. & Zambrana, R. (1985). Methodological approaches to reach on Hispanics. *Social Work Research & Abstracts, 2,* 42-49.

Caetano, R. (1989). Alcohol use among Hispanic groups in the United States. *American Journal of Drug and Alcohol Abuse, 14,* 293-308.

Casement, M.R. & Roberts, F. (1989). The Federal role in alcoholism treatment and prevention for minority populations. In T.D. Watts & R. Wright (Eds.). *Alcoholism in minority populations* (pp. 159-175). Springfield, IL: Charles C. Thomas Publisher.

Comas-Diaz, L. (1986). Puerto Rican alcoholic women: Treatment considerations. *Alcoholism Treatment Quarterly, 3,* 47-57.

Davila, R.D. (1987). The history of Puerto Rican drinking patterns. In M. Singer, L. Davison & F. Yalin (Eds.). *Alcohol use and abuse among Hispanic adolescents* (pp. 1-18). Hartford, CT: Hispanic Health Council.

Delgado, M. (1996a). Implementing a natural support system AOD project: Administrative considerations and recommendations. *Alcoholism Treatment Quarterly, 14.*

Delgado, M. (1996b). Puerto Rican food establishments as social service organizations: Results of an asset assessment. *Journal of Community Practice, 3.*

Delgado, M. (1995a). Hispanic/Latinos. In J. Philleo & F.L. Brisbane (Eds.). *Cultural competence for social workers: A guide for alcohol and other drug abuse prevention professionals working with ethnic/racial communities* (pp. 43-67). Rockville, MD: U.S. Department of Health and Human Services.

Delgado, M. (1995b). Natural support systems and AOD services to communities of color: A California case example. *Alcoholism Treatment Quarterly*, 13, 13-24.

Delgado, M. (1995c). Community asset assessment and substance abuse prevention: A case study involving the Puerto Rican community. *Journal of Child & Adolescent Substance Abuse*, 4, 57-77.

Delgado, M. (1995d). Hispanic natural support systems and alcohol and other drug services: Challenges and rewards for practice. *Journal of Multicultural Social Work*, 12, 17-37.

Delgado, M. (1994). Hispanic natural support systems and the AODA field: A developmental framework for collaboration. *Journal of Multicultural Social Work*, 3, 11-37.

Dorrington, C. (1995). Central American refugees in Los Angeles: Adjustment of children and families. In R.E. Zambrana (Ed.). *Understanding Latino families: Scholarship, policy, and practice* (pp. 107-129). Thousand Oaks, CA: Sage Publications.

Fernandez-Pol, B. Bluestone, H., Missouri, C., Morales, G. & Mizruchi, M.S. (1986). Drinking patterns of inner-city Black Americans and Puerto Ricans. *Journal of Studies on Alcohol*, 47, 156-190.

Fernandez-Pol, B., Bluestone, H. & Mizruchi, M.S. (1985). Cultural influences and alcoholism: A study of Puerto Rican alcoholism. *Clinical and Experimental Research*, 9, 443-446.

Gaston Institute (1992). *Latinos in Lawrence*. Boston, MA: University of Massachusetts.

Gilbert, M.J. (1993). Intracultural variation in alcohol-related cognitions among Mexican Americans. In R.S. Mayers, B.L. Kail & T.D. Watts (Eds.). *Hispanic substance abuse* (pp. 51-64). Springfield, IL: Charles C. Thomas Publisher.

Gilbert, M.J. (1989). Hispanic Americans: Alcohol use, abuse and adverse consequences. In T.D. Watts & R. Wright, Jr. (Eds.). *Alcoholism in minority populations*. Springfield, IL: Charles C. Thomas Publisher.

Glick, R. & Moore, J. (Eds.). (1990). *Drugs in Hispanic communities*. New Brunswick, NJ: Rutgers University Press.

Gordon, A.J. (1989). State-of-the-art review: Caribbean Hispanics and their alcohol use. In D. Spiegler, D. Tate, S. Aitken & C. Christian (Eds.). *Alcohol use among U.S. Ethnic minorities* (pp. 135-146). Rockville, MD: U.S. Department of Health and Human Services.

Hacker, G.A., Collins, R. & Jacobson, M. (1987). *Marketing booze to Blacks*. Washington, D.C.: Center for Science in the Public Interest.

Halter, M. (Ed.). (1995). *New migrants in the marketplace: Boston's ethnic entrepreneurs*. Boston, MA: University of Massachusetts Press.

Herd, D. (1989). The epidemiology of drinking patterns and alcohol-related problems among U.S. Blacks. In D. Spiegler, D. Tate, S. Aitken & C. Christian (Eds.). *Alcohol use among U.S. Ethnic minorities* (pp. 3-50). Rockville, MD: U.S. Department of Health and Human Services.

Hoffman, F. (1987). An alcoholism program for Hispanics. *Clinical Sociology Review*, 5, 91-101.

Inclan, J. & Hernandez, M. (1992). Cross-cultural perspectives and codependence: The case of poor Hispanics. *American Journal of Orthopsychiatry*, 62, 245-255.

Kane, G.P. (1981). *Inner-city alcoholism: An ecological analysis and cross-cultural study*. New York: Human Sciences Press.

Kitano, H.H.L. & Chi, I. (1989). Asian Americans and alcohol: The Chinese, Japanese, Koreans, and Filipinos in Los Angeles. In D. Spiegler, D. Tate, S. Aitken & C. Christian (Eds.). *Alcohol use among U.S. ethnic minorities* (pp. 373-382). Rockville, MD: U.S. Department of Health and Human Services.

Levitt, P. (1995). A todos les llamo primo (I call everyone cousin): the social basis for Latino small businesses. In M. Halter (Ed.). *New migrants in the marketplace* (pp. 120-140). Boston, MA: University of Massachusetts Press.

Marin, G. (1993). Defining culturally appropriate community interventions: Hispanics as a case study. *Journal of Community Psychology*, 21, 149-161.

Maxwell, B. & Jacobson, M. (1989). *Marketing disease to Hispanics: The selling of alcohol, tobacco and junk foods*. Washington, D.C.: The Center for Science in the Public Interest.

Mayers, R.S. & Feazell, C.S. (1985). Prevention and treatment of Black alcoholism in the workplace. In R. Wright, Jr. & T.D. Watts (Eds.). *Prevention of Black alcoholism: Issues and strategies* (pp. 168-181). Springfield, IL: Charles C. Thomas Publisher.

Moran, J.R. & May, P.A. (1995). American Indians. In J. Philleo & F.L. Brisbane (Eds.). *Cultural competence for social workers: A guide for alcohol and other drug abuse prevention professionals working with ethnic/racial communities* (pp. 3-39). Rockville, MD: U.S. Department of Health and Human Services.

Panitz, D.R., McConchie, R.D., Sauber, S.R. & Fonseca, J.A. (1983). Role of machismo and the Hispanic family in the etiology and treatment of alcoholism in Hispanic American males. *American Journal of Family Therapy*, 11, 31-44.

Rebach, H. (1992). Alcohol and drug abuse among American minorities. In J.E. Trimble, C.S. Bolek & S.J. Niemcryk (Eds.). *Ethnic and multicultural drug abuse* (pp. 23-57). New York: The Haworth Press, Inc.

Sarason, Y. & Koberg, C. (1994). Hispanic women small business owners. *Hispanic Journal of Behavioral Sciences*, 16, 355-360.

Segura, D. (1992). Walking on eggshells: Chicanos in the labor force. In S.B. Knouse, P. Rosenfeld & A.L. Cubertson (Eds.). *Hispanics in the work force* (pp. 173-193). Newbury Park, CA: Sage Publications.

Sims, C. (November 29, 1992). Under siege: Liquor's inner-city pipeline. *The New York Times*, Section 3, p. 1, 6.

Singer, M., Davison, L. & Yalin, F. (1987). *Alcohol use and abuse among Hispanic adolescents*. Hartford, CT: Hispanic Health Council.

Swift, C.F. & Beverly, S. (1985). The utilization of ministers as alcohol counselors and educators: Increasing prevention and treatment resources in the Black community. In R. Wright, Jr. & T.D. Watts (Eds.). *Prevention of Black alcohol-*

ism: *Issues and strategies* (pp. 182-198). Springfield, IL: Charles C. Thomas Publisher.

Triandis, H.C., Lisansky, J., Marin, G. & Betancourt, H. (1984). Simpatia as a cultural script of Hispanics. *Journal of Personality and Social Psychology*, 47, 1363-1375.

Watts, T.D. & Wright, Jr., R. (Eds.). (1989). *Alcoholism in minority populations*. Springfield, IL: Charles C. Thomas Publisher.

Williams, M. (1985). Blacks and alcoholism: Issues in the 1980s. In R. Wright, Jr. & T.D. Watts (Eds.). *Prevention of Black alcoholism: Issues and strategies* (pp. 13-31). Springfield, IL: Charles C. Thomas Publisher.

Wright, Jr., R. & Watts, T.D. (Eds.). (1985). *Prevention of Black alcoholism: Issues and strategies*. Springfield, IL: Charles C. Thomas Publisher.

Professional Development
of AODA Practice with Latinos:
The Utility of Supervision,
In-Service Training and Consultation

Betty Garcia, PhD

SUMMARY. The scope and complexity of the issues faced by practitioners providing services to Latinos necessitates that practitioner
skills must increasingly demonstrate multicultural competency. This
article addresses the use of three methods as a means of providing
ongoing learning of cross cultural competencies for practice with
Latinos Receiving AODA services. *[Article copies available for a fee
from The Haworth Document Delivery Service: 1-800-342-9678. E-mail
address: getinfo@haworth.com]*

The scope and complexity of the issues faced by practitioners providing
services to Latinos necessitates that practitioner skills must increasingly
demonstrate multicultural competency. The absence of a systematic[1] integration of multicultural content into academic professional training programs identifies a void in practitioner cross cultural competency preparation. However, the use of supervision, inservice training and consultation
can be utilized within human service agencies and within a variety of
organizational structures in the public and private sectors to provide ongo-

---

Betty Garcia is Associate Professor, Department of Social Work and Education, California State University at Fresno, 5310 Campus Drive, Fresno, CA
93740-0102.

[Haworth co-indexing entry note]: "Professional Development of AODA Practice with Latinos:
The Utility of Supervision, In-Service Training and Consultation." Garcia, Betty. Co-published simultaneously in *Alcoholism Treatment Quarterly* (The Haworth Press, Inc.) Vol. 16, No. 1/2, 1998, pp. 85-
108; and: *Alcohol Use/Abuse Among Latinos: Issues and Examples of Culturally Competent Services*
(ed: Melvin Delgado) The Haworth Press, Inc., 1998, pp. 85-108. Single or multiple copies of this article
are available for a fee from The Haworth Document Delivery Service [1-800-342-9678, 9:00 a.m. - 5:00
p.m. (EST). E-mail address: getinfo@haworth.com].

85

ing cross cultural competence learning for practitioners. This article will address the use of these three methods as a means of providing ongoing learning of cross cultural competencies for practice with Latinos receiving AODA services. The discussion will first focus on substance abuse assessment and treatment considerations, the relevance of integrating ethnicity factors into treatment, and on specific substance abuse issues related to Latinos. A review of the characteristics and functions of supervision, inservice training and consultation and their application as resources for cross cultural skill learning will be presented.

Substance abuse issues raised in relation to the Latino population are significant by virtue of the growing presence of Latinos. The growth of the Latino population between 1980 and 1990, was especially dramatic in that it increased by 53% percent, from 14.6 million to 22.4 million, constituting nine percent of the nation's population, with Latinos of Mexican origin representing the largest group at 60% (U.S. Bureau of the Census, 1993). Current projections indicate that the Latino population could reach 39 million by 2010, and potentially 59 million by 2030. Considerable evidence suggests that Latinos are at risk for alcohol and substance abuse compared to non-Hispanic populations (Brunswick & Messeri, 1984; Caetano & Kaskutas, 1995; Maddihian, Newcomb & Bentler, 1985).

Research findings indicate that there is a significant amount of alcohol drinking prior to adolescence (Caetano, 1986; Malone, 1986), drug use has increased dramatically among Latinos in the past few decades (Orlandi, 1992), and the stability of heavy drinking is greater among Hispanic men compared to white men (Caetano & Kaskatas, 1995, p. 558). Also, Latinos have shown greater at risk status for alcohol related injuries compared to other groups (Cherpitel, 1992, p. 1075) and Latino males have been found to abuse alcohol five to six times more than do non-Latino whites (Caetano, 1985; Valdez, Delgado, Cervantes & Bowler, 1993).

There are also notable findings related to generation in the United States and level of acculturation. Immigrant Latino males drinking patterns have been found to change from low frequency and high quantity to both high frequency and high quantity after immigration (Cervantes, Gilbert, Salgado de Synder & Padilla, 1991), and U.S. born and higher acculturated men and women show higher levels of drinking (Alcocer, 1993; Austin & Gilbert, 1989; Golding, Burnam, Wells & Benjamin, 1993; Padilla & Morrissey, 1993).

AODA ASSESSMENT AND INTERVENTION

Much of the discussion on assessment and intervention planning in AODA reflects an ecosystemic perspective regarding the significance of various factors in creating AODA and in developing effective treatment plans. Treatment for alcoholism is found in several settings that include mental health, chemical dependency and nonprofessional settings (Brown, 1995). Although there is a lack of agreement regarding the etiology of alcohol and other drug abuse, a wide range of factors that include biochemical, genetic, familial and environmental are viewed as potentially having a role in creating and or maintaining addictive behaviors (Brown, 1995; Straussner, 1993). Other situational factors, such as extreme stress and cultural shock, are believed to have a role in stimulating alcohol abuse because of its capacity to strain coping responses and social resources, as well as increase negative affect (Brown, Vik, Patterson, Grant and Schuckit, 1995). More recently there is greater emphasis on examining the individual's transactions with his or her environment as a means for understanding motivation for change, rather than regarding motivation only as a personal quality (Miller, 1995), and therefore potentially psychologizing a complex multifaceted process.

Assessment skills are needed at both the screening and testing levels. Screening assists in detecting potential at risk status (Cooney, Zweben, & Fleming, 1995; Miller, Westerberg, & Waldron, 1995), while testing assists with diagnosis and comprehending the specifics of the individual's unique situation (Miller, Westerberg, & Waldron, 1995). Assessment at all levels is essential because of the high incidence of faulty assessments that risk unsuitable treatment (Freeman, 1990), which sometimes occurs due to lack of awareness of the role of AODA in the presenting problem. Also, the ubiquitous presence of stereotypes about AODA can interfere with recognizing addiction (Liftik, 1995; Straussner, 1993). For example, the class based image of addictive behavior being primarily associated with underemployed, undereducated, low-income populations needs to be examined more closely.

Thorough assessment of AODA necessitates examining how the family system presents their difficulties in order to identify relevant treatment (Flores-Ortiz & Bernal, 1990; Straussner, 1993), and constructing an intergenerational assessment, and gathering information on drinking history, including reviewing quantity, quality, and frequency of use (Liftik, 1995). Careful evaluation of risk factors involves reviewing events and conditions in their life that may be connected to the development of alcoholism and/or possibly promote its abuse, and checking for direct indicators of abuse (Liftik, 1995). For example, "growing up in an alcoholic home," peer pressure or "poor psychosocial adjustment and lack of psychological resources" are all potential indicators of risk (Liftik, 1995, p. 63)

Process skills are essential in creating emotional safety, while balancing feedback and allowing the client to lead (Amodeo, 1995b), conveying to the client that s/he has deceived you and feels "support to reveal the truth to themselves and to you" (Liftik, 1995 p. 77). In this context, rather than being immobilized by feeling threatened, the client "can tolerate more and more of the discomfort that goes along with relinquishing denial and defensiveness" (Liftik, 1995, p. 62).

Appropriate client matching with treatment options requires thoughtful review of possible realms of client functioning (Mattson, Allen, Longabaugh, Nickless, Connors & Kadden, 1994) that include problem severity, cognitive style, social stability, client preferences for treatment, family history, patterns of alcohol use and motivational status (Connors, Allen, Cooney, DiClemente, Tonigan & Anton, 1994, p. 94), client demographics and interpersonal functioning (Mattson et al., 1994). Mattson et al. (1994) estimate that there are at least 23 types of programs that are cognitive in their orientation, emphasize relational interventions or pitch to higher levels of processing. Hester and Miller (1995) provide an extensive review of models that are in use.

Practice in AODA finds the practitioner involved in a myriad of assessment and treatment activities that require a broad variety of skills regarding interactional process skills, self awareness about potential countertransferential concerns, and appreciation for the client's tasks at various points of his or her recovery. For example, the distinct efforts needed for working with the treatment phase, stabilization, rehabilitation and relapse prevention (Straussner, 1993, p. 352) entails recognizing the unique tasks needed at each point and a process orientation that views both treatment and relapse prevention as ongoing processes (Straussner, 1993; Tommasello, Tyler, Tyler & Zhang, 1993). Moreover, there is support for the view that effective strategies are those that work with change strategies (Miller, 1995), teach coping skills, mobilize community forces, instill values toward prosocial behavior (McCrady & Delaney, 1995; Miller & Hester, 1986; Monti, Rohsenow, Colby, & Abrams, 1995), and provide supportive environments, rather than present threats (Tommasello, Tyler, Tyler & Zhang, 1993).

Key qualities that have been identified as indicators of practitioner mastery in substance abuse services include personal work with the filters derived from personal and family experiences that can lead to stereotypic thinking about clients (Amodeo, 1995a), familiarity with the variety of tasks and client's needs at various stages of recovery (Brown, 1995), and ability to facilitate client toleration of increasing levels of discomfort associated with the abandonment of denial (Brown, 1995). Amodeo

(1995) proposes that it is essential in the drinking stage not to force the client with excessive confrontational interventions, work with denial as a predictable dynamic and pace raising client anxiety with the awareness that, initially, clients cannot tolerate more than 10 to 15 minutes at a time (p. 114). Such work also requires self assessment regarding the potential for colluding with the client (Liftik, 1995).

Skilled efforts in ongoing treatment and with relapse prevention require the flexibility to take multiple roles as therapist, educator and coach through the drinking and transitional stages (Amodeo, 1995, p. 97), an orientation that approaches relapse with a perspective of limiting the "slip or relapse as quickly as possible and . . . resume[ing] the change process" (Miller, 1995, p. 92). Katz and Ney (1995) view relapse as the event of resuming substance use in a "context of a complex process—often with identifiable signs, such as the progressive deterioration of prorecovery behaviors, thoughts and feelings" (p. 232). Others propose that effective work requires a goal of educating the client about the relapse process so that s/he can identify indicators of possible relapse and secure needed resources for oneself (Straussner, 1993), and, a clear understanding of the family context, both immediate and extended (Flores-Ortiz & Bernal, 1990).

ETHNICITY AS CONTEXT FOR PRACTICE

Cross Cultural Competency and Ethnicity

Awareness of the need for cross cultural competency in human services is based on the appreciation for the uniqueness of individuals, their assumptive worlds, and their social and cultural history. Effective practice in a context of changing demographics and increasing diversity makes it imperative for all practitioners to be prepared to utilize interventions that demonstrate sensitivity to cultural difference and ethnic diversity (Applewhite, Wong & Daley, 1991; Brisbane, 1995; Delgado, 1995; Langrod, Alksne, Lowinson & Ruiz, 1981; Manoleas, 1994).

Cross culturally sensitive practice is characterized by the recognition that culture is dynamic and in a constant process of change, awareness of the heterogeneity within a culture and of the cultural beliefs related to perceptions of well being (Bellah, Madsen, Sullivan, Swidler & Tipton, 1985). Culture represents "an historically transmitted pattern of meanings embodied in symbols, a system of inherited conceptions expressed in symbolic form by means of which [persons] communicate, perpetuate and develop their knowledge about and attitudes toward life" (Geertz, 1973,

p. 89). The minority status[2] of Latinos in the U.S. also introduces a need for practitioners to be cognizant of the social meaning of difference in this society and the effects of this meaning on the individual (i.e., social identity), as well as the presence of multiple ethnicities and therefore, multiple social identities. Phinney (1996) has proposed that culture is an inadequate focus for understanding ethnicity precisely because of the heterogeneity within groups based on socioeconomic class, level of acculturation and other factors. She goes on to propose three factors that are helpful in accounting for the psychological significance of ethnicity. Phinney proposes that rather than thinking about ethnicity as a category, it is best understood as three clusters, which are culture, ethnic identity[3] and minority status, which are "dimensions along which individuals vary" (p. 918). This author's perspective on cross cultural competency building utilizes ethnicity as the organizing concept. Most relevant for practice is the realization that the mere presence of difference in culture and ethnicity creates a context of different meanings that can result in disparate perceptions regarding what problems exist and expectations regarding how to resolve those problems (Longres, 1991).

Chau (1991) identifies two concepts that are integral for effective culturally competent practice. First is sociocultural dissonance (Chau, 1987 cited in Chau, 1992) which refers to the stress created by cultural difference as a significant source of difficulties. Second, is dislocation (De Hoyos, De Hoyos & Anderson, 1986) which refers to the escalation of social disconnection that individuals experience as a result of a lack of access to opportunity and with discrimination. In general, culturally relevant practice is based on a view that culture is a strength and needs to be validated in treatment (Cheung, 1991a; Oetting & Beauvais, 1991). Such practice gives particular attention in assessment to the exploration of factors related to the immigration transition process, generation in the U.S., acculturation (Chau, 1991, 1992; Longres, 1991; Orlandi, 1992; Padilla & Salgado de Synder, 1995), and to gender status (Padilla & Salgado de Synder, 1992; Straussner, 1993; Terrell, 1993). A culturally sensitive assessment will also examine factors related to the stress of coping with two cultures (Chau, 1992), and the strengths, assets and needs that exist on an individual, family and community level (Delgado, 1995).

Dungee-Anderson and Becket (1995) suggest that process skills are notably significant because a practitioner's skills can be limited by a lack of self awareness that can potentially lead to countertransference or societal projection (Pinderhughes, 1989), and/or flawed application of competencies. However, the development and maintenance of such self reflective practice is dependent on a practice context (i.e., organizational structure) that appreciates the role of culture and its influence on adaptive coping (Cross, Bazron, Dennis & Isaacs, 1989; Daniels, Wodarsky, & Davis, 1987).

In substance abuse practice settings, more specific concerns with cross cultural competency have been raised. Public Health Service statistics (as cited in Orlandi, 1992, p. 9) indicate that ethnic/racial groups are "over-represented among injected drug abusers and among those people treated for drug abuse-related illnesses." While there is some support for a relationship between ethnicity and substance abuse in relation to beliefs about substance abuse, and the presence of cultural factors that might contribute to high or low usage (Cheung, 1991a; Delgado, 1989; Heath, 1991; Straussner, 1993; Terrell, 1993), there remains a need to more thoroughly examine the relationship between ethnicity and substance abuse (Cheung, 1991b). For a comprehensive review of literature on ethnocultural factors and substance abuse see Terrell (1993) for a discussion of the relationship between acculturation, stress, coping, social support and beliefs about substance abuse.

Some direction for applying cross culturally sensitive practice with ethnic groups has been provided in relation to assessment and intervention. For one, Amodeo and Jones (in press, p. 34) provide a framework for conducting a cultural AOD assessment for evaluating an individual's vulnerability to AOD problems and the potential for those individuals to receive culturally appropriate interventions. Key questions in this evaluation include "what types of individuals are most likely to be stigmatized?", "to what extent must individuals go against cultural norms to identify themselves as in need of services?", "what cultural events may constitute high risk situations for relapse?", and "to what extent would an individual or family have to go against cultural norms to achieve permanent behavioral change?" (pp. 25-31). Other proposals are premised on the significance of not limiting interventions to any one individual factor (Yin, Zapata & Katims, 1995) and implementing multilevel interventions with the individual and the family (Comas-Diaz, 1986), as well as engage in community networks and promote the development of interagency collaboration (Delgado, 1995). Such broad-based interventions whose purpose is to address the uniqueness of individuals and their communities has, in fact, been seen as enhancing the responsiveness of clients to the agency by increasing its credibility and relevance (Terrell, 1993).

Practice implications identified in the literature on ethnicity provide a context for looking more specifically at substance abuse considerations that are identified in relation to the Latino/Hispanic population.

WORKING WITH LATINO POPULATIONS

Latino Sociodemographics

Current sociodemographics of the Latino population indicate that a significant proportion of Latinos continue to deal with economic hardship. For example, in 1991 about 27% of all Latinos were living in poverty, and Latino single female heads of household with children under the age of 18 had a higher rate of poverty (60%) than any other group. Moreover, in 1990 only half of all Latino adults, age 25 and over, had attained a high school degree (U.S. Bureau of the Census, 1993).

Population demographics take on particularly significant meaning in light of proposals that individual and environmental pressures, such as individual stress, familial conflict, familial disruption, dislocation, and acculturation processes, are associated with greater vulnerability to substance abuse (Delgado, 1994; Schinke, Moncher, Palleja, Zayas & Schilling, 1988). Special concerns have been identified in regards to contemporary trends. For one, the changing role of women (Padilla & Salgado de Synder, 1995; Ortiz, 1995) resulting from their increasing participation in the labor force, increasing level of education and their acculturation process (Vazquez-Nuttall, Romero-Garcia, & De Leon, 1987) has direct implications for adjustments families must confront. The increasing numbers of single Latino heads of household, rates of divorce (Padilla & Salgado de Synder, 1992), and numbers of single, separated, divorced or widowed Latino women are particularly alarming in light of the reality that female headed families have lower incomes and tend to be more poor compared to other families (Ortiz, 1995, p. 36).

Second, greater attention is needed to the experiences of immigrants in their transition to this country, experiences with acculturation (Padilla, 1980), and with the intergenerational conflicts that often arise as children adapt more quickly to the new host culture (Szapocznik & Kurtines, 1980). Awareness of the importance of addressing Latino substance abuse issues in relation to the cultural context (Delgado, 1995; Langrod, Alksne, Lowinson, & Ruiz, 1981; Terrell, 1993; Tucker, 1985) has led to recommendations regarding the need for practitioners to develop cross cultural competency (Terrell, 1993), intervention planning that addresses the effects of substance abuse on the family, and the availability of natural support systems as a resource (Delgado, 1995; Straussner, 1993).

THE UTILITY OF SUPERVISION, INSERVICE TRAINING AND CONSULTATION AS RESOURCES FOR THE ONGOING DEVELOPMENT OF CROSS CULTURAL COMPETENCIES

Supervision, inservice training and consultation are three vehicles for ongoing learning in agency settings that are available as forums for the acquisition and further development of cross cultural competencies. These three represent a continuum of learning activities that can be generally said to range from high learner accountability (supervision), medium accountability (inservice training) and low accountability (consultation). The following will discuss central aspects of each regarding definition, functions, process assumptions, and goals.

Supervision

Supervision is an ongoing interactional process between two practitioners, where there is an assignment or designation of a supervisor to assist the worker in activities that benefit the client and is typified by clear expectations of accountability by both (Walsh, 1990). Powell (1993) proposes that the process is characterized by the transformation of principles into skills with four overlapping foci: administrative, evaluative, clinical and supportive (p. 9). While the inception of supervision was instituted to respond to a low level of professionalization (Kutzik, 1977; Perlmutter, 1972 as cited in Hardcastle, 1992), in the 1980s the emphasis shifted to technique, solution, and task-oriented (Powell, 1993). Supervision has been proposed both as a consultative, collaborative process that is closer to consultation (Caplan, 1970). It is also perceived as an activity that moves through developmental stages that evolve into mutual dialogue and address organizational, work coordination and teaching issues (Taibbi, 1995).

In relation to functions, Holloway and Brager (1989) make the distinction between two activities: (1) that of providing structure as those activities that include role and purpose clarification, developing supervisory contracts and coordinating worker's actions, and (2) the presence of support, as the affective dimension of supervision that relates to the presence of trust, respect and concern for the worker's welfare (p. 86). Hardcastle (1992) suggests supervisory functions can be problematic in that supervisors often are not trained or skilled to perform all of the functions (p. 64) such as dealing with organizational issues, teaching, work coordination and linkage with higher management levels.

Supervisory activities that enhance practitioners foremost are based on a well-developed supervisory relationship (Friedlander & Ward, 1984; Powell, 1989; Walsh, 1990), and focus on pertinent content such as individual and professional development of the practitioner (Powell, 1993), clarity about expectations and responsibilities (Taibbi, 1995), parallel process (Laveman, 1994, Taibbi, 1995), beliefs about how people change (Powell, 1993), and psychodynamic as well as organizational issues related to ethnicity and racism (Chandler & Hunt, 1980; Peterson, 1991). These efforts can be realized through various formats that include conjoint (Braver, Graffin & Holahan, 1990; Lenihan & Kirk, 1992), peer group (Hardcastle, 1992; Powell, 1993), mutual aid (Breashears, 1995), or group supervision (Holloway & Johnson, 1985; Sansbury, 1982; Wilbur, Roberts-Wilbur, Morris, Betz & Hart, 1991). As a role model (Deveaux & Lubell, 1994), the supervisor provides direction on an organizational level (Walsh, 1990), should be open to feedback, and assists the practitioner in feeling open and relaxed (Powell, 1989).

Inservice Training

Inservice training is distinguished by several features that include its didactic quality (Reid & Beard, 1980), value on the adult learner model (Knowles, 1970; Kopfstein, 1994; Rycus, 1978), the advantage of disseminating information to practitioners (Pothast, 1988), activities such as orientation, skill development training, and continuing education (Nodell, 1977, p. 37), and its implementation through structured blocks of time (Amatea, Munson, Anderson & Rudner, 1980). Caplan (1970) distinguishes this learning medium by pointing out that practitioners are free to participate or not; however, once enrolled, s/he "undertakes to pay attention to the teacher, to do [the] exercises and to carry out the precepts of the teacher" (p. 23).

Zober, Seipel and Skinner (1982) have identified two general types of models with distinct formats: (1) the classroom model that integrates learning within a class time frame, and (2) the action-oriented model which engages the practitioner in identifying the implementation of learning in on-the-job performance (p. 23). The practitioners' involvement in the process of creating an individualized plan for change is proposed as a way to heighten their commitment to change (Gregoire, 1994; Zober, Seipel & Skinner, 1982).

The key functions of inservice training are to elevate the competence of all staff members, improve on-the-job performance (Nodell, 1977; Zober, 1980), and increase the practitioner's mastery and knowledge base regarding treatment and ethics (Houle, Cyphert & Boggs, 1987). Several key features that are found to promote the success of the training include staff involvement in the decision making regarding the inservice training (Marks & Hixon, 1986; Reid & Beard, 1980) and the establishment of rapport between the trainer(s) and the staff before competencies assessment takes place (Leitner, 1980, p. 49). Inservice training is also enhanced by content that is directly relevant to staff needs (Rycus, 1978; Vinokur-Kaplan, 1986), the distribution of sessions over a period of a few months, particularly weekdays (Leitner, 1980), and moving practitioners and supervisors into training roles, as trainers move into a consultant role (Reid & Beard, 1980). Reid and Beard also suggest that preparation for inservice training should meet three objectives: (1) identification of learning interests of both line and management staff, (2) determination of level of staff familiarity with inservice concepts, and (3) adaptation of the training to match the practice setting.

Consultation

Caplan's (1970) model of consultation, which deals with prevention and treatment of mental disorders, originally developed in the '60s, remains the principal model for consultation (Rosenbaum & McCarty, 1994). Although the title of consultant has been applied to any professional activity carried out by a specialist, it specifically refers to interaction between two professionals, the consultant (a specialist) and the consultee, who invokes his or her help in regard to work on a problem in an area which is the former's area of expertise on an ad hoc basis (Caplan, 1970). The consultant role traditionally involves a four step process that includes: (1) initial contact, (2) assessment and data gathering, (3) formulation, and (4) recommendations (Caplan, 1970).

The model for mental health consultation was developed with a focus on three areas: (1) provision of consultation to the community's practitioners in order to improve mental health service delivery, (2) the development of preventive services to reduce relapse (tertiary prevention), identification of high risk populations (secondary prevention), and reduction of the incidence of mental disorders (Werner & Tyler, 1993, p. 689). The model outlined a focus for consultation on four levels that included: (1) client-centered case consultation, (2) consultee-centered case consultation, (3) program-centered administrative consultation, and (4) consultee-centered administrative consultation (Caplan, 1970). Some criticism has been directed at the clinical emphasis and lack of systemic perspective in the model (Rapoport, 1963).

Unlike supervision, the consultant takes no responsibility for the interventions (Caplan, 1970; Kadushin, 1977). The advisory nature of the consultation leaves the consultee free to choose what aspects of the consultation he or she will utilize (Caplan & Caplan, 1993; Kadushin, 1977; Munson, 1983). More recently it is recommended that the focus of the consultation should focus on the provider and not the client, that the frame of reference be broadened to include dynamics related to interpersonal and institutional factors, and that a collaborative, partnership-oriented practice replace a consultative role in school-based settings (Caplan, Caplan & Erchul, 1995). In the collaborative model, the consultant engages in implementing the recommendations and takes some degree of responsibility for outcomes.

Other models of consultation emphasize a problem solving focus, social system orientation, group context for consultation (Kudushin, 1977) and whose model focuses on organizational problems (Argyris, 1976; Schein, 1969). Argyris points out that a potential dilemma for consultants arises from their role of initiating open communication about rational organizational issues, which potentially can trigger more sensitive communication on an interpersonal level and create discomfort. Argyris suggests that the goals of consultation should include the development of process skills to improve the staff's ability to give and take feedback, their ability to take responsibility for their feelings and the ability of the organization to solve similar problems in the future (p. 333).

Characteristics of consultation that appear to enhance its effectiveness include an action-oriented approach rather than simply didactic (Backer, 1992), follow-up contact to assure maintenance of the benefits of the consult (Harchik, Sherman, Shelson & Strouse, 1992), and the use of a theoretical framework as a conceptual basis for assessment, analysis and direction for strategies (Lange & Grieger, 1993). In addition, it is also proposed that successful consultation means being alert for theme interference, that is, aspects of the consultant's past that may trigger discomfort and oversensitivity to some issues in the consultation process (Caplan, 1970; Caplan & Caplan, 1993).

An overview of the singular contributions of supervision, inservice training and consultation as vehicles for ongoing professional development highlights some distinctions and overlap between them. The rigorous, ongoing nature of supervision that endows the supervisor with the authority to monitor and direct the practitioner's progress makes supervision a useful vehicle for identifying problematic issues, and for following up on issues identified through inservice training. In this regard inservice training can be extremely helpful in overall consciousness raising of the staff (Freeman, 1990). The utility of consultation as a time limited resource, that is used intermittently and whose applicability is concerned with a limited segment (Kadushin, 1977), highlights its value as a back up for practice issues identified in supervision (Rooney, 1985) and as an enhancement of professional growth (Taibbi, 1995).

SUMMARY AND RECOMMENDATIONS: THE APPLICATION OF SUPERVISION, INSERVICE TRAINING AND CONSULTATION FOR CROSS CULTURAL COMPETENCY DEVELOPMENT

Each of these three mediums embodies unique benefits and limitations as resources for agencies in the task of providing ongoing professional development of cross cultural competencies. Similarly, the use of these resources in the service of sharpening cross cultural competencies must be practiced within a conceptual framework that incorporates the content, values and processes related to working with Latinos in a substance abuse treatment setting that has been identified here.

Cross cultural competence goes beyond awareness of diversity issues and is the implementation of practices that reflect value and appreciation of the role of an individual's history and cultural identifications (Manoleas, 1994). In this paper I have asserted that such competence in working with substance abuse issues with Latinos results in awareness about (1) substance abuse issues as they pertain to the Latino community, for example in relation to gender, immigrant status and level of acculturation factors, (2) cognizance of the role and implications of psychosocial stress in relation to substance abuse, (3) the importance of conducting an assessment that incorporates cultural factors, family dynamics and social support resources, and (4) possible effects of the combination of stereotypes based on ethnicity and addictive behaviors. Cross cultural competence will also reflect awareness of the significance of ethnicity in the lives of individuals, curiosity regarding assumptive worlds and social identities derived from cultural identifications, and value on doing one's own personal work on feelings about diversity issues.

Emphasis has also been placed on working within a practice framework that is systemic and ecological in nature. Such an approach has implications for both assessment and process skills. Formulations and intervention targets should incorporate individual, family, social support and physical and social environmental factors (e.g., neighborhood, other human service agency providers, racism). Process skills are essential in engaging the client in the difficult and sensitive work of confronting denial, dealing with relapse prevention and actual relapse.

The following recommendations are presented as a means for effective-

ly utilizing supervision, inservice training and consultation for the acquisition and development of cross cultural competencies for AODA practice
with Latinos.

Supervision

1. Goals of supervision should have clarity in terms of expectations,
   incorporate specific cross cultural competencies and include implementation of interventions on multilevels (i.e., individual, family,
   group, social support, community).
2. Supervision should reflect a developmental progression of the practitioner taking increasing responsibility for initiating discussions on
   the role of ethnicity in relation to assessment, formulation and intervention planning.
3. The supervisor should encourage open communication and feedback on the management of sensitive supervisory and organizational
   issues related to Latino substance abuse issues. For example, the
   practioner should be encouraged to explore culturally sensitive perspectives and approaches, even when these issues (e.g., significance
   of ethnicity in the formulation, role of diverse ethncities in the helping relationship) appear to go beyond what is conventionally discussed or practiced in their agency setting.
4. Organizations will provide supervisors with the resources and support to receive training for managing diversity issues in supervision
   on cognitive and affective levels.
5. The agency will be open to a variety of supervisory formats for dealing with ethnicity and substance abuse that include supervisor-led
   group supervision and peer group supervision.
6. Supervisory discussions will address and support the practitioner
   participating in the development of cross cultural competencies by
   organizations and professional groups other than the agency.
7. The supervisor will encourage, be attuned to and participate in utilizing parallel process as a concept for dealing with dynamics that
   arise in relation to Latino clients, i.e., identify therapist-supervisor
   dynamics and tensions that originate in the client-therapist relationship.

Inservice Training

1. Both line staff and management will participate in decision making
   regarding the selection of topics and presenters on cross cultural
   competency.

2. From an adult learner perspective, practitioners will identify and take responsibility for their learning needs and implementation of learning about practice with Latinos.
3. The agency will integrate content on the value of cross cultural competency and appreciation of diversity in all inservice activities, such as orientation and skill building training.
4. The organization will provide leadership that values and appreciates difference, particularly as it applies to Latino client population concerns.
5. Inservice training will incorporate an action-oriented model that includes individualized plans for on-the-job implementation.
6. Inservice training will reflect both line staff and management cross cultural competency learning needs, and include follow up meeting(s) in order to consolidate and maintain the learning gains.
7. Inservice training will be structured so that it is distributed over a period of a few months in order to provide staff the opportunity to assimilate the concepts and apply them.

Consultation

1. Consultation will aim to focus on practitioner rather than client oriented concerns about culturally competent formulations and interventions.
2. Consultation will function within a systems, ecologically minded frame of reference that is mindful of the role of resources and obstacles contributed by culture, racism and mainstream society for Latinos dealing with substance abuse.
3. In relation to organizational consultations, the organization will be cognizant of the discomfort that can arise as the consultation moves from safe, rational organizational issues to more sensitive and difficult feelings that arise when individuals discuss ethnic differences. Commitment to learning about practice and/or organizational factors that may obstruct culturally competent practice will provide the motivation to pursue and resolve these issues.
4. The agency will review possible consultants with the purpose of selecting individuals who have dealt on a personal and professional level with diversity issues. All consultants, regardless of specialization should be expected to manage dealing with diversity issues as they arise.
5. The agency will provide follow-up to the consultation in order to consolidate the gains of the consultation.

The above recommendations are presented with a perspective of high-lighting the unique benefits and resources provided by each medium as a method for change and the development of cultural competencies. While each offers specialized benefits, it is important to bear in mind the utility of developing a program that employs all three of these resources in a way that they complement each other. It is recommended that there be greater development of agency policy that supports experimentation with supervisory, inservice and consultative activities that stimulate and support all agency staffs development of cross cultural competencies. While much has been written regarding the functions of supervision, inservice training and consultation, there is a lack of literature on the use of these three methods for the acquisition and maintance of cross cultural competency in practice with Latinos in substance abuse. Additional research is needed that links these three methods in a systematic and thoughtful way for purposes of staff development.

NOTES

1. Mandates for multicultural curriculum have been instituted in several disciplines such as social work, psychology, and counseling psychology; however, there is yet a tremendous amount of work that is needed to assure the presence of both specialized multicultural courses and its inclusion in a substantive way in all courses.

2. Minority status is used synonymously with minority group which refers to a subordinate group whose members have significantly less control or power over their own lives than the members of a dominant or majority group (Schaefer, 1984).

3. Ethnic identity represents an "enduring, fundamental aspect of the self that includes a sense of membership in an ethnic group and the attitudes and feelings associated with that membership" (Bernal & Knight, 1993; Keefe, 1992; Phinney, 1990 cited in Phinney, 1996).

REFERENCES

Aguilar, M.A., DiNitto, D.M., Franklin, C., Lopez-Pilkinton, B. (1991). Mexican-American families: A psychoeducational approach for addressing chemical dependency. *Child and Adolescent Social Work, 8*(4), 309-325.

Alcocer, A.M. (1993). Patterns of alcohol use among Hispanics. In Mayers, R. Kail, B. and Watts, T. (Eds.). *Hispanic substance abuse.* Springfield, IL: Charles C. Thomas Publisher.

Amatea, E., Munson, P., Anderson, L. and Rudner, R. (1980). A short-term training program for caseworkers in family counseling. *Social Casework: The Journal of Contemporary Social Work, 61*, 205-213.

Amodeo, M. (1995a). The therapist's role in the drinking stage. In Brown, S. and Yalom, I. (Eds.). *Treating alcoholism.* San Francisco: Jossey-Bass Publishers.

_____ (1995b). The therapist's role in the transitional stage. In Brown, S. and Yalom, I. (Eds.). *Treating alcoholism.* San Francisco: Jossey-Bass Publishers.

Amodeo, M. and Jones, L.K. (in press). Viewing alcohol and other drug use cross-culturally: A cultural framework for clinical practice. *Journal of Families in Society.*

Applewhite, S., Wong, P. and Daley, J. (1991). Services approaches and issues in Hispanic agencies. *Administration and Policy in Mental Health, 19*(1), 27-37.

Argyris, C. (1976). Explorations in consulting-client relationships. In Bennis, W., Benne, K., Chin, R. and Corey, K. (Eds.). *The planning of change.* (3rd ed.). New York: Holt, Rinehart and Winston.

Austin, G.A. & Gilbert, M.J. (1989). Substance abuse among Latino youth. In *Prevention Research Update,* No. 3. Portland, OR: Western Center for Drug-Free Schools and Communities.

Backer, T.E. (1992). Gerald Caplan's approaches and consultation with public mental health organizations in the 1990's. *Consulting Psychology Journal 44,* 11-17.

Bellah, R.N., Madsen, R., Sullivan, W.M., Swidler, A., and Tipton, S.M. (1985). *Habits of the heart.* New York: Harper & Row, 1985.

Brashears, F. (1995). Supervision as social work practice: A reconceptualization. *Social Work, 40*(5), 692-699.

Braver, M., Graffin, N. and Holahan, W. (1990). Supervising the advanced trainee: A multiple therapy training model. *Psychotherapy, 27*(4), 561-567.

Brisbane, F.L. (1995). Introduction. In Philleo, J., and Brisbane, F.L. (Eds.). *Cultural competence for social workers: A guide for alcohol and other drug abuse prevention professionals working with ethnic/racial communities.* CSAP Cultural Competence Series. Washington, DC: U.S. Department of Health and Human Services.

Brown, S. (1995). A developmental model of alcoholism and recovery. In Brown, S. and Yalom, I. (Eds.). *Treating alcoholism.* San Francisco: Jossey-Bass Publishers.

Brown, S., Vik, P., Patterson, T., Grant, I. and Schuckit, M. (1995). Stress vulnerability and adult alcohol relapse. *Journal of Studies on Alcohol, 56*(5), 538-545.

Brunswick, A.F. and Messeri, P. (1984). Causal factors in onset of adolescents' cigarette smoking: A prospective study of urban Black youth. *Advances in Alcohol and Substance Abuse, 3,* 35-52.

Caetano, R. (1985). Drinking patterns and alcohol problems in a national sample of U.S. Hispanics. *Alcohol use among U.S. ethnic minorities.* Proceedings of a conference on the epidemiology of alcohol use and abuse among ethnic minority groups. Rockville, MD: U.S. Department of Health and Human Services.

Caetano, R. (1986). Patterns and problems of drinking among U.S. Hispanics. In T.E. Malone (Ed.), *Report of the Secretary's Task Force on Black and Minority Health, Volume VII: Chemical Dependency and Diabetes,* pp. 141-186. GPO

Publication #491-313/44709. Washington, DC: U.S. Government Printing Office.

Caetano, R., and Kaskutas, L. (1995). Changes in drinking patterns among Whites, Blacks and Hispanics, 1984-1992. *Journal of Studies on Alcohol, 56*(5), 558-565.

Caplan, G. (1970). The theory and practice of mental health consultation. New York: Basic Books, Inc., Publishers.

Caplan, G. and Caplan, R. (1993). *Mental health consultation and collaboration.* San Francisco: Jossey-Bass Publishers.

Caplan, G., Caplan, R. & Erchul, W.P. (1995). A contemporary view of mental health consultation: Comments on "Types of mental health consultation" by Gerald Caplan (1963). *Journal of Educational and Psychological Consultation, 6*, 23-30.

Carnes, B. (1992). Caring for the professional caregiver: The application of Caplan's Model of consultation in the era of HIV. *Issues in Mental Health Nursing, 13*, 357-367.

Cervantes, R., Gilbert, M.J., Salgado de Synder, N., and Padilla, A. (1991). Psychosocial and cognitive correlates of alcohol use in younger adult immigrant and U.S.-born Hispanics. *The International Journal of the Addictions, 25* (5a & 6a), 687-708.

Chandler, M. & Hunt, P. (1980). Counseling Blacks: Training and supervision of beginning counselors. In Ohlsen, M. (Ed.). *Introduction to counseling.* New York: Peacock Press.

Chau, K. (1991). Social work practice with ethnic minorities: Practice issues and potentials. *Journal of Multicultural Social Work, 1*(1), 23-39.

_____ (1992). Needs assessment for group work with people of color: A conceptual formulation. *Social Work with Groups, 15*(2/3), 53-66.

Cherpitel, C. (1992). Acculturation, alcohol consumption, and casualties among United States Hispanics in the emergency room. *The International Journal of the Addictions, 27*(9), 1067-1077.

Cheung, Y. (1991a). Ethnicity and alcohol/drug use revisited: A framework for future research. *The International Journal of the Addictions, 25*(5a & 6a), 581-605.

_____ (1991b). Overview: Sharpening the focus on ethnicity. *The International Journal of the Addictions, 25*(5a & 6a), 573-579.

Comas-Diaz, L. (1986). Puerto Rican alcoholic women: Treatment considerations. *Alcoholism Treatment Quarterly, 3*, 47-57.

Connors, G., Allen, J., Cooney, N. DiClemente, C., Tonnigan, J.S., and Anton, R. (1994). Assessment issues and strategies in alcoholism treatment matching research. *Journal of Studies on Alcohol,* Supplement 12, 92-100.

Cooney, N., Zweben, A. and Fleming, M. (1995). Screening for alcohol problems and at-risk drinking in health-care settings. In Hester, R. and Miller, W. (Eds.). *Handbook of alcoholism treatment approaches: Effective alternatives.* (2nd ed.). Boston: Allyn and Bacon.

Cross, T., Bazron, B.J., Dennis, K.W. and Isaacs, M.R. (1989). *Towards a cultur-*

ally competent system of care. Washington, DC: CASSP Technical Assistance Center, Georgetown University Child Development Center.

Daniels, M., Wodarski, J.S. and Davis, K. (1987). Education for community mental health practice with minorities. *Journal of Social Work Education*, *23*(1), 40-47.

De Hoyos, G., De Hoyos, A. and Anderson, C.B. (1986). Sociocultural dislocation: Beyond the dual perspective. *Social Work*, *31*(1), 61-67.

Delgado, M. (1989). Treatment and prevention of Hispanic alcoholism. In Watts, T.D. & Wright, R. (Eds.). *Alcoholism in minority populations*. (pp. 77-92). Springfield, IL: Charles C. Thomas.

Delgado, M. (1994). Hispanic natural support systems and the AODA field: A developmental framework for collaboration. *Journal of Multicultural Social Work*, *3*(2), 11-37.

Delgado, M. (1995). Hispanics/Latinos. In *Cultural competence for social workers: A guide for alcohol and other drug abuse prevention professionals working with ethnic/racial communities*. Rockville, MD: U.S. Department of Health and Human Services.

Deveaux, F. and Lubell, I. (1994). Training the supervisor: Integrating a family of origin approach. *Contemporary Family Therapy*, *16*(4), 291-299.

Dimeoff, L. and Marlatt, G.A. (1995). Relapse prevention. In Hester, R. and Miller, W. (Eds.). *Handbook of alcoholism treatment approaches: Effective alternatives*. (2nd ed.). Boston: Allyn and Bacon.

Dungee-Anderson, D. and Beckett, J. (1995). A process model for multicultural social work practice. *Families in Society: The Journal of Contemporary Human Services*, *76*, 459-467.

Epstein, J., Botvin, G., Diaz, T. and Schinke, S. (1995). The role of social factors and individual characteristics in promoting alcohol use among inner-city minority youths. *Journal of Studies on Alcohol*, *56*(1), 39-46.

Flores-Ortiz, Y., and Bernal, G. (1990). Contextual family therapy of addiction with Latinos. In Saba, G., Karrer, B., Hardy, K.V. (Eds.). *Minorities and family therapy*. New York: The Haworth Press, Inc.

Freeman, E. (1990). Assessment of substance abuse problems: Implications for clinical supervision. *The Clinical Supervisor*, *8*(2), 91-108.

Freeman, E., McRoy and Logan, S. (1987). Strategies for teaching the differential use of alcoholism treatment approaches. *Journal of Social Work Education*, *3*, 29-36.

Friedlander, J. and Ward, L. (1984). Development and validation of the Supervisory Styles Inventory. *Journal of Counseling Psychology*, *31*(4), 541-557.

Geertz, C. (1973). *The interpretation of cultures*. New York: Basic Books.

Golding, J., Burnam, M.A., Wells, K., and Benjamin, B. (1993). Alcohol use and cultural characteristics in two Mexican-American samples. *The International Journal of the Addictions*, *28*(5), 451-476.

Gordon, A. (1991). Alcoholism treatment services to Hispanics: An ethnographic examination of a community's services. *Family Community Health*, *13*(4), 12-24.

Gray, M. (1993). Relapse prevention. In Straussner, S. (Ed.), *Clinical work with substance-abusing clients*. New York: The Guilford Press.

Gregoire, T. (1994). Assessing the benefits and increasing the utility of addiction training for public child welfare workers: A pilot study. *Child Welfare, 73*(1), 69-81.

Hall, S. (1987). Cultural studies: Two paradigms. In Bennett, T., Martin, G., Mercer, C. and Woollacott, J. (Eds.). *Culture, ideology and social process: A reader*. London: B.T. Batsford Ltd in association with The Open University Press.

Harchik, A., Sherman, J. Sheldon, J. and Strouse, M. (1992). Ongoing consultation as a method of improving performance of staff members in a group home. *Journal of Applied Behavior Analysis, 25*, 599-610.

Hardcastle, D. (1992). Toward a model of supervision: A peer supervision pilot project. *The Clinical Supervisor, 9*(2), 63-76.

Heath, D. (1991). Uses and misuses of the concept of ethnicity in alcohol studies: An essay in deconstruction. *The International Journal of the Addictions, 25* (5a & 6a), 607-628,

Heather, N. (1995). Brief intervention strategies. In Hester, R. and Miller, W. (Eds.). *Handbook of alcoholism treatment approaches: Effective alternatives*. (2nd ed.). Boston: Allyn and Bacon.

Holloway, S. and Brager, G. (1989). *Supervising in the human services: The politics of practice*. New York: The Free Press.

Holloway, E.L. and Johnson, R. (1985). Group supervision: Widely practiced but poorly understood. *Counselor Education and Supervision, 24*, 332-340.

Houle, C., Cyphert, F. and Boggs, D. (1987). Education for the professions. *Theory into Practice, 26*(2), 87-93.

Kadushin, A. (1977). *Consultation in social work*. New York: Columbia University Press.

Katz, R.S. and Ney, N.H. (1995). Preventing Relapse. In Brown, S. and Yalom, I. (Eds.) *Treating alcoholism*. San Francisco: Jossey-Bass Publishers.

Knowles, M. (1970). *The modern practice of adult education: Andragogy versus pedagogy*. New York: Association Press.

Kopfstein, R. (1994). *Inservice education for interdisciplinary teamwork: Training and evaluating teams*. Unpublished doctoral dissertation, City University of New York.

Kutzik, A.J. (1977). The social work field. In F.W. Kaslow (Ed.) *Supervision, consultation and staff training in the helping professions*. San Francisco: Jossey-Bass Publishers.

Lange, A. and Grieger, R. (1993). Integrating RET into management consulting and training. *Journal of Rational-Emotive and Cognitive-Behavior Therapy, 11*(1), 51-57.

Langrod, J. Alksne, L., Lowinson, J. and Ruiz, P. (1981). Rehabilitation of the Puerto Rican addict: A cultural perspective. *The International Journal of the Addictions, 16*(5), 841-847.

Laveman, L. (1994). The multi-level supervision model and the interplay between clinical supervision and psychotherapy. *The Clinical Supervisor, 12*(2), 75-91.

Leitner, M. (1980). Competency-based in-service training in senior day care. *Activities, Adaptation and Aging, 1*(1), 41-51.

Lenihan, G. and Kirk, W. (1992). Conjoint supervision with beginning trainees: The model and it's effectiveness. *The Clinical Supervisor, 10*(1), 35-50.

Liftik, J. (1995). Assessment. In Brown, S. and Yalom, I. (Eds.). *Treating alcoholism*. San Francisco: Jossey-Bass Publishers.

Longres, J. (1991). Toward a status model of ethnic sensitive practice. *Journal of Multicultural Social Work, 1*(1), 41-56.

Maddihian, E., Newcomb, J.D. and Bentler, P.M. (1985). Single and multiple patterns of adolescent substance use: Longitudinal comparisons of four ethnic groups. *Journal of Drug Education, 15*, 311-326.

Malone, T.E. (1986). *Report of the Secretary's Task Force on Minority Health: Volume I: Executive Summary*. GPO Publication No. 487-637/QL3. Washington, DC: U.S. Government Printing Office.

Manoleas, P. (1994). An outcome approach to assessing the cultural competence of MSW students. *Journal of Multicultural Social Work, 3*(1), 43-57.

Marks, J. and Hixon D. (1986). Training agency staff through peer group supervision. *Social Casework, 67*(7), 418-423.

Mattson, M., Allen, J., Longabaugh, R., Nickless, C., Connors, G. and Kadden, R. (1994). A chronological review of empirical studies matching alcoholic clients to treatment. *Journal of Studies on Alcohol*, Supplement 12, 16-29.

McCready, B. and Delaney, S. (1995). Self-help groups. In Hester, R. and Miller, W. (Eds.). *Handbook of alcoholism treatment approaches: Effective alternatives*. (2nd ed.). Boston: Allyn and Bacon.

Miller, W. (1995). Increasing motivation for change. In Hester, R. and Miller, W. (Eds.). *Handbook of alcoholism treatment approaches: Effective alternatives*. (2nd ed.). Boston: Allyn and Bacon.

Miller, W., Brown, J. Simpson, T., Handmaker, N. Bien, T., Luckie, L., Montgomery, H., Hester, R. and Tonigan, J.S. (1995). What works? A methodological analysis of the alcohol treatment outcome literature. In Hester, R. and Miller, W. (Eds.). *Handbook of alcoholism treatment approaches: Effective alternatives*. (2nd ed.). Boston: Allyn and Bacon.

Miller, W. and Hester, R. (1986). The effectiveness of alcoholism treatment: What research reveals. In W.R. Miller and N.K. Heather (Eds.). *Treating addictive behaviors: Processes of change*. (pp. 121-173). New York: Plenum.

Miller, W. and Hester, R. (1995). Treatment for alcohol problems: Toward an informed eclecticism. In Hester, R. and Miller, W. (Eds.). *Handbook of alcoholism treatment approaches: Effective alternatives*. (2nd ed.). Boston: Allyn and Bacon.

Miller, W., Westerberg, V. and Waldron, H. (1995). Evaluating alcohol problems for adolescents. In Hester, R. and Miller, W. (Eds.). *Handbook of alcoholism treatment approaches: Effective alternatives*. (2nd ed.). Boston: Allyn and Bacon.

Monti, P., Rohsenow, D. Colby, S. and Abrams, D. (1995). In Hester, R. and Miller, W. (Eds.). *Handbook of alcoholism treatment approaches: Effective alternatives.* (2nd ed.). Boston: Allyn and Bacon.

Munson, C. (1983). *An introduction to clinical social work supervision.* New York: The Haworth Press, Inc.

Nodell, C. (1977). Why inservice education. *Long Term Care and Health Services Administration Quarterly, 1*(1), 33-44.

Oetting, E. and Beauvais, F. (1991). Orthogonal cultural identification theory: The cultural identification of minority adolescents. *The International Journal of the Addictions, 25*(5a & 6a), 655-685.

Orlandi, M. (1992). Defining cultural competence: An organizing framework. In *Cultural competence for evaluators: A guide for alcohol and other drug abuse prevention practitioners working with ethnic/racial communities.* Rockville, MD: U.S. Department of Health and Human Services.

Ortiz, V. (1995). The diversity of Latino families. In Zambrana, R. (Ed.) *Understanding Latino families.* Thousand Oaks, CA: Sage Publications, Inc.

Pabon, E., Rodriguez, O. and Gurin, G. (1992). Clarifying peer relations and delinquency. *Youth and Society, 24*(2), 149-165.

Padilla, A. (1980). The role of cultural awareness and ethnic loyalty in acculturation. In Padilla, A.M. (Ed.), *Acculturation: Theory, models and some new findings.* Boulder, CO: Westview Press.

Padilla, A. & Morrissey, L. (1993). Place of last drink by repeat DUI offenders: A retrospective study of gender and ethnic group differences. *Hispanic Journal of Behavioral Sciences, 15*, 357-372.

Padilla, A. and Salgado de Snyder, N. (1995). Hispanics: What the culturally informed evaluator needs to know. In *Cultural competence for evaluators: A guide for alcohol and other drug abuse prevention practitioners working with ethnic/racial communities.* Washington, DC: U.S. Department of Health and Human Services.

Pinderhughes, E. (1989). *Understanding race, ethnicity and power.* New York: The Free Press.

Peele, S. (1991). What works in addiction treatment and what doesn't: Is the best therapy no therapy? *The International Journal of the Addictions, 25*(12a), 1409-1419.

Peterson, F. (1991). Issues of race and ethnicity in supervision: Emphasizing who you are, not what you know. *The Clinical Supervisor, 9*(1), 15-31.

Phinney, J.S. (1996). When we talk about American ethnic groups, what do we mean? *American Psychologist, 51*(9), 918-927.

Pothast, H. (1988). In-service training on practice research. *School Social Work Journal, 13*, 23-29.

Powell, D. (1989). Clinical supervision–A ten year perspective. *The Clinical Supervisor, 7*(2/3), 139-147.

Powell, D. (1993). *Clinical supervision in alcohol and drug abuse counseling.* New York: Lexington Books.

Powell, T., Gospel, M. and Williams, A.L. (1992). Attitudes toward the clinical supervisory model: Results from inservice training. *The Clinical Supervisor*, *9*(2), 53-62.

Rapoport, L. (1963). Consultation: An overview. In Lydia Rapoport (Ed.). *Consultation in Social Work Practice*. New York: National Association of Social Workers.

Reid, W., and Beard, C. (1980). An evaluation of in-service training in a public welfare setting. *Administration in Social Work*, *4*(1), 71-85.

Rooney, R. (1985). Does inservice training make a difference? Results of a pilot study of task-centered dissemination in a public social service setting. *Journal of Social Service Research*, *3*(3), 33-50.

Rosenbaum, M. and McCarty, T. (1994). The relationship of psychosomatic medicine to consultation-liaison psychiatry. *Psychosomatics*, *35*(6), 569-573.

Rycus, J. (1978). Essentials of inservice training for child welfare workers. *Child Welfare*, *57*(6), 346-354.

Sansbury, D.L. (1982). Developmental supervision from a skills perspective. *Counseling Psychologist*, *10*(1), 53-57.

Schaefer, R.T. (1984). *Racial and ethnic groups*. (2nd ed.). Boston: Little, Brown and Company.

Schein, E. (1969). *Process consultation: Its role in organizational development* Reading, MA: Addison-Wesley Publishing Co.

Schein, E. (1976). Process consultation. In Bennis, W., Benne, K., Chin, R. and Corey, K. (Eds.). *The planning of change*. (3rd ed.). New York: Holt, Rinehart and Winston.

Schinke, S., Moncher, M., Palleja, J. Zayas, L., and Schilling, R. (1988). Hispanic youth, substance abuse, and stress: Implications for prevention research. *The International Journal of the Addictions*, *23*(8), 809-826.

Straussner, S. (1993). Assessment and treatment of clients with alcohol and other drug abuse problems: An overview. In *Clinical work with substance-abusing clients*. New York: The Guilford Press.

Sullivan, W. (1991). Technical assistance in community mental health: A model for social work consultants. *Research on Social Work Practice*, *1*(3), 289-305.

Sullivan, W. and Rapp, C. (1991). Improving client outcomes: The Kansas Technical Assistance Consultation Project. *Community Mental Health Journal*, *27*(5), 327-336.

Szapocznik, J., and Kurtines, W. (1980). Acculturation, biculturalism, and adjustment among Cuban Americans. In Padilla, A.M. (Ed.). *Acculturation: Theory, models, and some new findings*. Boulder, CO: Westview Press.

Taibbi, R. (1995). *Clinical supervision: A four-stage process of growth and discovery*. Milwaukee, WI: Families International, Inc.

Terrell, M.D. (1993). Ethnocultural factors and substance abuse: Toward culturally sensitive treatment models. *Psychology of Addictive Behaviors*, *7*(3), 162-167.

Tommasello, A., Tyler, F., Tyler, S. and Zhang, Y. (1993). Psychosocial correlates of drug use among Latino youth leading autonomous lives. *The International Journal of the Addictions*, *28*(25), 435-450.

Tracy, E., and Farkas, K. (1994). Preparing practitioners for child welfare practice with substance-abusing families. *Child Welfare*, 73(1), 57-68.

Tucker, M.B. (1985). U.S. ethnic minorities and drug abuse: An assessment of the science and practice. *International Journal of the Addictions*, 20, 1021-1047.

U.S. Bureau of the Census. (1991). *Statistical yearbook*. Washington, DC: Immigration and Naturalization Service.

U.S. Bureau of the Census. (1993). *Hispanic Americans today*. Current Population Reports, P-23-183. Washington, DC: U.S. Government Printing Office.

Valdez, R., Delgado, D., Cervantes, R. and Bowler, S. (1993). *Cancer in the U.S. Latino communities: An exploratory review*. Santa Monica, CA: RAND.

Vazquez-Nuttall, E., Romero-Garcia, I. and De Leon, B. (1987). Sex roles and perceptions of feminity and masculinity of Hispanic women: A review of the literature. *Psychology of Women Quarterly*, 11, 409-426.

Vinokur-Kaplan, D. (1986). National evaluation of in-service training by child welfare practitioners. *Social Work Research and Abstracts*, 22, 13-18.

Walsh, J. (1990). From clinician to supervisor: Essential ingredients for training. *Families in Society: The Journal of Contemporary Human Services*, 71(2), 82-87

Wetchler, J. (1990). Solution-focused supervision. *Family Therapy*, 17(2), 129-138.

Werner, J. and Tyler, J.M. (1993). Community-based interventions: A return to community mental health centers' origins. *Journal of Counseling and Development*, 71, 689-692.

Wilbur, M., Roberts-Wilbur, J., Morris, J., Betz, R. and Hart, G. (1991). Structured group supervision: Theory into practice. *The Journal for Specialists in Group Work*, 16(2), 91-100.

Williams, L. (1994). A tool for training supervisors: Using the supervision feedback form (SFF). *Journal of Marital and Family Therapy*, 20(3), 311-315.

Wise, T.N. (1995). Consultation-liaison research: The use of differing perspectives. *Psychotherapy and Psychosomatics*, 63, 9-21.

Yin, Z., Zapata, J. and Katims, D. (1995). Risk factors for substance use among Mexican American school-age youth. *Hispanic Journal of the Behavioral Sciences*, 17(1), 61-76.

Zober, M.A. (1980). A systematic perspective on the staff development and training evaluation process. *Aretae*, 6(2), 51-70.

Zober, M.A., Seipel, M.M. and Skinner, V. (1982). Action-oriented training and evaluation: Motivating and measuring change in job performance as a result of in-service training in departments of social service. *Journal of Continuing Social Work Education*, 2(1), 23-41.

Evaluating Hispanic/Latino Programs: Ensuring Cultural Competence

Richard C. Cervantes, PhD
Cynthia Peña, MA

SUMMARY. This article will provide a summary of existing information related to the evaluation of alcohol and other drug (AODA) treatment and prevention programs for Hispanics/Latinos. In addition, the authors provide an overview of recent survey data which examined actual evaluation practices in a national sample of federally funded substance abuse prevention projects targeting Hispanic/Latino high risk youth and families. *[Article copies available for a fee from The Haworth Document Delivery Service: 1-800-342-9678. E-mail address: getinfo@haworth.com]*

INTRODUCTION

The practice of program evaluation is a rapidly growing discipline that draws on research design approaches and methods found in the social and

Richard C. Cervantes is Senior Research Associate, Behavioral Assessment, Inc., 291 South La Cienega Boulevard, Suite 308, Beverly Hills, CA 90211. Cynthia Peña is a doctoral student at the University of California, Los Angeles, CA 90095.
The authors wish to extend their appreciation to Araceli Santos who helped throughout the preparation and research for the manuscript. The authors also wish to express thanks to members of the SAMHSA/CSAP Hispanic High Risk Youth Cluster, including the Cluster Liaison Eladio Perez, for support and guidance in this project.
Funding for the survey was provided under Contract No. 93MF07806601D from SAMHSA/CSAP to the first author.

[Haworth co-indexing entry note]: "Evaluating Hispanic/Latino Programs: Ensuring Cultural Competence." Cervantes, Richard C. and Cynthia Peña. Co-published simultaneously in *Alcoholism Treatment Quarterly* (The Haworth Press, Inc.) Vol. 16, No. 1/2, 1998, pp. 109-131; and: *Alcohol Use/Abuse Among Latinos: Issues and Examples of Culturally Competent Services* (ed: Melvin Delgado) The Haworth Press, Inc., 1998, pp. 109-131. Single or multiple copies of this article are available for a fee from The Haworth Document Delivery Service [1-800-342-9678, 9:00 a.m. - 5:00 p.m. (EST). E-mail address: getinfo@haworth.com].

109

behavioral sciences. The ability to determine the effectiveness of community based alcohol and substance abuse prevention and treatment programs becomes increasingly important to maintain private and public funding opportunities. While the field of evaluation grows, there unfortunately has been little attention paid to the issues and challenges faced when evaluating programs for culturally and linguistically distinct groups. In this article we will provide a summary of existing information related to the evaluation of alcohol and other drug (AODA) treatment and prevention programs for Hispanics/Latinos. In addition we will provide an overview of recent survey data which examined actual evaluation practices in a national sample of federally funded substance abuse prevention projects targeting Hispanic/Latino high risk youth and families. Through the review of literature and analysis of survey data results we provide a set of guidelines that may be useful in ensuring the development and implementation of culturally competent evaluation practices for Hispanic/Latino alcohol and substance abuse treatment and prevention programs.

The projected growth of the Hispanic/Latino population exceeds that of any other ethnic group in the United States. Currently, Hispanics/Latinos number approximately 22 million, representing 9% of the total population (U.S. Census, 1990). This heterogeneous group of persons share some communalities although distinctions exist between subgroups. Many Mexican Americans, Cubans, Puerto Ricans, and Central and South Americans share a basic "Hispanic" cultural heritage (language, religion, personal and family beliefs, and attitudes). At the same time, these groups differ on historical, political, economic, and immigration factors. Mexican Americans are the largest Hispanic group, accounting for 60% of the population, Puerto Ricans 12%, Cubans 5%, and a rapidly growing group of "Other Hispanics" (Central and South Americans) represents 22% (Chapa & Valencia, 1993).

In addition to their rapidly growing numbers, Hispanics are a youthful group with a median age of 26 compared to 33.5 for all other groups. Mexican Americans are the youngest (median age 24.1) and Cubans the oldest (39.1). Population projections estimate that the age group below 17 years will triple by 2020, where Hispanic youth will comprise 25% of all youth in the country. In addition, educational attainment for this ethnic groups is lower than non-Hispanics. Not surprisingly 1 in four Hispanics lives in poverty (37.6% of Hispanic children live below poverty level compared to 17.3% non-Hispanic children). The annual average family income for White non-Hispanics is $29,400 which is almost double that of Hispanic families ($15,800). Per capita income is considerably lower for Hispanics given the larger average family size.

HISPANICS/LATINOS
AND ALCOHOL AND OTHER DRUG ABUSE (AODA)

In contrast to the dearth of AODA treatment and/or treatment effectiveness research with Latinos, there is a growing body of work that has specifically addressed drinking patterns and the prevalence of alcohol related problems. In one of the few comprehensive reviews, Gilbert and Cervantes (1987) found that Mexican American men show a distinctive pattern of alcohol consumption when compared to other groups. Mexican American men have been shown to follow a pattern of drinking in which large quantities of alcohol are consumed with high frequency when compared to non-Latino and Latino groups as well. Unlike trends in the White population, these problems are not concentrated in young men but continue to plague Mexican American men well into middle age (Caetano, 1988; Gilbert & Cervantes, 1987).

Epidemiological research suggests that the proportion of later generation Mexican American males considered "very heavy drinkers" is as large as one third of the population. A characteristic drinking pattern of heavy (drinking to intoxication) and frequent drinking has been observed in young Mexican American men and women (Cervantes, Gilbert, Salgado de Snyder & Padilla, 1990-1).

Reviewing the literature specific to alcohol treatment, a paucity of information particularly related to Latinos is obvious. Closely related is the lack of studies in alcohol treatment literature on the efficacy of ethnically oriented treatment approaches (Collins, 1993). However, some studies such as that by Caetano (1993) suggest that Hispanics receiving treatment for alcohol related problems present a distinct demographic profile when compared to members of other ethnic groups, show different drinking patterns and drinking related problems, and also differ when compared on treatment outcomes. Hispanic clients are usually younger, married, less educated and have lower incomes. Although results on social disadvantage are inconsistent, compared to other minorities Hispanics tend to have less social disadvantage but when compared to Whites have more. Generally, Hispanics tend to report excessive drinking for longer periods of time than Whites, and report more physical problems related to drinking than Blacks. A slightly different client profile of Southwest Mexican Americans is presented by Gilbert and Cervantes (1987), in which they describe the population receiving alcohol treatment as mostly male, married, employed with greater economic stability, and receiving outpatient rather than inpatient or detoxification services. Gilbert and Cervantes (1987) have also noted that there is an overrepresentation of these Hispanics in treatment settings when compared to the proportion of the population which they represent.

Demographic characteristics alone place many Hispanic/Latino youth at high risk for alcohol and other drug related problems. The rapid growth of Hispanic/Latino youth over the next two decades, as well as the multiple antecedent risk factors, clearly suggests that substance abuse prevention and treatment must be a leading priority in Hispanic/Latino communities. Despite the paucity of research and information on substance abuse prevention available for Hispanics/Latinos, information available from researchers who have documented the incidence and prevalence of substance abuse in Hispanic youth (De La Rosa, Khalsa & Rouse, 1989) as well as adults, are cause for serious concern. National surveys and others (NIDA, 1985, 1988; Padilla, Padilla, Morales, Olmedo, & Ramirez, 1979) indicate Hispanic males 12 to 17 years of age were more likely to have ever used cocaine and just as likely to have used prescription drugs when compared to non-Hispanic Whites. Also indicated in these surveys is an increase in the amount of drugs ingested by Hispanic youth and variety of substances used over a longer lifetime of use as compared with other groups. Similar patterns of substance use have been reported more recently in various Southwest communities by Chavez, Oetting, and Beauvais (1986).

The most recent data from the National Household Survey on Drug Abuse (U.S. Dept. of Health and Human Services, 1994) describes the perceived availability and risk of harm of using drugs by a large, randomly selected sample of persons representative of the national population who were surveyed in 1992. This national survey confirms the relationship between attitudes and beliefs about drugs and drug use. Higher rates of drug use are associated with those who report high perceived availability and low risk of using drugs. Respondents were surveyed regarding a variety of illicit drugs such as marijuana, cocaine, LSD, PCP, and heroin. Regarding perceived availability, the overall population reporting that marijuana was "easy to get" was lower in 1992 (59%) when compared to 1991 (62%). Fewer also reported that cocaine was easy to get (40%, 44%) in the same time period. The perceived availability of drugs was little changed with regard to LSD, PCP and heroin. When broken down by ethnicity, the percentage of Blacks reporting that drugs were easily available was consistently higher when compared to Whites and Hispanics. The percentage of Hispanics perceiving drugs to be available was usually the lowest of the three ethnic group percentages. Marijuana was perceived as easily available by more than half of the respondents in each of the ethnic groups (64% for Blacks, 59% for Whites, 54% for Hispanics). Blacks also perceived LSD to be more available (30%) when compared to Whites (24%) and Hispanics (25%). Larger proportions in each group perceived cocaine or crack to be easily available (59% Blacks, 40% Hispanics, 38% Whites). Heroin was perceived as easily available by 39% of Black respondents, 28% Hispanics, and 25% of Whites. Overall, the percent of those reporting that drugs were easy to get was highest in younger age groups (18-25 and 26-34) which also have higher rates of drug use.

This survey also asked respondents to report the level of risk they perceived with a list of drug use activities such as "smoking marijuana occasionally," "trying cocaine once or twice," "trying heroin one or twice," and "smoking more than a pack of cigarettes per day." Fewer people perceived smoking marijuana as risky in 1992 (45%) compared to 1988 (50%). The same trend is observed with cocaine use, 68% to 71% in 1992 and 1988, respectively. Little change was seen with regard to heroin use, cigarette smoking. Whites had the lowest percentage (42%) reporting great risk associated with marijuana use (55% Blacks, 59% Hispanics). A slightly different trend was reported for cocaine use (Whites 67%, Blacks 76%, and Hispanics 72%) and for cigarette smoking (Whites 63%, Blacks 64 %, and Hispanics 73%) (DHHS, 1994).

Data from the 1992-1993 Monitoring the Future Study reveal important patterns of drug use among Latino youth. Among eighth grade students, Latinos have the highest prevalence for the use of marijuana, hallucinogens, LSD, cocaine and tranquilizers. It appears that Latino youth initiate drug use earlier than other ethnic groups. Latino youth also appear to show higher rates of use of dangerous drugs, such as heroin, crack and cocaine. Among alcohol use, Latinos show a high prevalence rate similar to White non-Latinos which is higher than the prevalence rate for Black youth (Amaro, Messinger, and Cervantes, 1996).

Existing research provides us with an idea about the extent of alcohol and other drug related problems experienced in the Hispanic/Latino community. Although sparse and with inherent methodologic limitations, these studies point to the urgent need for effective AODA prevention and treatment efforts targeting Hispanic/Latino youth. The size and growth of the Hispanic/Latino youth population underscores the need to develop and consistently utilized a culturally competent model of program evaluation and clinical practice with Hispanics presenting substance abuse risks or problems.

Both cursory and comprehensive reviews (Collins, 1993; Gilbert & Cervantes, 1987) point to the lack of prevention and treatment outcome studies. Development of effective substance abuse prevention and intervention programs is severely hindered by a lack of research, inadequate evaluation procedures and lack of documentation of existing program models. Further, there has been a lack of culturally relevant and appropriate Hispanic-targeted programs (Isaacs & Benjamin, 1991) in spite of the documented effects of culture on treatment and prevention outcomes (Ames & Mora, 1988; Freeman, 1994).

The body of literature examining the underlying factors of drug use and abuse in adolescents has long addressed the important relationships between personality, peer groups, and family factors (Brook, & Brook, 1987; Brook, Whiteman, Gordon, 1983; Brook, Whiteman, Cohen, Shapiro, & Balka, 1995; Jessor, Chase, & Donovan, 1980; Kandel, 1980). However, this body of literature remains limited in that its focus is not on Latino youth. The area of literature focusing on Latino youth has examined these same variables but does so while examining the effect of ethnicity, race, and culture. Findings suggest that parental attitudes and parental drug use play an important role in the alcohol and drug use of adolescents (Biafora, Warheit, Vega, and Gil, 1994; Gfroerer & De La Rosa, 1993; Vega, Zimmerman, Warheit, Apospori, and Gil, 1993; Warheit et al., 1995). In addition, other problem behaviors such as school dropout, psychosocial stress, and delinquency have been examined as they relate to AODA use (Biafora, Warheit, Vega, and Gil, 1994; Beauvais et al., 1996; Chavez, Oetting, and Swaim, 1994; Epstien, Botvin, Diaz, & Schinke, 1995).

CONDUCTING CULTURALLY COMPETENT EVALUATION

Effective evaluation of prevention and treatment programs for Hispanics/Latinos depends heavily on our understanding of the role which culture plays in the development of AODA use, misuse, and abuse. Understanding cultural factors is not only important in the development of effective prevention and treatment programs, but plays an equally critical role in the evaluation of such programs. The ability of evaluators to incorporate cultural factors such as language, acculturation, family values, and community attitudes into evaluation designs has been termed "cultural competence" (Orlandi, 1992). The use of culturally relevant instrumentation is an important component of culturally competent research and evaluation for Hispanics (Cervantes & Acosta, 1992). Failure to consider important demographic, socio-cultural, and psychological factors specific to Hispanic/Latino populations can result in inappropriate conclusions about the effectiveness of programs.

Inaccurate conclusions regarding program outcomes can also result from limited basic evaluation skills, knowledge, or experience (Casas, 1992). As AODA prevention and treatment efforts increase with the Latino population, many professionals may face the challenge of developing and evaluating culturally specific programs without having a full understanding of cultural issues or basic evaluation expertise.

Orlandi (1992) and Casas (1992) have provided frameworks to enhance the level of cultural competence and basic evaluation competence for those involved in evaluating prevention efforts. Both authors stress the need to foster a comprehensive understanding of target populations (particularly with regard to cultural characteristics) as well as developing basic, rigorous, and appropriate evaluation procedures.

BASIC EVALUATION CONCEPTS WITHIN A CULTURALLY COMPETENT FRAMEWORK

The accurate and comprehensive evaluation of any AODA program cannot be overemphasized. Program decisions, management, future funding and other decisions vital to the life and continuation of any program often rest on the results gathered from program evaluation procedures. Positive evaluation outcomes can result in the widespread application of proven prevention activities and treatment interventions.

Given the important role of evaluation, the authors present basic evaluation concepts that are central to most evaluation activities and when properly applied can result in sound rigorous evaluation plans. These components are recommended for the evaluation of high risk youth program funded by the Center for Substance Abuse Prevention which has a long history of funding demonstration projects with strong evaluation components. Additionally, many of these demonstration projects have targeted youth of culturally distinct groups. The components for effective evaluation include three major areas of evaluation: (1) management of evaluation; (2) process evaluation; and (3) outcome evaluation. The focus will be placed on process and outcome evaluation although management of the evaluation is discussed briefly. Using these evaluation concepts we intend to build on what Orlandis (1992) has termed "cultural competence" by presenting and how cultural factors should be incorporated into the evaluation of a program so that the result is a "culturally competent evaluation strategy."

Management of Evaluation

A comprehensive evaluation program requires efficient management. Areas to be monitored include resources, management of time, division of responsibilities between project staff and the evaluator, and clear definition of roles between all individuals.

Most importantly, to maximize management of a culturally competent evaluation, there must be an adequate budget to conduct the evaluation and allow for strategies that may not normally be included in evaluations of programs targeting non-Latinos. For example, with hard to reach populations it is good practice and often necessary to provide incentives to participants and participant families to ensure attendance and minimize attrition.

Equally important are the evaluator's qualifications and experience. The evaluator must be qualified to conduct an evaluation with a culturally distinct group, being aware of the issues that present as important (which will be elaborated in the following) and be able to suggest alternative approaches that are appropriate to the population.

In the design of the evaluation plan, evaluation activities, and the presentation of evaluation feedback and results, it is beneficial to include line staff who know the population; dividing the evaluation tasks with program staff and including them in the evaluation plan not only enhances their knowledge of and sensitivity to evaluation, but also provides the evaluation team with practical information regarding the feasibility of the evaluation.

Finally, the scheduling/time line for the evaluation plan, from start to finish, meeting reporting requirements and other obligations, should be realistic reflecting knowledge about the population being targeted. Many Latino youth are "hard to reach" and at times difficult to recruit, keep involved, and track. If families are involved in the evaluation or program, it may be difficult to bring an entire family together because of work schedules or resistance from some family members. A culturally competent evaluation should be aware of these potential barriers, allow for them, and offer creative solutions to overcoming them.

Process Evaluation

Process evaluation attempts to provide information on program planning, development, and administration. This level of evaluation describes successes, failures, barriers, and the "process" by which the project is administered. It includes the evaluation of staff and interventions with subsequent feedback. By identifying such points, the day-to-day mechanism of the project can be assessed. The value in this type of information is that it provides feedback that guides the program as the program itself evolves. The relative lack of experience in planning and implementing AODA prevention projects in Hispanic/Latino communities makes process data invaluable to projects who are still in their infancy (Casas, 1992). The assessment of program staffing issues, assessment of interventions, and adequate documentation of the feedback process are all relevant to adequate process evaluation procedures.

Program Staffing. It is important that the staff and their qualifications are appropriate for the project, that they be experienced in their roles and responsibilities, have a working knowledge of the community, and be aware of the multiple psychosocial, economic, and institutional issues confronting the target population. In the event that they are not, staff should receive the necessary training. For staff who are not ethnically matched with the community, training that exposes them to the population must be provided. When staff are experienced with the target population, have experience with interventions and are sufficiently qualified for their position, they should continue to receive training that will keep them abreast of the issues developing in their field, exposing them to other programs and interventions, presenting trends in their community, or even exposing them to new technologies that may enhance their performance. Training should continue as a regular, ongoing process.

Interventions. In the design of a program, whether it is a prevention program or a treatment program, interventions should be selected based on past research or success with the population. If interventions are new, there should be an established line of logic that suggests the intervention will be efficacious with the population. With Latino populations, given the limited research, it may be difficult to find evidence that an intervention has been successful with the population. Further, whether the interventions reso-nated with the culture, and was appropriate to acculturation levels. Casas (1992) provides a detailed discussion regarding the effects of sociocultural issues on intervention strategies.

Documenting the process by which interventions are delivered is criti-cal to the evaluation. Often interventions designed for other populations are modified by staff who are aware of the special needs of the target population. It is necessary to capture the changes in the delivery of the intervention however, subtle. This can be done at the planning stage of the program (developing curriculum, intervention guidelines, or activity de-scriptions) or during periodic recording of the delivery of activities/ser-vices (process and dosage documentation). Staff should also document the language in which the services was delivered and the utilization of cultural specific concepts (e.g., *personalismo*, *respeto*, etc.).

Feedback. Feedback from all involved in the program is useful not only to the program but to the evaluation as well. This should be systematically collected throughout the evaluation. It allows the evaluation to be more able to provide appropriate interpretations of evaluation results. Participants should always be asked to provide feedback regarding the interventions or services.

Feedback from members outside the program is important. Information provided by the community is also may provide insights to recruitment and retention barriers or successes, and is vital to integrating the program into the community. The community will also be able to articulate their view on the program and its interventions. This information is useful if incorporated into the program so that it becomes sensitive to the community, its needs and perceptions of its problems. This in turn empowers the community creating effects beyond those of the participants. The evaluation should include the development and activity of community advisory boards and assessments of community interactions, such as documenting community meetings attended by the program staff and interviews with key leaders, among others.

Documentation. Process evaluation procedures should also document important demographic variables such as age, gender, ethnicity, and family income level/occupation. However, it is also important to include other variables which often operate as moderating variables such as language preference and proficiency, level of acculturation, migration history, generation level and reading ability. Other facets important to Latino populations are natural support systems, extended family, and cultural identity.

In order to have useful information it is important to have these variables systematically measured and documented. For example, some variables such as acculturation and psychosocial stress may be assessed using an instrument that has been designed and used with the population (Acculturation Rating Scale for Mexican Americans, Hispanic Stress Inventory, respectively). This information will allow evaluators to gauge how appropriate some outcome measures may be for the participant or group. Assessment of the other variables will lend similar information that guides not only the program but the evaluation design, modifications, and result interpretations.

Outcome Evaluation

In contrast to process evaluation, outcome evaluation is primarily concerned with the effectiveness of a program. Outcome evaluation measures the attainment of program objectives as observed in measurable changes. That is, has the program effected a change in a proposed attitude or behavior which it set out to accomplish? Outcome evaluation addresses questions related to the "scientific soundness" of the evaluation plan.

Outcome questions should be clearly stated and relate clearly and logically to the project's objectives. The outcome evaluation design must be appropriate and valid. Often times it is at this point that some evaluations of Latino programs encounter problems. Many established measures designed to assess outcomes are not valid nor are they appropriate for Latino populations. Most likely they are not normed or validated with a culturally distinct group. However, there are some exceptions, and these have been reviewed in detail by the authors (Cervantes and Peña, in press).

One alternative to this problem is to develop measures specific to the program. In this case what is required are extensive procedures to assure that the newly developed instrument is psychometrically sound. This calls for additional resources which are not likely to be available.

An important related feature of instrumentation is the mode of administration. For Latino populations it is important that the administration procedures be designed such that reliable and valid data is collected. This may entail small group administrations based on different reading, comprehension, and language proficiency levels. Reading of each of the items for the group may be required as well as developing rating scales that are simple, clear, and non-abstract.

In the design of the outcome evaluation methodology it is important to have a control or comparison group. The control/comparison group should be comparable to the target population in terms of not only ethnicity, but age, gender, and socioeconomic status as well as community/neighborhood. The more comparable, the stronger the data regarding differences in outcomes. It is important to be aware that maintaining the involvement of the comparison group in the evaluation will also require resources as it is likely that the comparison population may be as "hard to reach" as the target population. This should be considered at the planning and design stage of the evaluation.

Attrition levels should be documented for both the program participants and the comparison groups. Attempts should be made to contact program or comparison dropouts and inquire into the reasons for terminating. If willing they can also be asked to complete the exit assessment and receive any incentives that were built into the program. This information can provide valuable insight into the cultural responsiveness of the program or evaluation and can also make interpretations more accurate. It is always likely that those that drop out from the program are distinct from those that continue. Having data that reflects these differences could yield valuable information for service delivery.

The community should be encouraged to participate and approve of two key aspects of the evaluation (this is apart from their involvement at the program design level): the design and instrumentation. The role of evaluation which is to systematically inquire and document the program activities may be viewed as intrusive not only to participants but to the community as a whole. In order to minimize this intrusion, the community should be made to feel as part of the evaluation, being fully informed of the process and having the opportunity to shape the process as they deem appropriate. Because it is often necessary to use modifications of established instruments or develop new ones, it is important that they also be able to review instruments and approve items that comprise the instruments.

FROM EVALUATION THEORY TO PRACTICE

In the section above, we have attempted to give a general overview of important evaluation concepts and strategies. These concepts have drawn on evaluation theory and what might be considered important aspects of culturally competent evaluation. In an attempt to examine the utilization of a culturally competent framework in the evaluation of programs targeting Hispanic youth, the authors surveyed a number of operating, federally funded programs designed to prevent and/or treat alcohol and other drug abuse.

The respondents of the telephone survey were directors and evaluators of operating Hispanic/Latino High Risk Youth Programs funded by the Center for Substance Abuse Prevention. Out of 23 fully operational programs, a total of 22 were contacted nationwide, including Puerto Rico. Twenty-two directors (from a possible 23) and 18 evaluators (from a possible 24) were contacted and completed the survey. The overall response rate was slightly above 85% for the total sample.

A 64 item survey was constructed specifically for this study. The goal was to design an instrument that would provide information on a wide range of evaluation issues, including management of evaluation, process evaluation, outcome evaluation design, and relevance of evaluation to culture. Respondents were asked to rate the overall usefulness of and success of evaluation efforts. Successful and innovative strategies, in addition to significant obstacles, were also assessed.

Management of Evaluation

Directors and Evaluators were asked to respond to items which provide information on the effectiveness and efficiency of the evaluation component. Directors and Evaluators felt the program evaluation component was "very much" to "extremely" important for their programs (X = 3.65, SD = .91, and X = 3.61, SD = .59 respectively). However, when responding to the overall usefulness of the evaluation information, Directors reported the information to be only "somewhat" useful (X = 2.60, SD = 1.05) as compared to Evaluators who reported the information as being "very" useful (X = 3.17, SD = .70). Directors also rated the effectiveness of Evaluators as X = 2.82, SD = .87 while Evaluators rated their effectiveness slightly higher (X = 3.33, SD = .66). The overall success of evaluation efforts was also rated by both Directors and Evaluators. Overall, both Directors and Evaluators perceived evaluation efforts as "somewhat" successful (X = 2.59, SD = .93 and X = 3.0, SD = .61 respectively).

Involvement of program staff in evaluation activities was also assessed. Both Directors and Evaluators reported program staff members as being "very" involved in the evaluation of the program (X = 2.91, SD = .97 and X = 3.27, SD = .65 respectively). Directors of the majority of programs (55%) said they had an evaluation committee or advisory group while 44% do not.

Process Evaluation

Staffing Patterns, Training, and Program Documentation. In an effort to assess the cultural responsiveness of each HRY program, staffing patterns were examined in terms of sociocultural and demographic variables. Based on the self-reports of Directors, 23% classified themselves as Anglo American, 27% as Hispanic, 14% as Mexican American, 1% as Cuban, 18% as Puerto Rican, and 1% as Other. In sharp contrast, the self-report ethnicity of Evaluators was 61% Anglo American, 11% Hispanic, 11% Cuban, and 17% Puerto Rican. A large number of Directors (77%) reported being bilingual, speaking both English and Spanish. A smaller number (23%) spoke English only. An equal number of Evaluators spoke English only (38%) or both English and Spanish (38%), and 22% spoke English and another language such as French or German.

Evaluators report that staff training on evaluation incorporated culturally specific topics "some of the time" (X = 2.52, SD = .60). In terms of the evaluation teams familiarity with Latino/Hispanic cultural issues, on average Evaluators reported themselves or their teams to be "very to extremely" familiar (X = 3.29, SD = .82) with these issues. However, when Directors were asked to respond to this same item, they perceived the evaluation teams as being only "somewhat to very" familiar with Latino/ Hispanic cultural issues (X = 2.72, SD = .94). When asked to rate the overall responsiveness of the evaluation methodology to Latino/Hispanic culture, on average Directors perceived it as "somewhat to very" responsive (X = 2.86, SD = .99) while Evaluators reported the methodology as being "very" responsive (X = 3.17, SD = .86).

In evaluating HRY programs targeting distinct cultural groups some important preliminary steps should be taken to insure that the evaluation component is appropriate for the target population. Evaluators were asked to respond to items assessing the process evaluation component of their program. Evaluators for 67% of programs conducted an initial needs assessment of the target community while 17% did not. A large proportion of the Evaluators (83%) reported assessing the ethnic demographic make-up of the community prior to implementing evaluation activities while 11% did not.

Process evaluation procedures should not only include the assessment of important demographic variables such as age, gender, reading level, and SES, but should also document other variables such as migration history, language preference and generational level. In addition, it is important that process evaluation procedures include the documentation of interventions which are culturally specific to Latino/Hispanic groups. Interventions which incorporate natural support systems, extended family, cultural identity and other factors relevant to Latino/Hispanic high risk youth should be carefully documented. Along these lines, Evaluator responses to these process evaluation inquiries are presented in Table 1.

For the programs surveyed, it can be seen that while most process evaluation procedures document basic demographic characteristics, only a small percentage of the programs formally assess important cultural vari-

TABLE 1. Demographic Variables Assessed by Hispanic High Risk Youth Programs

VARIABLE	% OF PROGRAMS EVALUATING
Age	100
Gender	100
Nationality/Ethnicity	88
Migration History	33
Language Preference	55
Generational Level	38
Reading Level	22
Family Dynamics	78
Extended Family	39
Acculturation	39

ables such as migration history, extended family characteristics, and level of acculturation. Also of note is the small number of programs that assess the reading level of program participants (either youth or family members), although low literacy (Spanish or English) remains a critical barrier to the evaluation of many programs. Seventy-one percent of the programs report experiencing problems in assessment procedures due to the low literacy of participants.

Outcome Evaluation

As reported by Evaluators 78% of the programs included a comparison or control group design and 22% did not. Pre- and post-test designs were conducted by all the programs (100%). Repeated measures designs were conducted by 78% of the programs and 22% were not. Case study and ethnographic designs were conducted by 39% of the programs while 61% reported not including this design in the outcome evaluation.

As expected, all (100%) of the programs measure changes in AODA knowledge, behavior, and involvement. A large number of programs (61%) identified self-esteem as the next important variable assessed in the outcome evaluation. Academic performance and family dynamics were also assessed by 39% of the programs. Outcome variables and the instruments used by the programs surveyed are presented in Table 2.

With respect to the validity of instruments used in the evaluation of the program, Evaluators for 89% of the programs reported consulting experts on instrumentation while 11% did not; eighty-three percent conducted pilot testing of instruments and 17% did not; ninety-four percent of the programs chose to design instruments within the community and target population to ensure their validity.

Evaluators reported conducting a variety of activities to ensure the reliability of the instruments used in the outcome evaluation. Internal consistency estimates were calculated by 30% of program evaluators; standardization of assessment procedures was reported by 30%; test-retest reliability estimates (10%), split half (5%), and factor analytical procedures (10%) were also performed. A few evaluators also reported consulting experts (5%) and administering measures of social desirability (5%) as reliability checks.

Program Directors and Evaluators were also asked to report innovative strategies employed in successful evaluations as well as barriers confronted through the course of the program. When asked to report specific successful strategies, Directors included appropriate instrumentation of outcome variables. This also involved modifying or developing instruments specific to the populations being targeted. Rigorous evaluation de-

TABLE 2. Outcome Variables Assessed by Hispanic High Risk Youth Programs

OUTCOME	% OF PROGRAMS EVALUATING	INSTRUMENTS	LANGUAGE
AODA Reduction	100	Adolescent Drug Abuse Diagnosis	Eng & Sp
		Utah State School Survey	Eng Only
		Adolescent Alcohol Involvement Sc.	Eng Only
		AODA Knowledge Test	Eng & Sp
		Michigan's Monitoring the Future Sc.	Eng & Sp
		Basic Drug Info Quest.	Eng & Sp
		Chemical/Substance Abuse Survey	Eng & Sp
		Southwest Inhalant Abuse Quest.	Eng & Sp
		Personal Experiences Screening Quest.	Eng & Sp
		Logan Square Student Survey	Eng & Sp
Self Esteem	61	Culture Free Self-Esteem Inventory	Eng & Sp
		Rosenberg Self-Esteem Sc.	Eng & Sp
		Multiattitude Screening Quest.	Eng Only
		Cooper-Smith Modification	Eng & Sp
		Peirs-Harris Self Concept Sc.	Eng & Sp
		Cooper's Self Esteem Sc.	Eng & Sp
		Dept. Soc. Serv. Self Concept Sc.	Eng & Sp
		Index of Self Esteem	Eng & Sp
Academic Performance	39	Gottfreds Effective School Battery	Eng Only
		School Environment Scale	Eng & Sp
		Career Aspirations Scale	
		California Social Competency Scale	Eng & Sp
		Denver Developmental Screening Test	
Family Dynamics	39	Structured Family Style	Eng & Sp
		Moos FES	Eng Only
		Project HiPath	Eng Only
		Niger's Family Resiliency Quest.	Eng Only
		Mother/Daughter Communication	Eng & Sp
		Parent/Family Pride Scale	Eng & Sp
		Hispanic Pride Scale	Eng & Sp
		FACES II	Eng & Sp
		Conner's Teacher Rating Scale	Eng & Sp
		California Social Competency Scale	Eng & Sp
		Adult Adolescent Parenting Inv.	Eng & Sp
Behavior Problems/ Peer Relations	28	Behavior Problem Checklist	Eng & Sp
		Target Behavioral Rating Scale	Eng Only
		Index of Peer Relations	Eng & Sp
		Revised Behavior Problem Cklst	Eng & Sp
		Level of School Discipline Form	Sp Only

OUTCOME	% OF PROGRAMS EVALUATING	INSTRUMENTS	LANGUAGE
Cultural Awareness/ Identification	22	Tri-ethnic Research Center Quest.	Eng & Sp
Gang Membership/ Identification	17	Gang Membership Inv. Gang Component Quest.	Eng & Sp Eng & Sp
Communication Skills	17	Mother Daughter Communication Scale	Eng & Sp
General Development/ Psychopathology	17	DISC Healthy Character Development Scale CES-D	Eng & Sp Eng & Sp Eng & Sp
Peer Relations	11	Index of Peer Relations	Eng & Sp
Delinquency	11	Revised Behavior Problem Chkl. Reynolds Adolescent Depression Sc.	Eng Only Eng Only
Problem Solving	11	General Gains Scale	Eng & Sp

sign and analysis of the data collected ensured the successful evaluation of some programs. Along these lines, advanced computer systems were noted as vitally important. In terms of administration of the program, using the ongoing evaluation to shape and modify the administration and goals of the program, as well as regular site visits by administration, were also reported as helpful.

Evaluators reported similar strategies in ensuring the successful evaluation of the programs with which they were working. Rigor in design (longitudinal design, comparison groups, and reliability analysis) and the utilization of process evaluation methodologies were the strategies most frequently reported by Evaluators. Also reported as important were presenting results to program staff and effective communication between the evaluation team and the program staff or agency.

When asked to report the barriers facing the evaluation of Hispanic High Risk Youth Programs, both Directors and Evaluators were consistent in their responses. Frequently mentioned obstacles included the limitations of instruments currently available for the target population, troublesome pre- and post-test implementation, a cumbersome and bureaucratic model of implementation, and high personnel turnover (either program staff or the evaluator/evaluation team).

CONCLUSIONS AND RECOMMENDATIONS

First and foremost, our work on this project suggest that generally there exists a small body of literature related to the evaluation and research of alcohol and drug prevention and treatment programs for Hispanic/Latino adults and youth. There is a significant literature on the epidemiology of AODA among Hispanics/Latinos yet we continue to know very little about antecedent risk and resiliency factors for this population group. A small but growing number of studies have examined behavioral problems as well as family dynamics among Hispanics/Latinos. Unfortunately, these research studies have been somewhat peripheral to AODA. There is a critical need for more research on alcohol, tobacco, and drug abuse and related issues within the Hispanic/Latino population, and more specifically as related to Hispanic/Latino youth.

In view of the review of the literature, compendium of instruments, and survey of CSAP evaluators, several recommendations must be made. These recommendations may serve as a set of general guidelines; however, it is important to recognize there is no simple "formula" for evaluating any treatment or prevention program, especially those programs where culture and language are prominent factors in program activities.

1. At the time of the evaluation telephone survey, nationally 39% of all evaluators of High Risk Programs were Hispanic/Latino. This is in sharp contrast to the 80% of directors who were reported to be Hispanic/Latino. Efforts must be made on the part of grantees to seek and hire qualified, bicultural/bilingual Hispanic/Latino evaluators and other evaluation staff. In the absence of well-qualified Hispanic/Latino evaluators, grantees should carefully select an evaluation team with a track record in providing culturally competent evaluation services. Although only a small percent of Hispanics/Latinos hold advanced degrees, efforts should be made to train and support Hispanic/Latino program staff that desire more involvement in evaluation activities. Supervisory staff can also encourage Hispanic/Latino line staff to receive specialized evaluation training that is often offered at local and regional conferences and workshops.

   It is also critical that academicians involved in the evaluation of these programs develop course materials which are specific to community based research and cultural factors as they relate to program evaluation.

2. Training on Hispanic/Latino cultural issues is important for both program staff and evaluation staff. Based on survey findings, training which specifically addresses cultural issues occurs only "some

of the time." To the extent that the evaluation team is not qualified to conduct training on cultural issues, consultants with this expertise should be brought in to provide technical assistance. Training all staff on Hispanic/Latino cultural issues will help to ensure culturally responsive evaluation design and implementations.

3. With respect to community sensitivity, evaluators must first understand the social and demographic characteristics of the population they will be targeting. Our survey findings reveal that not all programs conducted initial community needs assessments prior to implementing their programs. Use of existing census data reports or other local needs assessment information may be particularly useful for evaluators who may not reside in the vicinity of the project site. Such needs assessments need not necessarily involve new data collection efforts but should include information that assists in understanding the demographic and social characteristics of target communities.

4. Evaluators must recognize the tremendous heterogeneity that exists within the Hispanic/Latino population and must therefore be sensitive to the dimensions of individual variability for each Hispanic/Latino program participant. With this sensitivity and awareness of individual variability, the evaluation team is better prepared to formulate a strategy for selecting the appropriate assessment tools and evaluation design. For example, if participants are first or second generation Hispanic/Latino, a rating scale could be utilized (e.g., Cuellar, Harris, & Jasso, 1980) to help specify the group level of acculturation. Use of such a scale would allow the evaluator to determine which existing instruments would be most culturally relevant for the program participant. This acculturation assessment would also be helpful for ascertaining the usefulness of program activities for distinct groups of participants based upon cultural factors such as language preference and ethnic identity.

5. Along these lines, it is also important to assess non-traditional demographic characteristics of program participants once the program has been established. Having a thorough demographic assessment of the target group will aid evaluation efforts in assessing the overall effectiveness of programs. This is particularly true since a program may have different effects on demographically distinct groups of people. An encouraging note is that all programs surveyed assessed age and gender; however, far fewer assessed variables such as ethnicity, migration history, language preference, generational level, reading level, or acculturation.

6. Because language use is an inherently critical factor in the assessment of Hispanic/Latino program participants, the language use of program participants should be considered in all aspects of the evaluation of the program. For example, the evaluation team should make no assumptions about the degree of fluency, comprehension and literacy that a bilingual Hispanic/Latino participant may have. These variables, as mentioned above, should be formally assessed. The evaluation of any program targeting Hispanic/Latino populations should include questions such as "What is the language spoken in your home?", "What is the language that *you* now speak at home?," "What is the language you speak with your close friends?", "Do you feel more at ease speaking English or Spanish?" so that the evaluation team will gain information about language proficiency and preference. Beyond this, it goes without saying that in nearly all cases, translation of evaluation instruments will be necessary. A team approach to instrument translation as suggested by Brislin (1986) is strongly recommended.

   In addition, community members play an extremely important role and become a valuable resource to evaluation staff in designing and implementing evaluation activities. Their input is important in tasks such as developing appropriate instruments, helping establish rapport with participants and collecting data. In return they may receive training and experience that will be of later use.

7. To ensure culturally appropriate evaluation design, it is important to have an open flow of communication between program staff, community members, and evaluation staff. One successful approach noted in our findings is the use of community advisory groups or evaluation committees that provide a link between program and evaluation.

8. A positive aspect of the outcome evaluation is that program evaluation teams are involved in a variety of activities that ensure the validity and reliability of the instruments they use. A large percentage of programs consult experts, pilot test instruments, and design instruments within their own communities to ensure the validity of their assessment instruments. Activities to ensure the reliability of the instruments are less frequently conducted. We recommend that evaluators attempt to achieve an acceptable level of scientific rigor in the evaluation design which may include pre- and post-test designs, longitudinal designs, and using a comparison or control group. In addition it is recommended that evaluators also compute reliability estimates for the instruments they use and that they at-

tempt to standardize administration procedures as much as possible. In terms of data analysis it is also suggested that the appropriate rigor be utilized.

9. Finally, it is also important that evaluators and directors be involved in the dissemination of the information they obtain during the course of their program. This information becomes invaluable to others who are beginning their programs or facing obstacles in current programs. We encourage evaluators, directors and qualified staff to formally present their findings and submit them to professional journals.

REFERENCES

Amaro, H., Messinger, M., & Cervantes, R.C. (1996). The health of Latino youth and challenges for prevention. In M. Kagawa-Singer, P.A. Katz, D.A. Taylor and J.H.M. Vanderryn (Eds.) *Health Issues for Minority Adolescents* (pp. 80-115). University of Nebraska Press: Lincoln, NE.

Ames & Mora (1988). Alcohol problem prevention in Mexican American populations. In M.J. Gilbert (Ed.) *Alcohol Consumption Among Mexicans and Mexican Americans: A Binational Perspective*. Los Angeles, CA: Spanish Speaking Mental Health Research Center.

Beauvais, F., Chavez, E.L., Oetting, E.R., Deffenbacher, J.L., & Cornell, G.R. (1996). Drug use, violence, victimization among white American, Mexican American, and American Indian dropouts, students with academic problems, and students in good standing. *Journal of Counseling Psychology, 43*(3), 292-299.

Biafora, F.A., Warheit, G.J., Vega, W.A., & Gil, A.G. (1994). Stressful life events and changes in substance abuse among a multiracial/ethnic sample of adolescent boys. *Journal of Community Psychology, 22*, 296-311.

Brislin, R.W. (1986). A culture general assimilator: Preparation for various types of sojourns. Special Issue: Theories and methods in cross-cultural orientation. *International Journal of Intercultural Relations, 10*(2) 215-234.

Brook, J.S., Whiteman, M., & Gordon. A.S. (1983). Stages of drug use in adolescence: Personality, peer, and family correlates. *Development Psychology, 19*(2), 269-277.

Brook, J.E., & Brook, J.S. (1987). A developmental approach examining social and personal correlates in relation to alcohol use over time. *The Journal of Genetic Psychology, 149*(1), 93-110.

Brook, J.S., Whiteman, M., Cohen, P., Shapiro, J., & Balka, E. (1995). Longitudinally predicting late adolescent and young adult drug use: Childhood and adolescent precursors. *Journal of the American Academy of Child and Adolescent Psychiatry, 34*(9), 1230-1238.

Caetano, R. (1988). Alcohol use among Hispanic groups in the United States. *American Journal of Drug and Alcohol Abuse, 14*, 293-308.

Casas, J.M. (1992). A culturally sensitive model for evaluating alcohol and other drug abuse prevention programs: A Hispanic perspective. In M.A. Orlandi (Ed.) *Cultural Competence for Evaluators*. Washington, DC: Office of Substance Abuse Prevention.

Cervantes, R.C. & Peña, C. (In Press) *The Hispanic/Latino Evaluation Handbook*. Washington, D.C.: SAMHSA/CSAP.

Cervantes, R.C. & Acosta, F.X. (1992). Psychological testing for Hispanic Americans. *Applied and Preventive Psychology, 1*, 209-219.

Cervantes, R.C., Gilbert, M.J., Salgado de Snyder, N.S., & Padilla, A.M. (1990-1). Psychosocial and cognitive correlates of alcohol use in young adult immigrant and U. S. born Hispanics. *International Journal of the Addictions, 25*(5A & 6A) 687-708.

Chapa, J. & Valencia, R.R. (1993). Latino population growth, demographic characteristics, and educational stagnation: An examination of recent trends. *Hispanic Journal of Behavioral Sciences, 15*, 165-187.

Chavez, E.L., Oetting, E.R., & Beauvais (1986). Drug use by small town Mexican American youth: A pilot study. *Hispanic Journal of Behavioral Science, 12*(1), 76-82.

Chavez, E.L., Oetting, E.R., & Swaim, R.C. (1994). Dropout and delinquency: Mexican American and caucasian non-Hispanic youth. *Journal of Clinical Child Psychology, 23*(1), 47-55.

Collins, R.L. (1993). Sociocultural aspects of alcohol use and abuse: Ethnicity and gender. *Drugs & Society, 8*(1), 89-116.

Cuellar, I., Harris, L., & Jasso, R. (1980). An acculturation scale for Mexican American normal and clinical populations. *Hispanic Journal of Behavioral Sciences, 2*, 199-217.

De La Rosa, M.R., Khalsa J.H., & Rouse, B.A. (1990). Hispanics and illicit drug use: A Review of recent findings. *International Journal of the Addictions, vol.* 26, 665-691.

Epstein, J.A., Botvin, G.J., Diaz, T., & Shcinke, S. (1995). The role of social factors an individual characteristics in promoting alcohol use among inner-city minority youth. *Journal of Studies on Alcohol, 56*, 39-46.

Gfroerer, J. & De La Rosa, M. (1993). Protective and risk factors associated with drug use among Hispanic youth. *Journal of Addictive Diseases, 12*(2), 87-107.

Gilbert, M.J., & Cervantes, R.C. (1987). *Mexican Americans and alcohol* (Monograph No. 11). Los Angeles, CA: Spanish Speaking Mental Health Research Center.

Isaacs, M.R., & Benjamin, M.P., (1991). *Towards a Culturally Competent System of Care: A Monograph on Programs Which Utilize Culturally Competent Principles*. (Volume II). Washington, D.C.: CASSP Technical Assistance Center, Georgetown University Child Development Center.

Jessor, R., Chase, J.A., & Donovan, J.E. (1980). Psychosocial correlates of marijuana use and problem drinking behavior in a national sample of adolescents. *American Journal of Public Health, 70*, 604-613.

Kandel, D.B. (1980). Drug and drinking behavior among youth. *Annual Review of Sociology, 6,* 235-286.

NIDA. (1985). *1985 National Household Survey on Drug Abuse: Population Estimates.* DHHS Pub. No. (ADM)87-1539. Rockville, MD: U.S. Government Printing Office.

NIDA. (1988). *1987 National Household Survey on Drug Abuse: Population Estimates.* DHHS Publication, Rockville, MD: U.S. Government Printing Office.

Orlandi, M.A. (Ed.). (1992). *Cultural Competence for Evaluators.* Washington, D.C.: Office of Substance Abuse Prevention.

Padilla, E., Padilla, A., Morales, A., Olmedo, E., & Ramirez, R. (1979). Inhalant, marijuana, and alcohol abuse among barrio children and adolescents. *International Journal of Addictions, 14*(7), 945-964.

U.S. Bureau of the Census (1990). U.S. population estimates by age, sex, race and Hispanic origin: 1989. *Current Population Reports,* Series P-25, No. 1057, Washington D.C., U.S. Government Printing Office.

U.S. Department of Health and Human Services. (1994). *Perceived availability and risk of harm of drugs: Estimates from the National Household Survey on Drug Abuse.* Advanced report #5 (March, 1994).

Vega, W.A., Zimmerman, R.S., Warheit, G.J., Apospori, E.A., & Gil, A.G. (1993). Risk factors for early adolescent drug use in four ethnic and racial groups. *American Journal of Public Health, 83,* 185-189.

Warheit, G.J., Biafora, F.A., Zimmerman, R.S., Gil, A.G., Vega, W.A., & Apospori, E. (1995). Self-Rejection/Derogation, peer factors, and alcohol, drug, and cigarette use among sample of Hispanic, African-American, and White non-Hispanic adolescents. *The International Journal of Addictions, 30*(2), 97-116.

GROUP SPECIFIC

The Drug Free Workplace
in Rural Arizona

Juan Paz, PhD

SUMMARY. The topic of alcohol, tobacco, and other drug use is of great importance nationally with important implications for the workplace. This paper will review the results of an exploratory research project that focused on the extent of ATOD problems in the workplace. *[Article copies available for a fee from The Haworth Document Delivery Service: 1-800-342-9678. E-mail address: getinfo@haworth.com]*

INTRODUCTION

The recent round of congressional budget cuts in substance abuse funding in rural areas together with rising concern regarding the entry of drugs into this country has brought renewed focus to issues of drug abuse in the workplace. The rural communities in the corridors along the U.S.-Mexico

Juan Paz is Assistant Professor, Arizona State University School of Social Work, Tucson Component, 2424 East Broadway, Suite 100, Tucson, AZ 85719.

[Haworth co-indexing entry note]: "The Drug Free Workplace in Rural Arizona." Paz, Juan. Co-published simultaneously in *Alcoholism Treatment Quarterly* (The Haworth Press, Inc.) Vol. 16, No. 1/2, 1998, pp. 133-145; and: *Alcohol Use/Abuse Among Latinos: Issues and Examples of Culturally Competent Services* (ed: Melvin Delgado) The Haworth Press, Inc., 1998, pp. 133-145. Single or multiple copies of this article are available for a fee from The Haworth Document Delivery Service [1-800-342-9678, 9:00 a.m. - 5:00 p.m. (EST). E-mail address: getinfo@haworth.com].

133

border and between Phoenix and Tucson have been identified as an area of concern regarding the growth of the drug problem. Data regarding alcohol, tobacco and other drug abuse problems in rural areas with high concentrations of Hispanic populations has up to this point been non-existent.

A review of the literature revealed that while a great deal of research has been conducted on the drug free workplace among the white population, no research has been conducted with Hispanic populations. A recent site visit with the Administracion de Servicios de Salud Mental Y Contra Addicion (The Mental Health and Anti-Addiction Services Administration) in Puerto Rico uncovered that fact that the majority of the literature they used in the Programa de Ayuda Ocupacional (The Workplace Program) was literature that had been translated into Spanish from studies conducted on non-Hispanics (Center for Substance Prevention, 1994).

The most significant literature on the Drug Free Workplace with Hispanic populations is the conceptual paper written by Sanchez Mayers, Souflee, and Feazell (1993). They point out the centrality of the family and how the family must be included at any attempts at providing treatment or prevention services for Hispanic workers. There must be a cultural fit between the culture of the worker and that of the helping professional.

RESEARCH QUESTIONS

The goal of this exploratory research project was to lay a foundation for the development of a body of knowledge regarding the use of drugs in the rural workplace among Hispanic workers. The research questions sought to answer: To what extent are alcohol, drugs and tobacco a problem in the workplace? Do rural businesses have policies and practices that help them address these problems? The final question was: How do these businesses cope with these problems?

BACKGROUND

The Drug Free Workplace project was funded in 1994 by the Center for Substance Abuse Prevention as a component to the Adelante Juntos Community Empowerment Partnership (AJCEP). The partnership was funded to develop alcohol, tobacco and other drug abuse prevention strategies for rural communities in southern Arizona. The purpose of the Drug Free Workplace project is to increase the capacity of businesses to initiate, develop and expand substance abuse prevention programs in the workplace for their employees.

A research plan was developed to survey businesses in 15 rural communities. During August, 1994, a group of interviewers participated in a training session designed to teach them basic knowledge on how to conduct personal interviews and gather data using structured research instruments in both English or Spanish. The selection criteria for the interviewers were: (1) they had to reside in the community in which they were to collect surveys, (2) they had to be fluent in both English and Spanish, and (3) possess extensive geographical knowledge of their assigned community.

METHODOLOGY

The unit of analysis was individual business owners or managers. Due to the small size and extensive social networks in rural communities, the sample was selected using a purposive sampling plan using the snowball effect. Using this approach, the interviewers were instructed to interview as many businesses as possible. They began on collecting data on each main street. After completing their first interview, the participant was asked to recommend another businessperson who would be asked to participate in the study. This approach proved effective to gain entry into the business community. The data collection process took place during the month of September, 1994. A total sample of 188 participants were collected from five partnership regions.

A total of fifteen rural communities along the southern Arizona corridor were the sites where the data were collected (see Table 1). The total population for these fifteen communities was 59,551. The communities were divided into five areas. They varied from predominantly agri-business communities to mining communities. The smallest community (Winkelman) has a population of 410 persons while Casa Grande has over 20,335. The communities have a diverse ethnic mix, except for New and Old Pascua which are predominantly Yaqui (an Indio-Latino tribe) with only a handful of businesses.

These communities comprise a network of rural towns along Interstate Highway 10, between Phoenix and Tucson. Historically, this part of the U.S.-Mexico border has been identified as an area of heavy drug traffic. (This continued to be true during the 1996 presidential race which identified the need to stem the flow of traffic along the border as a priority of national drug control policy.)

The research instrument was divided into five sections. These included: (1) a demographic section that identified the number of employees and type of business; (2) information that identifies whether or not the business has policies attempting to control the use of alcohol and drugs in the

TABLE 1. Communities Participating in Study

Community	Population Size	Unemployment
Casa Grande	20,335	5.0%
Coolidge	7,035	6.0%
San Manuel	4,193	4.3%
Oracle	3,192	1.8%
Mammoth	1,920	7.3%
Hayden	910	11.8%
Winkelman	410	8.7%
Kearney	2,440	3.0%
Eloy	7,680	11.7%
Eleven Mile Corner	400	N/A
Picacho	1,877	2.6%
South Tucson	5,520	11.3%
New Pascua	3,174	23.0%
Old Pascua	465	23.0%

Total: 59,551   (Az Dept. of Commerce, 1995)

workplace; (3) identifies the types of assistance that businesses have in place; (4) the identification of the type and nature of problems businesses are having; and (5) whether or not the business owner is interested in receiving technical assistance to enhance their capacity to cope with drugs in the workplace.

LIMITATIONS OF THE STUDY

The study is non-random and consists of a purposive sample. As a result, it is not possible to conduct a test of a hypothesis or arrive at theoretical conclusions. All the data were collected using English language questionnaires. Spanish language questionnaires may have yielded some different data. However, the data collected was of excellent quality. Using the snowball effect, we were able to collect data from very small businesses along each town's main street.

The businesses participating in the study reflect a wide range of occupations. From the total sample, four different types of businesses arose most frequently. These included: (1) automotive = 22, (2) food and lodging = 24,

(3) retail = 35, and (4) service = 26. The remainder were distributed among 28 other different types of businesses. These included agriculture, construction, health care, manufacturing, processing, mining, finance, insurance and education. Most of the employers fell into the small business category. From the total sample, 43 had only one employee, 31 had two, 19 had three, 17 had four and 21 had five. From the remainder, 9 had six employees, 4 had fifteen employees and only one or two businesses had between 7 and 14 employees. The majority of these businesses had primarily Hispanic employees. In 60% of the agencies with one employee, that employee was Hispanic; for the remainder 70% of those with two employees or more had Hispanic employees.

POLICY ON ALCOHOL, DRUGS, AND TOBACCO

One very important result from this survey is that the majority, 125 businesses (67.2%), had no written drug policies while the remaining third (32.8%) of businesses did. For tobacco, the data reveals 130 businesses (69.0%) had no written tobacco policies while only 30.1% did.

In the policy area, only 31.9% had employee assistance program policies and 14.9% had policies which assisted their employee's families (see Chart 1). This indicates that few rural businesses provided any form of assistance to their employees and their families. This is significant because in rural areas, drug treatment and prevention services are scarce for both employees and their families. In other words, individuals who have alcohol, tobacco and other drug problems in the workplace would not have resources to access for themselves and their families.

Regarding drug testing, only 17.1% of businesses had a policy requiring pre-employment drug testing while 80% did not (see Chart 2). Random drug testing policies were in place in only 24.3% of businesses. A total of 18.6% of businesses had a policy requiring drug testing after accidents occurred in the workplace. Discussion of these issues with the project's advisory board uncovered that few businesses had drug free workplace policies and procedures in place. The cost of drug testing and the urban location of drug testing facilities creates financial and logistical obstacles to most rural businesses. Drug testing would burden the businessperson with having to pay for the testing as well as pay for the cost of transporting the tests or sending employees to urban medical testing facilities.

Most businesses carry out their prevention efforts in the workplace. When business people were asked how they informed their workers about drug policies, more than half (54.4%) of the businesses indicated they

CHART 1. Do you assist the families of employees?

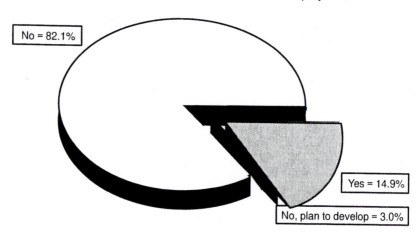

No = 82.1%

Yes = 14.9%

No, plan to develop = 3.0%

CHART 2. Do you conduct pre-employment drug testing?

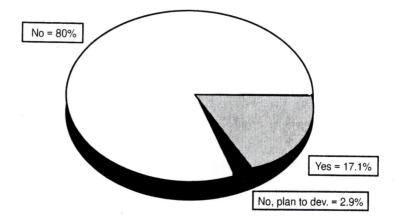

No = 80%

Yes = 17.1%

No, plan to dev. = 2.9%

inform their employees about their drug policies during the hiring process, 5.9% inform their workers at meetings, and 16.2% in the company manual (see Chart 3). The remaining 23.5% indicated they do not inform their employees about drug policies. This finding is indicative that most employers inform their employees at the workplace where they are in control of the setting. In addition, the cost associated with these practices is minimal when compared to the cost of drug testing and services outside their businesses.

CHART 3. How do you inform your workers about policies?

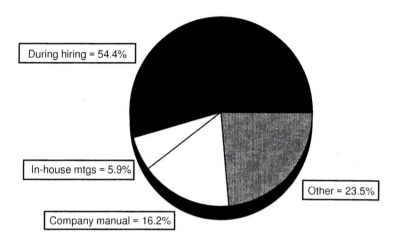

During hiring = 54.4%

In-house mtgs = 5.9%

Other = 23.5%

Company manual = 16.2%

One interesting point was that most had a basic awareness of services available to them. The majority (68.1%) of those participating in the survey indicated they were aware of services in their community which provide assistance to persons with alcohol, drugs, or tobacco problems.

TYPES OF ASSISTANCE AND INTERVENTIONS

The vast majority of businesses did not initiate any form of assistance to their employees. From the total population 11 referred employees to a telephone hotline, 23 provided counseling services, 14 provided follow-up, 23 had educational programs, 15 provided assistance for families, and 34 provided referral services. The single largest type of assistance offered their employees were referral services (22.2%). It is critical to consider that alcohol, drug treatment and prevention services are not available in every community. Most of these types of programs are located in urban areas.

The extent to which businesses took disciplinary action or terminated an employee was minuscule. Close to 95% of the respondents never took any of these actions. This may result from the fact that the majority of the businesses had small work forces with few employees available to replace another worker. Another finding is the fact that no disciplinary action or terminations were initiated because of tobacco abuse. In fact, tobacco use or abuse was not identified as a major problem area by *any* of the busi-

140   ALCOHOL USE/ABUSE AMONG LATINOS

nesses responding. The fact is that cigarette smoking is still fairly common along the U.S.-Mexico border and cigarette sales in the region are still unregulated. In addition, several of these communities are located near reservations where cigarette sales are heavy due to lower prices and lower taxes. In other words, tobacco is still neither seen as a drug nor a health hazard by the residents of this region.

PROBLEMS IN THE WORKPLACE

The results of this study provide conclusive evidence that the rural workplace like the urban workplace is experiencing an extraordinary amount of alcohol and drug related problems. Several respondents identified problems that are common in the workplace. Table 2 provides the percentages of the various types of problems businesses are experiencing due to alcohol and other drug abuse. For example, absenteeism was identified as the largest problem by 12.8% of the respondents. Preoccupation with family problems was the second largest problem identified by 11.98%. Conflict among employees was identified as the third largest problem by slightly over 10%. From the total sample 89.39% of the employers identified several problems related to alcohol and drug abuse.

Individual business owners and managers were hesitant to acknowledge the existence of an alcohol or drug problem in their workplace. Discussion of

TABLE 2. Problems with Alcohol and Drugs in the Workplace

a.	absenteeism	12.80%
b.	accidents/injuries on the job	3.70%
c.	conflict among employees	10.90%
d.	employee turnover	8.66%
e.	high health care costs	6.48%
f.	low morale	6.83%
g.	low productivity	8.30%
h.	poor quality products/services	6.80%
i.	preoccupation with family problems	11.98%
j.	theft	7.16%
k.	job performance	5.78%
Total		89.39%

such problems is considered taboo. Only 18 admitted that drugs were a problem in their businesses. To admit that a problem exists in their business would make the business owner feel vulnerable. In a small community, rumors of an alcohol or drug problem could have a devastating effect on business.

A larger number of participants (48) indicated that drugs were a problem in their business community. It may be less threatening for a businessperson to admit that such a problem exists in the town's small business community. Consequently, it is less complicated for businesspersons to admit that an alcohol and drug problem exists in the community overall. When discussing the impact of alcohol and drugs in their community, approximately 73% acknowledged the existence the problem in their community. This reflects the interdependent relationship businesses have with other members of their community.

TECHNICAL ASSISTANCE

When asked if they had ever received training to recognize alcohol, drug, and tobacco abuse in the workplace, only 76 (40.4%) respondents indicated they had received training. When asked if they were interested in technical assistance to establish Employee Assistance or Wellness Programs, (50) 27.1% expressed an interest. Finally, when asked if they would attend a half day workshop on how to develop drug abuse policies for their business, 60 businesses (31.9%) responded affirmatively.

CULTURALLY APPROPRIATE SERVICES

During the data collection process, the interviewers and staff identified business owners and managers interviewed to join a drug free workplace advisory board. This participatory approach was vital to the project because the advisory board members become stakeholders in the process. The board met once a month during the life of the project to (1) discuss alcohol, tobacco and other drug issues of mutual interest; (2) to form a network of small business owners interested in developing drug free workplace policies and services; and (3) to develop culturally appropriate literature for the Hispanic population in the region.

The significantly large percentage of Hispanic employees in the workplace requires businesses to utilize bilingual and bicultural literature. Numerous businesses have a difficult time identifying culturally relevant resources and speakers. In fact, members of the advisory board frequently invited project staff to conduct educational seminars to employees in their communities. Small businesses in the rural communities of Arizona have few resources available to help them develop appropriate drug free workplace policies and practices. The majority of the Spanish language literature available through the national drug information clearinghouses was often from other Hispanic cultural groups (i.e., Puerto Rico) with little relevance to the predominantly Mexican origin Hispanic population of the region. As a result, a great deal of the advisory group's activities was on developing culturally appropriate materials and resources that incorporated the regions' culture.

SUMMARY

Several major findings are important in the planning of drug free workplace services to businesses. In the policy arena, it was found that only one third (32.8%) of employers had any written form of alcohol, tobacco and other drug policies. One quarter (23.4%) indicated they do not inform their employees about their policies. Those that *do* inform them about drug policies focus mostly on the hiring process, at meetings and in the job manual. This is the traditional approach usually prevalent in most businesses. The results of this survey indicate that most employers (68.1%) are aware of services available in their community to assist their employees.

Few employers indicated they have ever taken disciplinary action or terminated their employees due to reasons of alcohol, tobacco, and other drug abuse. This may be indicative of rural employers' tolerance of alcohol and drugs or simply their inability to identify the symptoms of abuse. It was acknowledged that some employers may be reluctant to divulge this information. An additional factor is the fact that it is very costly to replace employees in most of the communities because unemployment is low. Hence, there is a reluctance to initiate actions toward employees. Unemployment is high in only two communities because of changes in the economic infrastructure. In Hayden, the local refinery has dramatically altered its production. In Eloy, a significant portion of the population are migrant farm workers following the cyclical migrant stream. In the Old and New Pascua communities, the unemployment parallels that of other tribes. Few businesses are located in either the Old Pascua village or the New Pascua reservation.

The data regarding alcohol indicates that small businesses are uninformed about the negative effects of alcohol on their employees health. This data suggests that the lack of action towards their employees is more a protective function of employers towards employees they value. Another perspective proposes that employers may be unaware of a wide range of actions and resources available to help their employees with alcohol, tobacco, and other drug abuse problems in lieu of taking punitive actions towards them. It is meaningful to recognize that in rural areas abuse of alcohol and other drugs is a strong taboo. Small businesses are more dependent on their community to succeed. In small communities, businesses are reliant on informal networks and have to be alert that negative information about their employees is not spread by word of mouth. This would have a negative impact on their business.

The data that measures the level at which businesses recognize alcohol and drugs as a problem marks a traditional pattern of denial in the workplace. At the respondents' immediate business level, only 10% of employers responded that drugs were a problem. The percentage increases when the level of the problem is focused on the business community. Four times (40%) the number of employees recognized the existence of a problem. When asked about the problem at the community level, the number of positive responses increased dramatically to 70%. This data reveals that most employers tend to deny the problem when it applies to their businesses. Yet, they are more open to admit that the alcohol and drug problem exists within other businesses and the community at large. This may either indicate a failure to recognize the problem as it occurs at their personal business or is clearly an attempt to protect their business interests.

Overall, the majority of employers responded they would not be interested in receiving technical assistance in the alcohol, tobacco and other drug area. Only 27% indicated they would accept technical assistance while 32% indicated a willingness to attend a workshop to learn more about the problem.

RESEARCH OUTCOMES

The immediate outcome of this survey was to initiate plans to provide technical assistance and conduct an educational workshop for those willing to participate. The educational content included basic information about alcohol, tobacco and other drug abuse and their impact on overall health. A special emphasis was made on recognizing that nicotine is a drug, and that smoking tobacco has numerous consequences on the body. An additional educational component taught participants to identify symptoms that an employee may be abusing alcohol or drugs in the workplace. Businesspersons received further training to identify new ways to deal with employees who abuse drugs. For example, methods that can be utilized separate from disciplinary action to prevent termination.

A second product that was created was the development of a directory of services that are available in the communities and region where they live. While it was not possible to create a directory in each community, technical assistance was provided to guide a group of community business leaders to take ownership and begin to outline a plan to educate their community about the problem. As part of an empowerment strategy, these leaders were provided with training materials and literature that included problem solving techniques and ways to access needed services.

RECOMMENDATIONS

Beyond providing technical assistance to businesses, a campaign to educate the general public in small communities about the nature of alcohol and drug problems and where to go for help is needed. Information of this nature is often unavailable or non-existent in small rural communities. This type of campaign can be carried out by asking each of the businesses participating in the workshop or who receives technical assistance to distribute the literature in each of their businesses. This type of campaign may include posters, pamphlets, fliers, and public service announcements on radio and television. The type of campaign also needs to be carried out in Spanish with the Spanish language communication media. In some of these communities, Spanish language newspapers, radio and television stations are reliable places to disseminate drug abuse literature. Other avenues of information dissemination could be in local churches, at banks, and grocery stores. Creative approaches could be used to develop publicity via t-shirts for youth in sports games, the distribution of key chains and pencils. One very valuable resource to assist in this type of endeavors is the Hispanic Latino Leadership Training in Prevention. This training used a trainer of trainers approach to educate individuals with knowledge and skills regarding prevention and Hispanic cultural issues.

The Arizona Prevention Resource Center in Tempe presently provides information on general prevention issues throughout the state. However, it should consider the creation of a toll free line that would provide information to businesses in rural areas regarding resources they need. In addition, training that teaches strategies to work with Hispanic families is needed. The large Hispanic work force in rural areas make it incumbent to link the workplace with the employees' families. Often the workplace is the only resource available to families in rural areas. In some of the rural areas included in this survey very few agencies provide services to families. The main institutions in these communities are the family, church, school and workplace. This survey strengthens the notion that the survival of these institutions is precarious under the onslaught of the drug crisis.

In sum, alcohol, tobacco and other drugs are a problem in all of the rural communities studied. A clear outcome of this survey is to recognize how small communities and businesses are protective of each other and need help in taking ownership of the drug and alcohol problem in their community. The empowerment philosophy certainly will be most helpful and practical in helping small businesses to help themselves.

REFERENCES

Arizona Dept. of Commerce (1995). Community Profile Reference Guide. Phoenix, Arizona.

Beattie, M.C., Longsbaugh, R. and Fava, J. "Assessment of Alcohol Related Workplace Activities: Development and Testing of Your Workplace." *Journal of Studies in Alcohol*, Vol. 53, pp. 469-475, 1992.

Blum, T.C. and Roman, P.M., "Drugs, the Workplace and Employee-Oriented Programming." *Treating Drug Problems*. Dean R. Gerstein and Hemrick J. Harwood (eds.) National Academy Press: Washington, D.C. Vol. 2, pp. 197-243, 1992.

Fetterman, D.M., Kaftarian, S.J. and Wandersman, A. (1996) *Empowerment Evaluation: Knowledge and Tools for Self-Management and Accountability*. Thousand Oaks, California: Sage Publications.

Harris, M.M. and Heft, L.L. "Alcohol and Drug Use in the Workplace. NIDA Monograph 91, pp. 271-286. Washington, D.C.: Supt. of Doc., U.S. Government Printing Office. 1989.

Sanchez Mayers, R., Kail, B.L., and Watts, T.D. (1993). *Hispanic Substance Abuse*. Springfield, Illinois: Charles C. Thomas Publishers.

Alcohol Use Among Latino Males: Implications for the Development of Culturally Competent Prevention and Treatment Services

Edgar Colon, DSW

SUMMARY. This paper examines the factors surrounding the use of alcohol among Latino males. Prevention and treatment strategies for the provision of culturally competent treatment services are proposed, based on an analysis of the literature. *[Article copies available for a fee from The Haworth Document Delivery Service: 1-800-342-9678. E-mail address: getinfo@haworth.com]*

The Latino population is an aggregation of several distinct subgroups: Mexican, Puerto Rican, Cuban, and Central and South American (Szacpocznik & Kurtines, 1980). Latinos comprise the most rapidly increasing ethnic group in the United States over the past decade. In 1990, there were approximately 22 million persons of Latino extraction, double the number in 1980 (U.S. Bureau of the Census, 1992). It is estimated that by the year 2000, there will be 29 million Latinos living in the United States (U.S. Bureau of the Census, 1988). Presently, Latinos constitute the second largest minority community behind the African American community.

Edgar Colon is Associate Professor of Social Work and Urban Studies, Southern Connecticut State University, 501 Crescent Street, New Haven, CT 06515-1355.

[Haworth co-indexing entry note]: "Alcohol Use Among Latino Males: Implications for the Development of Culturally Competent Prevention and Treatment Services." Colon, Edgar. Co-published simultaneously in *Alcoholism Treatment Quarterly* (The Haworth Press, Inc.) Vol. 16, No. 1/2, 1998, pp. 147-161; and: *Alcohol Use/Abuse Among Latinos: Issues and Examples of Culturally Competent Services* (ed: Melvin Delgado) The Haworth Press, Inc., 1998, pp. 147-161. Single or multiple copies of this article are available for a fee from The Haworth Document Delivery Service [1-800-342-9678, 9:00 a.m. - 5:00 p.m. (EST). E-mail address: getinfo@haworth.com].

147

Although Latinos are increasing in their proportion to other ethnic groups in the U.S., the health of the Latino community may be declining. This may be due to the increasing inequality in income and resource allocation in the United States since the mid-1970s (Engmann, 1976). Since 1973, low income Latino families have experienced an absolute decline in income. In particular, weekly wages and salary incomes for Latino males below the 90th percentile declined between 1979 and 1987.

Latinos are younger, earn less, and have fewer economic resources than the White population. The median age of Latinos is 26, compared to the total population median age of 34. One quarter of all Latino families were below the poverty line in 1990, compared to 9% of the non-Latino population. Household income among Latinos was about three quarters that of the non-Latino population in 1990 ($22,300 compared to $33,500). Household net worth or family assets of Latino families was $5,345 compared to White families' $44,408 (U.S. Bureau of the Census, 1992).

Research undertaken in the last decade has demonstrated that segments of the Latino male population are particularly heavy drinkers and are therefore at risk for alcohol related problems. It is estimated that Latino males tend to use alcohol to a greater extent than the general population (National Institute on Drug Abuse, 1987). Among Mexican American males, alcohol abuse has been identified as major social and health problem (Gilbert & Cervantes, 1986). Puerto Rican men were reported to drink more often and more heavily and to suffer more frequent blackouts and morning tremors than Anglo or African American men (Caetano, 1985). Gordon (1981) observed high drinking habits and alcoholism rates among Guatemalan, Dominican, and Puerto Rican migrants.

The purpose of this article is to examine the factors surrounding the use of alcohol among Latino males. On the basis of this analysis, alcoholism treatment strategies for the provision of culturally competent treatment services are proposed.

LATINO MALES AND THE USE OF ALCOHOL

The major thrust of alcohol related research conducted among Latino males has thus far been devoted to constructing an epidemiological portrait of alcohol use practices and associated social and health consequences (Newcomb, Maddahian, & Bentler, 1986). Less attention has been given to psychological and cognitive factors associated with ethnic and gender differences (Caetano & Medina-Mora, 1988). Recent studies have focused on quantity-frequency drinking patterns and attitudes towards drinking (Gilbert & Cervantes, 1987; Caetano, 1985).

A first major effort to understand the drinking patterns and practices of all U.S. Latinos was conducted by the National Institute on Drug Abuse (NIDA, 1987). The National Household Survey of Drug Abuse was the eighth study in a series of national surveys designed to measure the prevalence of drug and alcohol use among individuals in American households aged 12 and over. The survey estimated drug use prevalence, including alcohol use for a representative sample in the U.S. civilian, non-institutionalized population.

In this survey, 1,996 Latino adults were interviewed along with a sample of Blacks (n = 1,945) and Anglo-Americans (n = 3,949). Few differences were found in overall use rates (lifetime and past morbidity) when comparing Latino, Black and Anglo men. Conversely, female alcohol use rates showed a marked ethnic difference between Latina and Anglo women. Anglo women were found to have lifetime use rates (85.6%) which were considerably higher than Latinas (62.9%). Latinos in this national survey were not broken down by subgroup or generational status. Latino subgroups were not distinguished between immigrant individuals and individuals born in the United States.

Caetano (1985, 1988) conducted a more Latino group focused national survey to examine alcohol patterns in a representative national sample of U.S. born and immigrant Latinos. Because the sample was large enough, Latino subgroups could be assessed separately. Among the foreign born, Latin American (Central and South America) females were found to have the highest rates of abstention (75%) followed by Mexican American females (71%), Cuban females (48%) and Puerto Rican Females (45%). High rates of alcohol abstention among immigrant females have been reported by other researchers (Gilbert, 1987). Several studies have also reported that in the generations following immigration, Latinas were seen to move from abstention and very infrequent drinking to moderate drinking levels (Holck, Warren, Smith, & Rochat, 1984).

Research studies conducted on the cross generational alcohol use patterns of Latino men show a movement of Latino men from less high frequency drinking, defined as reaching the blood level of legal intoxication, to more frequent, high quantity drinking. Caetano (1988) found among Latino immigrants and U.S.-born men and women that Latina immigrants differed less from their U.S.-born counterparts than Latino immigrant men differed from U.S.-born men in the frequency and quantity of drinking.

ETHNIC AND GENDER DIFFERENCES

Ethnic differences in patterns of alcohol abuse do not appear to be as marked among females as among males, suggesting that gender could be more important in determining alcohol abuse profile than ethnicity. Several reasons for this are possible. First, although males experience more risk factors, females may possibly mediate and/or manifest this experience differently through the process of socialization and development of differential coping mechanisms for those risk factors. Second, females experience adolescence differently than males (Licht & Dweck, 1983).

Clinical studies have also noted significant gender and ethnic differences among alcohol abusers. Gilbert and Cervantes (1986) reported that Mexican Americans were overrepresented as alcohol service clients in several states and appeared to have poorer outcomes than Anglos (Mendalhall et al., 1989). Conversely, African Americans were found to frequent alcohol service programs at the same rate as non-African American clients and had the poorest treatment prognosis when compared with other ethnic and religious (Latino, Irish, Scandinavian, German, French, and Mormon) groups (Babor & Mendelsohn, 1983).

In related studies, gender and ethnic differences have also been reported among drug users, with Latinos being overrepresented in the percentage of admissions into drug treatment programs (De La Rosa, Khalsa & Rouse, 1990) In terms of outcome, African American substance abusers had higher dropout rates from a methadone maintenance program (Sorenson, Gibson, Berna & Dietch, 1985) than Latinos and Anglos, whereas female Mexican American drug abusers had poorer post-treatment social functioning than male Mexican American and Anglo patients (Anglin, Booth, Ryan & Hser, 1988). These studies suggest that ethnic and gender characteristics may affect prevalence rates and alcohol treatment outcomes.

Studies investigating the alcohol use patterns of adolescent Latino males have found that their patterns of alcohol use are clearly associated with degree of vulnerability, defined as the cumulative effects of risk factors, to such use (Clayton, 1992; Newcomb, 1992; Newcomb, Maddahian & Bentler, 1986). Therefore, the development of substance abuse treatment services must be comprehensive in scope and based on the use of multidimensional treatment approaches.

ADOLESCENT LATINO MALES AND THE USE OF ALCOHOL

Morales (1984) reviewed the literature on Latino adolescents and alcohol abuse. He reported that Mexican American youth from the lowest socioeconomic status levels (SES) tend to abuse substances. He suggested that SES plays a major role as a contributing risk factor for substance use among this population. Schinke, Moncher, Palleja, Zayas and Schiling (1988) argue that social milieu risk factors, specifically underemployment, racial discrimination and poverty, contribute to Latino male adolescent perceptions of helplessness, fatalism and low self-esteem. In an investigation of sixth and seventh graders, Vega et al. (1993) found a linear relationship between the cumulative number of risk factors (perceptions of helplessness, fatalism and poor self-esteem) and rates of alcohol abuse for Whites, Latinos and African American adolescents.

Alcohol use among Latino adolescent males may be attributed to a combination of risk factors. The number and complexity of risk factors present directly increase the likelihood of alcohol and drug use (Clayton, 1992; Newcomb, 1992). Moreover, individual attributes and environmental conditions may also serve to increase risk. Recent research studies on the sociobehavioral correlates of alcohol consumption suggest a number of potential explanations for understanding the complexity of risk factors affecting rates of alcohol use among adolescent and adult Latino males. These include: (a) age; (b) religious preference; (c) education level; (d) income potentials; and (e) degree of acculturation to American society.

ACCULTURATION AND THE MASCULINE ROLE

A topic in the social science literature that has garnered a significant amount of attention is acculturation (Stevens, 1985). Among Mexican Americans, acculturation measures have primarily been employed with the intention of measuring the degree to which one has experienced cultural change towards the majority culture. Numerous investigations have attempted to define, operationalize and measure acculturation among Mexican Americans (Cuellar, Harris, & Jasso, 1980). Padilla (1980) developed a degree assessment conception of acculturation scale. With it he examines a person's level of cultural awareness and ethnic loyalty and determines the type rather than degree of acculturation.

Caetano (1987) in an investigation of acculturation and Latino normative behaviors found that the more acculturated Latino men and women held more liberal views on drinking than those held by less acculturated Latinos. These behavioral norms were found to be related to the appropriate amounts and contexts of alcohol use for Latino men and women of various ages (Caetano, 1987). A number of studies have examined the relationship between problem drinking behaviors, Latino male cultural values and degree of acculturation.

Madsen (1964) studied problem drinking among acculturating Mexicans, noting that male interpersonal relations required alcohol consumption. Abad (1974), investigating the drinking problems of Puerto Rican men, cited Latino male cultural values as service barriers. Hoffman (1994)

noted that heterosexuality, assertiveness and reciprocity in relations between Latino men are central values in machismo as are responsibility to
the family, courage, pride and self control. Pleck, Sonenstein, and Ku
(1993) found that among adolescent males' strong endorsement of masculine ideology is associated with problem behaviors in four areas: school
difficulties, delinquency, sexual activity and substance abuse.

Therefore, as there appears to be a strong relationship between a strong
male gender identity and the willingness to seek help by Latino males,
there is a clear need to address the possible correlation between a macho
orientation, high risk behaviors and protective and risk factors. Protective
factors limit or reduce alcohol use and may encounter, buffer, neutralize
and interact with risk factors within or across time (Brook, Nomura &
Cohen, 1989a; Newcomb, 1991). These factors represent opposite ends of
the same continuum. That is, those who are not at risk are by default
protected.

PROTECTIVE AND RISK FACTORS

Certain protective and risk factors have been suggested to account for
Latino male alcohol use. Alcohol use by parents or older siblings (Estrada,
Rabow & Watts, 1982) and family disintegration (Delgado, 1990, Szapocznik & Kurtines, 1980) are often cited as substance abuse vulnerability
factors for Latino males. Frequent church attendance and religious affiliation also appear to buffer Latino males against alcohol abuse (Estrada et
al., 1982; Guinn, 1975). Low self-concept is another important correlate of
Latino male alcohol abuse (Perez, Ramirez, Ramirez, & Rodriguez, 1980).
Poverty, alcohol availability, poor school performance and peer drug use
are also correlated with Latino male drug use (Delgado, 1990).

Two important issues emerge when considering both risk and protective
influences on alcohol use by Latino males. The influence of protective
factors can be a distinct influence away from risk. Their effect on alcohol
use can have both direct and moderator effects. Substantively, the main or
direct effect of protection is to predict less alcohol use, whereas the direct
effect of risk is to predict increased alcohol use (Newcomb, 1992).

There are several interpretations of the role of risk and protective factors in understanding the use of alcohol by Latino males. First, although
Latino males experience more risk factors than Latinas, Latinas possibly
mediate and/or manifest differently the effects of these factors during the
process of socialization. Second, Latino males also may develop differential coping mechanisms for certain risk factors, mechanisms that may not
be available to Latinas. For example, when Latinas experience risk factors,

they may have fewer reference groups or models than males to help them deal with them. Third, Latina females experience adolescence differently than Latino males (Licht & Dweck, 1983). The relationship between protective and risk factors, cognitive expectation and levels of drinking is also important given the potency of reinforcing cognition as a potential determinant of drinking behavior (Cervantes et al., 1990).

ALCOHOL EXPECTANCIES

The examination of alcohol expectancies related to drinking among Latino males may have strong predictive power (Clark & Midinak, 1982). Welte and Barnes (1987) analyzed alcohol expectancies among Latino males and found that the alcohol expectancies held by Latino males and the process of acculturation, with its inherent stress, influenced drinking prevalence and the number of alcohol-related problems found among Latino males (Caetano, 1987; Cervantes, Gilbert, Synder, & Padilla, 1990).

Clark and Midanik (1982) found that Latino males tend to expect most of the expected results of drinking alcoholic beverages. They also found that the amount of alcoholic beverages consumed by Latino males was found to be related to the type of expectations held by the respondents and their acceptance of behavioral consequences to the consumption of alcoholic beverages.

Research with non-Latinos has tended to show that differences do indeed exist in the number and quality of alcohol expectancies for Latino males and for people in general (Leigh, 1989). Nevertheless, the high value placed in Latino cultures of group membership/activity versus individual membership/activity could be perceived as supporting the need to identify nonspecific and generalized expectancies because the social collective is often used as a behavioral and attitudinal referent by Latino males (Sabogal, Marin, Otero-Sagogal, Marin, & Perez-Stable, 1987). Therefore, the development of alcohol and other substance abuse treatment approaches requires the creation of social group centered approaches to the engagement and maintenance of Latino males in treatment.

The available research data cannot be perceived as definite in identifying the expectancies held by Latino males. In light of the role of the risk and protective factors associated with the consumption of alcohol by Latino males, early culturally competent prevention and intervention efforts need to occur before risk reaches a level at which time treatment intervention may have little or no impact.

THE DEVELOPMENT OF CULTURALLY COMPETENT TREATMENT SERVICES

Research on Latino males receiving alcohol related care is lacking in terms of treatment experience and effectiveness (Institute of Medicine, 1990). Furthermore, there have been no major studies to determine whether culturally competent alcohol related treatment produces different effects for Latino males than such treatment provided to them in mainstream programs (Gilbert & Cervantes, 1987). Research in these areas is important because significant differences exist among Latino subgroups (Caetano, 1988; National Center for Health Statistics, 1985). Each subgroup has a distinct cultural background that influences attitudes toward alcohol use and its treatment.

Santisteban and Szapocnick (1982) argue that alcohol treatment for Latino males must be culturally appropriate to be effective. They assert that two central issues need to be addressed in treatment. These issues are the relevance of the Latino family, and the problems produced by the process of acculturation. Scopetta et al., (1977) found that many Cuban male immigrants in Florida tended to cope with a difficult acculturation process by resorting to drinking.

The degree of acculturation of Latino males to American life has significant implications for the cultural appropriateness of treatment programs. Intervention programs must involve the Latino family and its affected male members and be based on recognition of the cultural and behavioral characteristics of each Latino subgroup (Markides, Ray, & Stroup-Benham, 1990; Perez-Stable et al., 1994).

The following brief example describes an alcohol treatment program that incorporates strategies based on recognition of the cultural and behavioral aspects of Latino male behavior.

CASE EXAMPLE: AN ALCOHOLICS ANONYMOUS (AA) GROUP MODEL FOR LATINO MALES

Hoffman (1994) noted that Alcoholic Anonymous groups for Latino males have existed in Los Angeles, California for many years. However, given the recent massive new Latino migration, a different approach to recovery involving "rough therapy" and rowdy behavior has become common in Los Angeles. He notes that meetings conducted in this "rough therapy" style lend themselves to expressions of machismo and aggressive male behavior. Moreover, he argues that these A.A. groups have adapted

to the machismo ethos in a way that leaves Latino males room for surren-
der to a higher power and still retain a sense of masculine assertiveness.
These Latino A.A. groups provide Latino males with companionship in
a positive alternative to the barroom. The A.A. meeting serves as a setting
for integration into the Latino culture and for acculturation into the dominant society. Overall, it is clear that the transcultural adaptational group
model has developed culturally appropriate ways of integrating the machismo value system into the discourse to confront drinking problems. The
"rough therapy" treatment approach has incorporated male boasting,
competitiveness and sexually aggressive behavior towards women as a
way to remove the barrier that machismo-related behaviors can be in
alcohol treatment with Latino males (Abad, 1988).

TREATMENT RECOMMENDATIONS

As Latino male members of Latino subgroups are exposed differential-
ly to risk factors, it is critical for treatment programs to consider the
influence of both risk and protective factors on Latino male alcohol use
patterns. Protective factors may exert a distinct influence from risk and its
effect on alcohol use can have both direct and moderator effects. Moreover, given the high prevalence of alcohol use by adolescent Latino males,
the development of culturally appropriate and age group specific early
alcohol prevention and treatment programs is of critical importance (Vega
et al., 1993).

Level of acculturation seems to have an important influence on the
alcohol use patterns of Latino males and the degree of self-efficacy to quit
drinking. Treatment providers should assess these factors in determining
their relevance to treatment planning. When analyzing the alcohol expectancies held by Latino males, the role of acculturation in the client's belief
system should be explored. The process of acculturation, with its inherent
stress, may influence drinking prevalence and the number of alcohol related problems (Caetano, 1987).

For alcohol treatment services to be culturally appropriate and sensitive, there is therefore a need for a close working alliance between practitioners and researchers to examine more closely the relationship between
Latino male endorsement of masculine ideology and alcohol and drug
abuse, violence, juvenile delinquency and adult crime and sexual activity.
From a help seeking perspective, there is evidence that Latino men with
strong male gender identity schema avoid all situations in which they
perceive themselves as helpless or weak (Heppner, 1981).

In the development of culturally sensitive and appropriate services,

156   ALCOHOL USE/ABUSE AMONG LATINOS

practitioners must intervene in a manner that promotes the removal of internalized barriers that impede access by Latino males to the therapeutic process. Alternative helping formats (i.e., workshops, seminars, or classes) may be rated more favorably by Latino men who are highly restrictive emotionally and highly oriented toward success, power, and competition. However, men with less traditional masculine ideologies may find both traditional psychological services and other alternative helping formats equally helpful (Robertson, & Fitzgerald, 1992).

CONCLUSION

Markides, Ray and Stroup-Benham (1990), and Perez-Stable et al. (1994) noted that to effectively promote healthy behaviors among ethnic and racial groups in the United States, intervention programs need to be based upon the specific cultural and behavioral characteristics of each group. Moreover, the ability of alcohol treatment programs to effectively meet the variety of needs of the heterogeneous Latino male clientele will have implications for resource allocation and program effectiveness. Meeting these distinct needs will require recognition that certain Latino male behaviors may affect patterns of alcohol use.

Furthermore, the degree of acculturation to American culture by Latino males may have significant implications for the appropriateness of treatment approaches (Rogler et al., 1987). The use of concepts of cultural variability and adaptation in the development of client centered alcohol treatment services for males in different Latino subgroups may lead to a more viable and acceptable form of treatment (Gilbert & Cervantes, 1986b). Sutro (1989) studied the cross-cultural adaptation of Alcoholics Anonymous groups in a remote Indian village in southern Mexico. He noted that the use of a nonchemical substitute dependency, ritual reminder of the pitfalls of drinking, repair of social and medical damage caused by drinking and restoration of self-esteem were four elements of successful treatment.

The delivery of alcoholism treatment to Latino males should not use a single factor approach. As suggested by Kandel (1978) there are complex, multiple pathways leading to the use of alcohol and prevention and treatment efforts should reflect this complexity. The focus of treatment and prevention to Latino males should be based on a reduction of the total number of risk factors in a given environment.

Clinical assessment of the alcohol expectancies held by Latino males should make possible the development of targeted prevention and treatment messages and modalities. As an example, the association between depression and alcohol expectancies and use strongly suggests that Latino males may be using alcohol as a coping mechanism. Therefore, prevention and treatment strategies that encourage and teach alternative coping techniques are required.

Although Latino males are similar to other groups in their perceptions of alcohol use, there are important gender and origin differences that need to be addressed in the development of alcohol prevention and treatment programs. Lastly, further research is needed to better understand the special alcoholism treatment needs of Latino male clients and to address them with culturally sensitive and appropriate treatment services.

AUTHOR NOTE

Edgar Colon is Associate Professor of Social Work and Urban Studies teaching in the areas of social welfare administration, research, human behavior, substance abuse practice, and social policy. In addition to his long standing academic career, Dr. Colon has served as Associate Director of Social Work and Discharge Planning at the Lincoln Medical and Mental Health Center, a 700-bed level 1 trauma center in New York City. During his tenure at Lincoln, he also served as the Director of the Children's Outpatient Psychiatric Service and Chief Psychiatric Social Worker while an Assistant Professor of Psychiatry on the faculty of New York Medical College, in Valhalla, New York. Presently, Dr. Colon consults to hospitals on issues of managed care practice and substance abuse treatment. He also has recently had several professional articles on program service delivery issues affecting Latino communities in the delivery of health and mental health services accepted for publication in the *Journal of Multicultural Social Work* and *Journal of Health and Social Policy*. His current professional memberships include NASW, the American Society of Public Administration, the National Network for Social Work Managers, the Council on Social Work Education, and the Connecticut Association of Latin Americans in Higher Education.

REFERENCES

Abad. V. (1988). *Machismo and Alcoholism Among Puerto Ricans.* Paper presented at the Annual Alcoholism Conference of the National Institute on Alcohol Abuse and Alcoholism, Washington, D.C.

Baron, R.M., & Kenney, D.A. (1986). *The moderator-mediator distinction in social psychological research: Conceptual, strategic, and statistical considerations.* Journal of Personality and Social Psychology, 51, 1173-1183.

Brook, J.S., Nomura, C., & Cohen, P. (1989a). *A network of influences on adolescent drug involvement: Neighborhood school, peer, and family.* Genetic, Social and General Psychology Monographs, 115, 125-145.

Brook, J.S., Whiteman, M., Gordon, A.S., & Cohen, P. (1986) *Dynamics of childhood and adolescent personality traits and adolescent drug use.* Developmental Psychology, 22, 403-414.

Caetano, R. (1983). *Drinking patterns and alcohol problems among Hispanics in the U.S.: A review.* Drug and Alcohol Dependence, 18, 1-5.

Caetano, R. (1985). *Drinking patterns and alcohol problems in a national sample of U.S. Hispanics.* Paper presented at the National Institute on Alcohol and Alcoholism Conference, Epidemiology of Alcohol Use and Abuse among U.S. Ethnic Minorities, Bethesda, MD.

Caetano, R. (1987b). *Acculturation and drinking patterns among U.S. Hispanics.* British Journal of Addictions, 82, 788-799.

Caetano, R., & Medina Mora, M.E. (1988). *Acculturation and drinking practices among people of Mexican descent in Mexico and the United States.* Journal of Studies on Alcohol, 49, 462-471.

Caetano, R., & Martinez, R.M. (1987). *Alcohol use in Madrid among U.S. Hispanics (Report Number C-47, prepared under contract for the National Institute on Alcohol Abuse and Alcoholism).* Berkeley. CA: Alcohol Research Group.

Cervantes, R.C., Gilbert, M.J., Synder, N.S., & Padilla, A.M. (1990-1991). *Psychosocial and cognitive correlates of alcohol use in younger adult immigrant and U.S. born Hispanics.* International Journal of the Addictions, 25, 687-708.

Clark, W.B., & Midanik, L. (1982). *Alcohol use and alcohol problems among U.S. adults.* in NIAAA (Ed), Alcohol consumption and related problems. Washington, D.C., Government Printing Office, 3-52.

Clayton, R.R. (1992). *Transition in drug use: Risk and protective factors.* In M. Glantz, & R. Pickens (Eds.), Vulnerability to Drug Abuse, Washington, D.C., American Psychological Association, 15-51.

Cuellar, I., Harris, L.C., Jasso, R. (1980). *An acculturation scale for Mexican normal and clinical populations.* Hispanic Journal of Behavioral Science, 2, 199-217.

De La Rosa, M.R., Khalsa, J.H., & Rouse, B. A. (1990). *Hispanics and illicit drug use: A review of recent findings.* International Journal of the Addictions, 25, 665-691.

Delgado, M. (1990). *Hispanic adolescents and Drug abuse: Implications for research, treatment, and prevention.* In A.R. Stiffman & L.E. Davis (Eds.) Ethnic Issues in Adolescent Mental Health, Newbury Park, CA: Sage.

Edmanson, H. (1975). *Mexican american alcoholism and deaths at LA-USC medical center.* Testimony before the Subcommittee on Alcoholism of the California Commission on Alcoholism of the California Senate Health and Welfare Committee, Sacramento, CA.

Engmann, D.J. (1976). *Alcoholism and alcohol abuse among Spanish speaking population in California: A needs and service assessment.* Sacramento, CA: California Commission on Alcoholism for the Spanish Speaking.

Estrada, A., Rabow, J., & Watts, R. (1982). *Alcohol use among Hispanic adoles-*

cents: A preliminary report. Hispanic Journal of Behavioral Sciences, 4, 339-351.

Fernadez-Pol, B., Bluestone, H., & Mizruchi, M.S. (1988). *Substance abuse patterns: A study of psychiatric inpatients.* American Journal of Alcohol and Drug Abuse, 14, 41-50.

Gilbert, M.J. (1987). *Alcohol consumption patterns on immigrant and later generation Mexican American women.* Hispanic Journal of Behavioral Sciences, 9, 299-313.

Gilbert, J.M., & Cervantes, R.C. (1987). *Mexican Americans and alcohol.* Monograph No. 11, Los Angeles, CA: Spanish Speaking Mental Health Center.

Gilbert, M.J., & Cervantes, R.C., (1986). *Alcohol services for Mexican Americans: A review of utilization patterns, treatment considerations and prevention activities.* Hispanic Journal of Behavioral Sciences, 8, 191-223.

Gordon, A.J. (1981). *The cultural context of drinking and indigenous therapy in three Migrant Hispanic cultures: An ethnographic report.* In D.B. Heath, J.O. Waddell & M.D. Tropper (Eds.) Cultural factors in alcohol research and treatment of drinking problems, 9, 217-240.

Heppner, P.P. (1981). *Counseling men in groups.* Personnel and Guidance Journal, 59, 249-252.

Hoffman, F. (1994). *Cultural adaptations of Alcoholic Anonymous to Hispanic service populations.* The Journal of the Addictions, 29(4), 445-460.

Holck, S.E., Warren, C., Smith, J., & Rochat, R. (1984). *Alcohol consumption among Mexican American and Anglo women: Results of a survey along the U.S. Mexico border.* Journal of Studies on Alcohol, 45, 149-153.

Institute of Medicine (1990). *Broadening the base of treatment of alcohol problems.* Washington, D.C.: National Academy Press.

Kandel, D.B. (1978). *Convergence in prospective longitudinal survey of drug use in normal populations.* In D.B. Kandel (Ed.), Longitudinal Research on Drug Use: Empirical Findings and Methodological Issues. NY: Halstead, 132-169.

Leigh, B.C. (1989) *In search of the seven dwarfs: Issues of measurement and meaning in alcohol expectancy research.* Psychological Bulletin, 105, 361-372.

Lex, B.W. (1985). *Alcohol problems in special populations.* In J.H. Mendelsohn & N.K. Mello (Eds.) The diagnosis and treatment of alcohol. NY: McGraw-Hill.

Licht, B.G., & Dweck, C.S. (1983). *Sex differences in achievement orientations: Consequences for academic choices and attainment.* In M. Marland (Ed), Sex differentiation and schooling. London: Heineman Educational Books.

Marin, G., Marin, B.V., Otero-Sabogal, R., Sabogal, F., & Perez-Stable, E.J. (1990). *The role of acculturation in the attitudes, norms, and expectancies of Hispanic smokers.* Journal of Cross Cultural Psychology, 20, 399-415.

Marin, G., Sabogal., F., Marin, B., Otero-Sabogal, R., & Perez-Stable, E.J. (1987). *Development of a short acculturation scale for Hispanics.* Hispanic Journal of Behavioral Sciences, 9, 183-205.

Markides, K.S., Ray, L.A. & Stroup-Benham, C.A. (1990). *Acculturation and alcohol consumption in the Mexican American population of the southwestern United States: Findings from HHANES 1982-1984.* American Journal of Public Health, 80 (sppl.), 20-26.

Mendenhall, C.L., Gartside, P.S., Roselle, G., A., Grossman, C, J, Weesner, R.E., & Chedid, A. (1989). *Longevity among ethnic groups in alcoholic liver disease.* Alcohol and Alcoholism, 24, 11-19.

Morales, A. (1984). *Substance abuse and Mexican American youth: An overview.* Journal of Drug Issues, 9, 279-311.

National Institute on Drug Abuse. (1987). *National Household Survey of Drug Abuse.* Washington, DC: Alcohol, Drug Abuse, and Mental Health Administration, 1987a.

National Center for Health Statistics (1985). *Plan and operation of the Hispanic health and nutrition examination survey, 1983-1984.* Vital Health Statistics (Series 1, No. 19, DHHS Publication No. [83-1321]). Washington, D.C.: Government Printing Office.

Newcomb, M.D. (1992). *Understanding the multidimensional nature of drug use and abuse: The role of consumption, risk factors, and protective factors.* In M.D. Glantz & R. Pickens (Eds.), Vulnerability to drug abuse. Washington, D.C., American Psychological Association.

Newcomb, M.D., Maddahian, E., & Bentler, P.M. (1986). *Risk factors for drug use among adolescents: Concurrent and longitudinal analyses.* American Journal of Public Health, 76, 525-531.

Padilla, A.M. (1980). *The role of cultural awareness and ethnic loyalty in acculturation.* In A.M. Padilla (Ed.) Acculturation: Theory, models, and some new findings. Boulder, CO: Westview.

Perez, R., A.M., Ramirez, A., Ramirez, R., Rodriguez, M. (1980). *Correlates and changes over time in drug and alcohol use within a barrio population.* American Journal of Community Psychology, 8(6), 612-636.

Pleck, J.H., Sonenstein, F.L., & Ku, L.C. (1988). *Problem behaviors and masculine ideology.* Journal of Counseling Psychology, 29, 113-126.

Robertson, J.M., & Fitzgerald, L.F. (1992). *Overcoming the masculine mystique: Preferences for alternative forms of assistance among men who avoid counseling.* Journal of Counseling Psychology, 39, 240-246.

Rogler, L.H., Malgady, R.G., Constantino, G., & Blumenthal, R. (1988). *What do culturally sensitive mental health services mean: The case of Hispanics.* American Psychologist, 42, 565-570.

Santisteban, D. (1979). *Toward a conceptual model of drug abuse among Hispanics.* In J. Szapocnik (Ed.), Mental Health and Drug Abuse: An Hispanic Assessment of Present and Future Challenges, Washington, D.C., National Coalition of Hispanic Mental Health and Human Services Organizations, 47-60.

Schinke, S.P., Moncher, M.S., Pajella, J., Zayas, L.H., Schiling, R.F. (1988). *Hispanic youth, substance abuse, and stress: Implications for prevention research.* International Journal of the Addictions, 809-826.

Scopetta, M.A., O.E., Szacpocnick, J. (1977). *Relationship between drug abuse* and effective treatment for Cuban Americans. National Institute on Drug Abuse, Research Contract No. 2, 110-120.

Sorenson, J.L., Gibson, L., & Bernal, G., & Deitch, D, (1985). Methadone applicant drop-outs: Impact of requiring involvement of friends or family in treatment, International Journal of the Addictions, 20, 1273-1280.

Stevens, G, (1985). Nativity, intermarriage, and mother tongue shift. American Sociological Review, 50, 70-83.

Sutro, L.D., (1989). Alcoholics Anonymous in a Mexican peasant-indian village, Human Organ, 48(2): 180-186.

Szapocznik, J., & Kurtines, W. (1980). Acculturation, biculturalism, and adjustment among Cuban Americans. In A.M. Padilla (Ed.), Acculturation: Theory, models, and some new findings, Boulder, CO: Westview, 139-157.

U.S. Department of Health and Human Services. (1993). National household survey on drug abuse: Main findings, 1991. (Public Health Services Publication No. 92-1887). Rockville, MD.

U.S. Bureau of the Census. (1988, 1991). The Hispanic population of the United States: March, 1988. In Current population reports (advance report), population characteristics (Series P-20, No. 431). Washington, D.C.: Government Printing Office.

Vega, W.A., Zimmerman, R.S., Warheit, G.J., & Gil, A.G. (1993). Risk factors for early adolescent drug use in four ethnic and racial groups. American Journal of Public Health, 83, 185-189.

Welte, J.W., & Barnes, G.M. (1987). Alcohol use among adolescent minority groups. Journal of Studies on Alcohol, 48(4), 329-336.

The Treatment
of Alcohol Dependency
Among Latinas:
A Feminist, Cultural
and Community Perspective

Juana Mora, PhD

SUMMARY. This paper explores the meaning of culturally competent and gender-specific programming for Latinas, and addresses the
impact of culture and gender on alcohol problems. In addition, it lays
out a rationale for the development of a theoretical framework for
the treatment of alcohol abuse and dependency among Latinas based
on feminist, cultural, and community perspectives. *[Article copies
available for a fee from The Haworth Document Delivery Service: 1-800-342-
9678. E-mail address: getinfo@haworth.com]*

INTRODUCTION

Although a decade of research on Latino drinking patterns has revealed
consistent evidence of increased alcohol use and abuse among some segments of the Chicana/Latina population (Caetano, 1985; Gilbert 1987,

---

Juana Mora is Associate Dean, College of Humanities and Professor of Chica-
na/Chicano Studies, California State University, Northridge, 18111 Nordhoff
Street, Northridge, CA 91330-8252.

[Haworth co-indexing entry note]: "The Treatment of Alcohol Dependency Among Latinas: A
Feminist, Cultural and Community Perspective." Mora, Juana. Co-published simultaneously in *Alcoholism Treatment Quarterly* (The Haworth Press, Inc.) Vol. 16, No. 1/2, 1998, pp. 163-177; and: *Alcohol
Use/Abuse Among Latinos: Issues and Examples of Culturally Competent Services* (ed: Melvin Delgado) The Haworth Press, Inc., 1998, pp. 163-177. Single or multiple copies of this article are available for a
fee from The Haworth Document Delivery Service [1-800-342-9678, 9:00 a.m. - 5:00 p.m. (EST). E-mail
address: getinfo@haworth.com].

163

1991; Canino, 1994), there is a serious lack of research and information on effective treatment approaches and modalities for Latinas (Gilbert & Cervantes, 1988). The current state of knowledge on substance abuse treatment for Latinas is based on reports from treatment professionals and reviews of local and state treatment statistics (Gilbert & Cervantes, 1988; Woll, In press; Mora & Gilbert, 1991). There are few empirical studies detailing the efficacy of various treatment approaches or modalities with this population. It is not known, for example, which forms of alcohol treatment are most effective or desirable for Latinas in general and for specific groups of Latinas, including Latina adolescents, Latina lesbians, and other Latinas who may be at risk for developing alcohol dependency problems.

There is currently not enough information available on the extent to which Latinas are at risk for developing alcohol dependency problems, which Latinas are most "at risk," or even the characteristics of Latinas in treatment. In fact, about the only information available is that Latinas are less represented in treatment programs than men (Gilbert & Cervantes, 1988) and face many barriers in securing adequate treatment (Beckman & Amaro, 1986). Latinas, for example, face a host of complicating factors and barriers to treatment, including stigma, fear of losing custody of children, lack of childcare while in treatment, and language and financial barriers (U.S. Department of Health and Human Services, 1995).

The lack of systematic and empirical studies of treatment effectiveness with Latinas is partially due to the failure of traditional treatment programs to reach this population. Studies on substance abuse, like mental health research, have found that Latinas are less likely than other persons to seek treatment and less likely to complete treatment (Finn, 1994). Research on women has also found that women with a drinking problem may not initiate or continue treatment in a program that misunderstands or ignores important aspects of her life (McCrady & Raytek, 1993).

This paper will explore the meaning of "culturally competent" and "gender-specific" programming for Latinas, address the impact of culture and gender on alcohol problems and argue for the development of a theoretical framework for the treatment of alcohol abuse and dependency among Latinas based on feminist, cultural, and community perspectives.

CONCEPTS AND DEFINITIONS

Research on the treatment of alcohol and other drug abuse among women indicates that programs that incorporate and address the unique experiences and needs of women have best results and outcomes (McCrady & Raytek, 1993; U.S. Department of Health & Human Services, 1995). Because of this link between the understanding of the lives of women and positive treatment outcomes, it is important for treatment providers who serve Latina women to move beyond a basic cultural awareness and sensitivity and make serious efforts to become "competent" in the culture of the women in treatment. The concept of "cultural sensitivity" refers to an awareness and appreciation of one's own and other cultures (Orlandi, 1992). However, one can be "sensitive" but lack knowledge about the history, values, art, and music of another culture and this lack of knowledge can be a barrier between the provider and the client. The concept of "cultural competence" refers to a set of cognitive, interpersonal skills, and deliberate actions that allow individuals to increase their understanding and appreciation of cultural differences (Orlandi 1992; Gilbert, 1993). In this paper, I argue that when working with Latina women, an important aspect of the "competence" providers must acquire to effectively work with this population is an understanding of the role of the Latina woman within traditional Latino culture and in contemporary U.S. society.

Traditionally, Latinas hold special but difficult roles in their families and communities. In Latino cultures, women are given special roles and are highly respected as the central figures in the extended family networks (Falicov, 1982). While this special cultural place gives women much prestige and cultural power, it is also a role that requires them to sacrifice their needs for the needs of others. In recent years, the traditional role of Latinas has gone through major modifications as a result of the large number of Latinas in the labor force and the influence of the women's movement (Padilla & Salgado de Snyder, 1995). Part of the change in the lives of Latina women is an apparent increase in alcohol use among some Latinas.

Because traditional treatment programs have not served Latinas well and this population is young and expected to grow, it is important to define and develop "gender-specific" and "culturally competent" alcohol treatment services and programs for Latinas (Beckman & Amaro, 1986; Hill, S.Y., 1994; Woll, in press; U.S. Department of Health and Human Services, 1995). Latinas, for example, represent 52% of the estimated 27 million Latinos living in the U.S. and it is anticipated that by the year 2010, Latinas will represent nearly 11% of the total U.S. female population. It is also important to address the potential for alcohol problems in this populations because Latinos are young, with nearly half (48%) of the population being under the age of 24 (Herrell, 1993; U.S. Bureau of the Census, 1994).

Effective treatment programs for Latinas must include an understanding of the traditional role of women in Latino culture, the changing lives of

Latina women in the U.S., the factors that contribute to the changes in their lives and how these play a role in the development of alcohol problems. An understanding of the dynamics of change, gender and culture in the lives of Latina women will help counselors and others reduce the risk of alcohol dependency and support Latinas in their recovery.

This paper will not address the efficacy of various treatment modalities, i.e., residential vs. outpatient. Instead, the focus will be on examining underlying and common themes related to the socio-cultural context of alcohol use and abuse among Latinas and how these can be utilized to design culturally sensitive and competent programming.

Due to a lack of empirical data on effective alcohol treatment approaches for Latinas, the ideas expressed in this paper are taken from and based on a variety of sources, including: (1) the Latino alcohol literature, (2) Chicana feminist literature, (3) women's alcohol literature, and (4) the experience of the author as a consultant on a 1990-1993 national cross-site evaluation of Pregnant and Postpartum Women and Their Infants (PPWI) Demonstrations program funded by the Center for Substance Abuse Prevention.

CHICANA/LATINA HETEROGENEITY

It is difficult to articulate what "culturally competent" programming means for Latinas because there is great heterogeneity both across Latina groups and within specific groups. Among Mexican American women there are differences in values, language and behaviors due to age, class, education, and generational status. Some Mexican American women are very recently immigrated to the U.S.; others are members of families who have lived in the U.S. for many generations. Generally, recently immigrated Latinas are less educated, work in lower paying jobs and are primarily Spanish speaking. Later generation or U.S.-born Latinas are more likely to be English speaking or bilingual and have various levels of education (Buriel, 1993).

The major Latino groups in the U.S. are Mexican Americans, Puerto Ricans, Cubans, and Central Americans. Each group has a unique history and special relationship with the larger society. Each group has a sense of its own identity but shares common linguistic, religious and family characteristics recognized across groups as "Latino."

Mexican Americans are the largest of the Latino groups in the U.S., representing more than half of all Latinos. The majority of Mexican Americans live in the South and midwestern parts of the U.S. The next largest group are Puerto Ricans who live primarily in or near the New York area followed by Cubans, who live primarily in the city of Miami, Florida.

In some regions, there is a growing number of Central American immigrants and other Latin American immigrants. In New York City, Dominican and Colombian immigrants are prominent and in Los Angeles there are large communities of Guatemalan, Salvadoran and Nicaraguan immigrants.

DIVERSITY AMONG LATINAS: IMPLICATIONS FOR TREATMENT

The diversity in language, values, and backgrounds encountered across and within Latina groups is sometimes perceived as an obstacle to developing culturally competent and effective treatment programs for Latinas. However, if the diversity in cultures and backgrounds is respected and validated and if common themes, values and experiences are identified and utilized in treatment, this approach can be a powerful method for helping Latinas address their common problems with alcohol. Validating cultural background can be a powerful tool in recovery. Mental health and cross-cultural counseling literature identifies cultural heritage and pride as positive tools for building self-esteem in culturally different clients (Sue, 1981). As program staff develop an understanding of the uniqueness in the cultural groups encountered in their service area, they can utilize this knowledge to build self-esteem and empower Latinas in treatment.

Two important common experiences across Latina groups which can be exploited for developing self-esteem and empowerment among Latina women in treatment is their similar gender socialization and acculturation experiences. Culturally, most Latinas grow up in patriarchal and authoritarian family environments that are reinforced and influenced by the Catholic church. In these settings, women are expected to nurture and care for others and to aspire to marriage and motherhood (Falicov, 1982; Williams, 1990). The significance for treatment is that although acculturated Latinas may reject these cultural expectations, the messages received in early childhood about the "proper" role of a "senorita" may remain very much a part of their cultural and personal identity. Stress and conflict associated with the integration of traditional cultural expectations with new cultural values, roles and expectations may form part of the basis for alcohol abuse and should be explored in the treatment and recovery process.

Another common experience is that Latinas living in the U.S. must adapt and adjust to new cultural surroundings as they strive to retain their ethnic identity (Blea, 1992). This process can be very difficult and stressful for some Latinas, particularly younger women. There is some evidence that cultural conflict contributes to substance abuse among Latina adolescents (Szapocznik et al., 1989; Vega, 1995). It is possible that at least among some Latinas, conflicts and questions regarding cultural identity, acculturation pressures, and perceived or real discrimination form part of the context for alcohol abuse and should also be incorporated into the treatment and recovery process.

Program staff should strive to understand the commonalities across Latina groups for building trust and support but should also acknowledge important differences. There are, for example, differences across all groups associated with generational status. Newly arrived or recent immigrant Latinas have unique language, employment, educational and psychological needs. These women are more likely to experience grief and loss associated with immigration and stress related to the lack of language and employment skills (Vargas-Willis & Cervantes, 1987; Vega, 1995). Later generation or U.S.-born Latinas have different language, education, employment, and psychological needs. These women are more likely to be bilingual or English dominant thus may experience less strain associated with lack of language skills, but may be more likely to experience other types of stressors associated with the process of adaptation to new cultural values and behaviors (Buriel, 1993). These differences contribute to a different set of vulnerabilities and problems associated with the onset of alcohol problems for these women.

ALCOHOL USE AMONG LATINAS:
WOMEN AT RISK

Several researchers have suggested, based on survey research studies, that some Latinas may be at risk for developing alcohol dependency and related problems (Gilbert, 1991; Roth, 1991; Ames & Mora, 1988; Canino, 1994). Epidemiological studies among Latinos have found differences in drinking patterns across Latino groups and by gender. For example, a 1984 national survey of drinking patterns among Latinos in the U.S. found that there is a higher proportion of Mexican American men who drink "heavily," defined as drinking 5 or more drinks at a sitting at least once a week or more often, followed by Puerto Rican and other Latino and Cuban men (Caetano, 1985). The same survey found that although the majority of Latina women in the U.S. have higher abstention rates than U.S. women (47% vs. 36%), Mexican American women report more "heavy" drinking (14%) than Cuban (7%) or Puerto Rican (5%) women (Caetano, 1985). Abstention rates were highest among Mexican American women (46%) and lowest for Puerto Rican women (33%). The abstention rate for Cuban women was higher than Puerto Rican women (42%) and similar to Mexican American women. In addition, Cuban women exhibited the most moderate drinking patterns among the three groups.

It seems paradoxical that Mexican American women have the highest rates of "heavy" drinking and also have high rates of abstention from drinking. This apparent paradox most likely reflects the large proportion of Mexican immigrant women in the population who are primarily abstainers compared to a smaller proportion of Mexican American women who are "heavy" drinkers.

High abstention rates among Latinas reflects the strict cultural sanctions against female drinking that are common in most Latin American cultures (Bacon, 1976). Drinking is viewed as primarily a male activity to be shared with other men. In the U.S. this pattern is maintained, particularly in immigrant families, where drinking is viewed as an activity to be shared by the men after work or on weekends. Traditionally, Chicanas and other Latinas report *less* and *less frequent* drinking compared to men (Caetano, 1985) and are more likely to prefer mixed drinks than beer or wine (Trotter, 1985; Munch et al., 1981). Latinas, particularly immigrant women, tend to drink lightly, infrequently and primarily at family gatherings and holidays (Gilbert, 1985; Canino, 1994).

Research indicates that a larger proportion of Latina women abstain from drinking alcohol compared to other women in the U.S. population. This means that Latina women, as they immigrate to the U.S., generally maintain their cultural norms and values regarding the proper role of women as occasional or non-drinkers. However, research also indicates that a small proportion of subsequent generations of Latina women, particularly Mexican American and Puerto Rican women, are beginning to drink alcohol in heavier quantities compared to immigrant women in their communities (Gilbert, 1987).

The important questions for treatment are: (1) To what extent are some of these women who are increasing their alcohol intake at risk for developing alcohol dependency? (2) Who are the Latina women who are most at risk and most likely to require treatment? (3) What are the factors that contribute to the increased risk and how can treatment programs help the women at greatest risk? The following sections will explore some of these questions in more detail.

ACCULTURATION AND ALCOHOL USE

Most studies of alcohol use among Chicanas/Latinas indicate that acculturation to U.S. culture is related to an increase in the *quantity* and *frequency* of alcohol use. In the first national survey of alcohol use among Latinos in the U.S., Caetano (1985) found that U.S. born and more highly acculturated women, particularly Mexican American women, had higher rates of "heavy" drinking (14%).

Acculturation into U.S. culture and society, more than any other factor, appears to have a direct effect on changes in drinking behaviors on Latinas. Acculturation theory, as it relates to modifications in alcohol use, proposes that over time the drinking patterns, norms, and behaviors of an immigrant population will look more like the patterns of the new culture than the culture of origin (Markides, Krause, & Mendes de Leon, 1988; Keefe & Padilla, 1987).

The degree to which Latinas acculturate to U.S. norms is usually influenced by the age of immigration to the U.S., degree of exposure to the new culture, individual willingness to explore new environments and self-confidence (Negy & Woods, 1992; Keefe & Padilla, 1987). Thus, degree and level of acculturation is highly variable and differs by individual experience.

For Latinas, a major acculturating force which has had an impact both on gender roles, family dynamics, and alcohol use is the large number of Latinas employed outside of the home (Zavella, 1987; Williams, 1990; Gilbert, 1991). Latina scholars argue that it is within the context of the workplace where traditional Latinas gain access to new sources of knowledge, information, and personal and economic power (Williams, 1990; Zavella, 1987). Working outside the home can thus form a major and important transformational experience for traditional Latina women. These changes associated with employment and being born or raised in the U.S. seem particularly important in lowering abstention and increasing rates of heavier drinking among Latina women. Holck et al. (1984), for example, found a link between education and greater alcohol consumption among Mexican American women in Texas. Burnam (1989) also reported higher levels of alcohol abuse and dependency among more highly educated Mexican American women in Los Angeles. However, higher levels of consumption are also found among younger, acculturated inner-city Latinas (Gilbert, 1989; Beauvais et al., 1996.)

Although increased alcohol use seems to be linked to education, acculturation is probably a stronger indicator of increased use both among highly educated and employed Latinas and younger, inner-city Latinas. In fact, there is increasing evidence that younger generations of Mexican American female adolescents are drinking more like their male counterparts or women in the general population than like their immigrant mothers (Gilbert, 1991). This has also been found among younger generations of Puerto Rican women who have rates of alcohol consumption similar to their male counterparts and show few differences between themselves and young men in terms of the onset of the first alcoholic symptom (Canino et al., 1987a).

If in fact employment and acculturation play key roles in the increased use of alcohol among some Latinas, what are the changes in the lives of Latinas that occur as a result of employment and acculturation that are related to increased alcohol use? And, what are the implications for treatment?

LATINAS: CONTEMPORARY LIFESTYLES AND CHANGES IN GENDER ROLE

Several researchers have proposed that employment outside of the home and changes in traditional gender roles increase the risk of alcohol dependency among Latinas (Canino, 1994; Gilbert, 1987; Corbett et al., 1991). Several important questions for treatment are: (1) what are the changes in traditional female roles that influence changes in drinking behaviors, (2) how do employment and education opportunities impact drinking behavior, and (3) how can treatment providers make sense of these changes in order to reduce the risk and support women in the process of change and recovery?

Employment for Latinas, as for all women in American society, creates some conflict and role transformation. For the Latina who is socialized within a traditional family structure that requires strict sex-role differentiation, there are numerous stressors related to sex role changes and accommodations that are part of working outside of the home (Vargas-Willis & Cervantes, 1987; Blea, 1992; Williams, 1990). Increasing employment among Latinas who would otherwise be involved in childrearing and other family obligations has significant personal and social implications. Working women have higher levels of social support, in part because they have income and are more likely to drive, but they may also experience rejection and resistance from spouses, children or other family members (Williams, 1990; Blea, 1992; Zavella, 1987). Kelly and Garcia (1989), for example, compared employed Mexican immigrant women in Los Angeles and Cuban immigrant women in Miami and found that working was a difficult experience that challenged them to continually negotiate and justify their actions to other members of the family.

The prevailing view about employment and women's drinking through the 1970s was that employment outside of the home has negative effects on women's mental health and drinking behavior, particularly when combined with marital or family roles. Explanations for the increased drinking associated with employment and/or with multiple roles include *stress-related* interpretations of role conflict as well as *environmental* explanations involving increased opportunities and more permissive drinking norms outside of the home (McCrady & Rayteck, 1993).

For Latinas, both *stress* and *environmental* explanations for alcohol abuse are possible. For example, acculturation stress and conflicts about new roles and expectations and the inability to meet these may form part of the onset and development of alcohol abuse among some Latinas. Other research has found that increased use of alcohol among some Latinas is due to environmental forces, including new opportunities to drink, greater exposure to public environments for drinking, and increased income (Gilbert, 1991; Mora, in press). However, changes in drinking behavior among Latinas cannot be attributed entirely to employment trends or changes in gender roles. These demographic and social changes are very complex and are part of larger social, economic and cultural forces impacting Latinas.

The current research literature does not provide sufficient information about how Chicana and Latina women balance two cultures, new careers, break old traditions, and refashion new identities and how these changes impact drinking behavior. We do know that the status and role of Latinas in the U.S. has been undergoing a process of change for several decades. Latinas are now not only more likely to work outside of the home, but they are having less children, pursuing higher education, working in the arts, business, medicine and politics (Blea, 1992; Williams, 1990). These changes are not necessarily negative and for many Latinas these experiences constitute positive new experiences in their lives. In addition we cannot disregard the fact that alcohol dependency in women is also related to individual risk factors including family background, childhood sexual abuse, low self-esteem, and depression (McCrady & Raytek, 1993).

In a discussion of gender-role conflict and drinking behavior, Hunter (1990) concluded that the intricate relationship between the women's movement and changes in women's roles to drinking behavior among women are complex and although it may be more acceptable for women to drink in public, drinking excessively is still less acceptable for women than for men. In fact, there is some indication that rates of drinking and heavier drinking among employed women varies considerably by the type of employment (professional/managerial vs. bluecollar), suggesting that there is not a single, simple effect of employment per se. For example, Gilbert (1991) and Mora (in press), in a study of nearly three hundred Latinas in Los Angeles, found that increased alcohol consumption was encountered among professional Latinas and not among bluecollar women.

It is too simplistic and problematic to suggest that the loss of traditional female roles lead to the development of drinking problems among women and consequently that the treatment and solution would be to help women accept traditional female gender roles. Feminist scholars suggest that it is in fact the lack of access to power within traditional families, including the power of choice and economic decision making, that cause feelings of powerlessness and a desire to relieve the strain by using or abusing alcohol (Bepko & Krestan, 1985). Beckman and Amaro (1984), for example, reported that alcoholic women are more likely to report drinking or feeling like drinking than are men when they feel powerless and inadequate.

If we frame alcohol problems among Latinas in a feminist and cultural perspective, the treatment of alcohol problems should not necessarily reinforce traditional and possibly oppressive cultural patterns for Latinas. Instead, treatment services and programs should be structured to support and empower Latinas to pursue new roles and make new choices, free of alcohol, guilt and stigma.

DIVERSITY AND CHANGE: TREATMENT IMPLICATIONS

The treatment implications of diversity and change in the Latina population is that in order for services to be fully competent and effective, they must move beyond simple notions of cultural sensitivity. Effective and competent programs must incorporate a realistic understanding of the contemporary cultural life of Latina women and the complex interaction between traditional culture, change and alcohol problems among Latina women.

Regardless of the modality utilized (inpatient vs. outpatient, etc.), the philosophical framework of a culturally competent program should be based on a complete understanding of the unique cultural and historical legacies of each Latina population served, of the traditional cultural expectations and changing lifestyles and roles of Latina women and how all of these interact with individual and family factors in the development of alcohol problems for each woman in treatment. Programs can avoid "ineffective" approaches and strategies by hiring bilingual/bicultural and recovering female staff who understand the traditional and ideal expectations of Latinas, the realities of contemporary Latina lifestyles and alcoholism.

The environment of "culturally competent" programs should be supportive, non-judgmental and empowering places where Latinas can find relief from stigma and guilt, find support for their choices from other

174 ALCOHOL USE/ABUSE AMONG LATINOS

women like themselves, find understanding and insight into their own behaviors, education and job training, childcare and parenting education and family involvement in their treatment and recovery.

The role of culturally competent alcohol treatment programs for Latinas should be to lessen the risk of alcohol problems associated with changes in gender roles and lifestyles, to reduce cultural and community stigma associated with female alcoholism, and empower Latinas to live better lives.

REFERENCES

Aguirre-Molina, M. (1991). Issues for Latinas: Puerto Rican Women. In Roth, P. (Ed.), *Alcohol and Drugs are Women's Issues*. New Jersey: Scarecrow Press.

Ames, G. & Mora, J. (1988). Alcohol Problem Prevention in Mexican American Populations. In Gilbert, M.J. (Ed.), *Alcohol Consumption among Mexicans and Mexican Americans: A Binational Perspective*. Spanish Speaking Mental Health Research Center, University of California, Los Angeles.

Bacon, M.K. (1976). Cross cultural studies of drinking: Integrated drinking and sex differences in the use of alcoholic beverages. In Everett, M.W., Waddell, J.O., & Heath D.B. (Eds.), *Cross-cultural approaches to the study of alcohol*. The Hague: Mouton.

Beauvais, F., Chavez, E., Oetting, G., Deffenbacher, J.L., Cornell, G.R. (1996). Drug Use, Violence and Victimization among White American, Mexican American, and American Indian Drop-outs: Students with Academic Problems and Students in Good Standing. *Journal of Counseling Psychology*, Vol. 43, No. 3, p. 292-299.

Beckman, L.J. & Amaro, H. (1986). Personal and social difficulties faced by women and men entering alcoholism treatment. *Journal of Studies on Alcohol*, 47, 2, 135-145.

Beckman, L.J. & Amaro, H. (1984). Patterns of Women's Use of Alcohol Treatment Agencies. In Wilsnack, S. & Beckman, L. (Eds.), *Alcohol Problems in Women*. New York: Guilford Press.

Blea, I. (1992). *La Chicana and the Intersection of Race, Class, and Gender*. Westport, Connecticut: Praeger Press.

Buriel, R. (1993). Childrearing Orientations in Mexican American Families: The Influence of Generation and Sociocultural Factors. *Journal of Marriage and the Family*, 55, 987-1000.

Burnam, A. (1989). Prevalence of alcohol abuse and dependence among Mexican Americans and Non-Hispanic Whites in the community. In Spigler, D.L., Tate, S.S., Aitken, and Christian (Eds.), *Alcohol Use among U.S. Ethnic Minorities*, NIAAA Research Monograph 18; DHHS Publication ADM 88-1435. U.S. Government Printing Office, Washington, D.C.

Caetano, R. (1985). Drinking Patterns and Alcohol Problems in a National Sample of U.S. Hispanics. In Spiegler, D., Tate, D., Aiken, S. & Christian, C. (Eds.), *Alcohol Use Among U.S. Ethnic Minorities*. Research Monograph No.

18, National Institute on Alcohol Abuse and Alcoholism. DHHS Publication No. (ADM) 89-1435. Washington, D.C.: U.S. Government Printing House, 147-162.

Canino, G. (1994). Alcohol Use and Misuse among Hispanic Women: Selected Factors, Processes and Studies. *International Journal of the Addictions 29, 9,* 1083-1099.

Canino, G., Bird, H., Shrout, P., Rubio, M., Geil, K. and Bravo, M. (1987a). The prevalence of alcohol abuse and/or dependence in Puerto Rico. In M. Garrison and J. Arana (Eds.), *Health and Behavior: Research Agenda for Hispanics.* The Research Monograph Series, Vol. 1. The University of Illinois Press, 127-144.

Corbett, K., Mora, J., & Ames, G. (1991). Drinking patterns and drinking related problems of Mexican American husbands and wives. *Journal of Studies on Alcohol,* 52, (3), 215-233.

Falicov, C.J. (1982). Mexican Families. In McGoldrick, M., Pearce, J.K., Girodano, J. (Eds.), *Ethnicity and Family Therapy.* New York: Guilford Press.

Finn, P. (1994). Addressing the needs of cultural minorities in drug treatment. *Journal of Substance Abuse Treatment,* 11, (4).

Gilbert, M.J. (1987). Alcohol consumption patterns in immigrant and later generation Mexican American women. *Hispanic Journal of the Behavioral Sciences,* 9, (3), 299-313.

Gilbert, M.J. (1989). Current information on drinking behavior among Hispanic youth. In R. Wright Jr. and T.D. Watts (Eds.), *Alcohol Problems of Minority Youth in America.* Interdisciplinary Studies in Alcohol Use and Abuse, Vol. 2, New York: The Edwin Mellon Press, Ltd.

Gilbert, M.J. (1991). Acculturation and Changes in Drinking Patterns Among Mexican American Women: Implications for Prevention. *Alcohol Health and Research World,* 15, (3), 234-238.

Gilbert, M.J. (1993). Anthropology in a multidisciplinary field: substance abuse. *Social Science and Medicine,* Vol. 37, p. 1-3.

Gilbert, M.J. & Cervantes, R. (1988). Alcohol Treatment for Mexican Americans: A Review of Utilization Patterns and Therapeutic Approaches. In Gilbert, M.J. (Ed.), *Alcohol Consumption Among Mexicans and Mexican Americans: A Binational Perspective.* Spanish Speaking Mental Health Research Center: University of California, Los Angeles.

Herrell, I.C. (1993). *Health Care Issues Affecting Hispanic Women, Infants, and Children.* U.S. Department of Health and Human Services, Health Resources and Services Administration. Washington, D.C.

Hill, S.Y. (1984). *Mental and physical health consequences of alcohol use in women.* Recent Developments in Alcoholism, Alcoholism and Genetics Research Program, Department of Psychiatry, University of Pittsburgh School of Medicine, Pittsburgh, PA.

Holck, S.E., Warren, C.W., Smith, J.C., & Rochat, R.W. (1984). Alcohol Consumption among Mexican American and Anglo Women: Results of a Survey Along the U.S.-Mexico Border. *Journal of Studies on Alcohol,* 45, 2, 149-154.

176 ALCOHOL USE/ABUSE AMONG LATINOS

Keefe, F.E. & Padilla, A. M. (1987). *Chicano Ethnicity.* Albuquerque, New Mexico: University of New Mexico Press.

Markides, K., Krause, N., & Mendes de Leon, C. (1988). Acculturation and Alcohol Consumption among Mexican Americans: A Three-Generational Study. *American Journal of Public Health,* 9, 1178-1181.

McCrady, B., & Raytek, H. (1993). Women and Substance Abuse: Treatment Modalities and Outcomes. In Lisansky-Gomberg, E.S., & Nirenberg, T.D. (Eds.), *Women and Substance Abuse.* Norwood, New Jersey: Ablex.

Mora, J. (In press). Learning to Drink: Early Drinking Experiences of Chicana and Mexicana Women. University of California, Davis.

Mora, J. & Gilbert, M.J. (1991). Issues for Latinas: Mexican American Women. In P. Roth (Ed.), *Alcohol and Drugs are Women's Issues.* New Jersey: Scarecrow Press.

Munch, N. et al. (1981). How Americans say they drink: Preliminary data from two recent national surveys. *Current Studies in Alcoholism,* 8, 233-251.

Negy, C. & Woods, D.J. (1992). The Importance of Acculturation in Understanding Research with Hispanic-Americans. *Hispanic Journal of Behavioral Sciences,* 14, 2, 224-247.

Orlandi, M.A. (1992). Cultural Competence for Evaluators: A Guide for Alcohol and Other Drug Abuse Prevention Practitioners Working with Ethnic/Racial Communities. U.S. Department of Health and Human Services, OSAP.

Padilla, A.M. & Salgado de Snyder, N.V. (1995). Hispanics: What the Culturally Informed Evaluator Needs to Know. In Orlandi, M.A., Weston, R. & Epstein, L.G. (Eds.), *Cultural Competency for Evaluators: A Guide for Alcohol and Other Drug Abuse Prevention Practitioners Working with Ethnic/Racial Communities.* Office of Substance Abuse Prevention Cultural Competence Series I. Office Of Substance Abuse Prevention, Rockville, Maryland.

Roth, P. (1991). Introduction. *Alcohol and Drugs are Women's Issues.* Roth, P. (Ed.). New Jersey: Scarecrow Press. VII-X.

Sue, D. (1981). *Counseling the Culturally Different: Theory and Practice.* New York: Wiley & Sons.

Szapocznik, J. & Kurtines, W.M. (1989). *Breakthroughs in Family Therapy with drug abusing and problem youth.* New York: Springer Publishing Co.

Trotter, R. (1985). Mexican Americans in South Texas: Differing Lifestyles and Alcohol. In L. Bennett & G. Ames (Eds.), *The American Experience with Alcohol: Contrasting Cultural Perspectives.* New York: Plenum Press, 279-296.

U.S. Bureau of the Census (1994). The Nation's Hispanic Population-1994, Statistical Brief. U.S. Department of Commerce, Washington, D.C.

U.S. Department of Health and Human Services (1995). White Paper: Effectiveness of Substance Abuse Treatment. Washington, D.C.

Vargas-Willis, G. & Cervantes, R. (1987). Consideration of Psychosocial Stress in the Treatment of the Latina Immigrant. *Hispanic Journal of Behavioral Sciences.* Vol. 9, No. 3, 315-329.

Vega, W.A. (1995). The Study of Latino Families: A Point of Departure. In

Zambrana, R.E. (Ed.), *Understanding Latino Families: Scholarship, Policy, and Practice.* Thousand Oaks, California: Sage.

Williams, N. (1990). *The Mexican American Family: Tradition and Change.* Dix Hills, New York: General Hall Press.

Woll, C. (In Press). What Difference Does Culture Make?: Providing Treatment to Women Different From You. In Underhill, B. (Ed.), *Chemical Dependency: Women at Risk.* New York: The Haworth Press, Inc.

Zavella, P. (1987). *Women's Work and Chicano Families: Cannery Workers of the Santa Clara Valley,* Ithaca, New York: Cornell University Press.

Latina Lesbians
and Alcohol and Other Drugs:
Social Work Implications

Migdalia Reyes, EdD, MSW

SUMMARY. Although studies on alcohol and drug abuse of heterosexual men of color, women, gay males and lesbians are becoming today more prevalent, there has been no documented research on alcohol consumption and drug related problems for Latina lesbians. The author in this article contributes to the limited existing knowledge by providing new data on substance abuse practices among Latina lesbians. This article presents research findings based on 35 ethnographic interviews. It brings forth information related to issues of substance abuse for Latina lesbians and suggests recommendations for research, policy and treatment. *[Article copies available for a fee from The Haworth Document Delivery Service: 1-800-342-9678. E-mail address: getinfo@haworth.com]*

INTRODUCTION

Because of ethnocentrism, racism, androcentrism and lesbophobia, Latina lesbians are an invisible substance abuse population that risk facing social and emotional problems. Historically, most research and treatment has focused on men, with some recent attention to African American and

Migdalia Reyes is Associate Professor, San Jose State University School of Social Work, 1 Washington Square, San Jose, CA 95192-0214.

[Haworth co-indexing entry note]: "Latina Lesbians and Alcohol and Other Drugs: Social Work Implications." Reyes, Migdalia. Co-published simultaneously in *Alcoholism Treatment Quarterly* (The Haworth Press, Inc.) Vol. 16, No. 1/2, 1998, pp. 179-192; and: *Alcohol Use/Abuse Among Latinos: Issues and Examples of Culturally Competent Services* (ed: Melvin Delgado) The Haworth Press, Inc., 1998, pp. 179-192. Single or multiple copies of this article are available for a fee from The Haworth Document Delivery Service [1-800-342-9678, 9:00 a.m. - 5:00 p.m. (EST). E-mail address: getinfo@haworth.com].

Latino men. Because of the AIDS epidemic, some attention has recently been given to exploring the treatment needs of gay males. Yet, Latina lesbians are one of the least researched population groups. Evidence of this exemplifies the fact that today in the United States few substance abuse institutions deliver special services toward Latina lesbian women. An example of a comprehensive approach is found in the Lapis Program of the Alcohol Center for Women in Los Angeles (personal communication, Susan Chacin, December 20, 1996).

LATINOS IN THE USA

Latinos in the USA are a heterogenous population. We may not speak of a homogeneous Latin American national or regional society of the 25 countries comprising Latin America: Mexico, Central America, South America and the Caribbean. However, some commonalities exist in the former Spanish colonies regarding history, culture and language (Bethell, 1987; Radcliffe et al., 1993). The essential feature of what is today Latin America originated in pre-Columbian, indigenous cultures along with the Spanish colonial social formation of the 1500s to the 1800s (Radcliffe et al., 1993). These cultural, linguistic and racial heritages contribute to the widely diverse formations of present Latin American national characteristics. For example, in contemporary Latin America, European and African ethnic-cultural elements converge to influence countries such as Brazil, Cuba and Haiti. Indigenous ethnic-cultural elements predominate within Andean countries (IADB, 1995), Central America and Mexico. These elements add to the great diversity of Latin Americans in the USA. Latinos in the USA comprise 22.4 million people (US Census, 1991). Clearly, this number does not include undocumented populations. USA-born Latinos, those who reside in the USA or who are immigrants, "comprise an aggregation of several distinct national origin subgroups and research has found differences among Puerto Ricans, Mexicans, Cuban, and South and Central Americans" (Vasquez, 1994, p. 119). According to Vasquez (1994), "various sociodemographic characteristics of Latinos are relevant to mental health, including educational attainment, employment, generation and immigration status, family income and size, and language status" (p. 119). There is no doubt that issues of economic depravation and lack of resources are of concern to social workers delivering services to Latinos, especially as they relate to anti-immigration and welfare reform legislation. Vasquez (1994) posits that Latina women are reported to have the highest poverty levels when compared to other marginalized populations. Greene (1994) suggests that broad descriptions of cultural realities may not be generalizable to include Latina lesbian women. Evidence shows that this social group is faced with triple jeopardy due to the marginalized status granted to them through dominant paradigms which view their ethnicity (race), gender and sexual/emotional orientation as unpreferred and inferior (Greene, 1994).

SUBSTANCE ABUSE:
LATINOS AND WOMEN

Substance abuse is a complex phenomena and thus the experiences of people who abuse alcohol and other drugs vary tremendously. Socioeconomic status, cultural consumption patterns, genetic and social conditions–especially oppression and depravation–have been flagged as indicators for substance abuse (Mayers-Sanchez et al., 1993). Variations among Latinos also exist in relation to habits of use (i.e., polydrug users) and drugs of choice.

According to Mayers-Sanchez et al. (1993), substance abuse among Latino men parallels that of other populations. The literature shows that acculturation and biculturation processes may lead some Latinos to change their patterns of alcohol consumption (Amaro et al., 1990). For example, Mayers-Sanchez (1993) indicates that Latinos tend to move from more frequent use to the USA cultural standards of "normative" restrictive use.

Some studies show that dependence on alcohol and other drugs among women is less predominant, especially for Latina women (Comas-Diaz & Greene, 1994). According to Bepko (1991), this is due to how "relatively little. . . . is known about the physiological and psychological effects of drugs and alcohol on women. . . . We know little about differential approaches that might address women's needs more effectively" (p. 1). Forth-Finegan (1991) posits that the fields of mental health and medicine have generated important research findings on alcoholism among women. According to the literature, many women tend to begin consuming alcohol because of the cultural normality of social use (De La Rosa et al., 1993; Peluso & Peluso, 1988). De La Rosa et al. (1993) indicate that a negative stigma is attached to women with substance abuse problems. Moreover, research and corresponding treatment programs often pose androcentric biases and damaging stereotypes about this population group. For example, some research findings report women to be sicker and harder to treat than men (Forth-Finegan, 1991). Others report that Latino women are more likely than men to resume drug or criminal activity after treatment (Mayers-Sanchez et al., 1993). Booth et al. (1990) state that an increased vulnerability to substance abuse in the home and within personal social support networks and multigenerational abuse are due to the influence of peer groups. Also, abuse is often more prevalent among those who began experimenting while in junior high school or high school. Inter-generational behavioral conflicts (deterioration of parental influence), emigration patterns, as well as value conflicts stemming from differences in levels of bi-culturalism may also contribute to abusing alcohol and other drugs.

Many Latinos may be exposed to dependency due to the influence of the environment in drug and crime infested areas (i.e., neighborhoods, schools, bars). Symptoms of family dysfunction, especially physical and sexual abuse, are important indicators for risk behavior as well. Child rearing practices and the protective nature of some parents toward their daughters because of *Marianismo* may also be significant indicators. For example, many women start using alcohol and other drugs once they have had the opportunity to become more independent or when they move from home to go to college. Becoming involved with partners who consume alcohol and other drugs is also an important cofactor. As with other ethnic groups, Latinos may use alcohol and other drugs for self-medication purposes and to numb feelings (Doweiko, 1996; Royce & Scratchley, 1996).

Nicoloff and Stiglitz (1987) and others (Peluso & Peluso, 1988) contend that alcohol abuse is more significant for the lesbian population than for heterosexual women. While these authors posit that lesbian women are not different to other population groups in terms of etiological influences of substance abuse, they suggest that social, political, economic and cultural factors, vis á vis the systematic and ongoing oppression of lesbian women in our society, play a major role upon lesbians who abuse alcohol and other drugs.

TRADITIONAL CULTURAL PRACTICES OF LATINOS

Familismo is a distinctive cultural tradition of Latino populations that places the family at the center (Delgado & Humm-Delgado, 1982; Vasquez, 1994). According to Delgado et al. (1982), loyalty, emotional closeness and interdependence are common overriding descriptors of the Latino family. This kinship network poses issues for women, especially lesbians who encounter family conflict because of sexism and lesbophobia. Moreover, the historical heritage of cultural androcentric values and traditions and practices of *machismo* and *Marianismo,* play a major role regarding the substance abuse practices of Latina women. A salient characteristic of the Latino culture assumes rigid delineations in how males and females are socialized. For example, one manifestation of *machismo* is that males tend to be socialized to be dominant and independent, while gender role expectations for women are different. For example, socialization of females falls within the *good-bad* dichotomy of *Marianismo*, which ultimately attempts to model behavior to harmonize with and represent the virtues of the Virgin Mary (Reyes, 1992). This value system places women in a position of power regarding the assumption that women are spiritually superior to men (Carrier, 1995). As such, *Marianismo* is critically linked to the cultural expectations of women marrying, having children in a heterosexual relationship and taking care of others in spite of their personal needs and requirements (Reyes, 1992). *Marianismo* may also be conceptually applied to the parents' protective position in regard to their daughter's abuse of alcohol and other drugs in order to maintain the honor of the family (Morales, 1984). Moreover, *Marianismo* is key to understanding lesbophobic values and doctrines of the Catholic church.

An interesting component of *Marianismo* is in relationships among women friends. According to Espin (1987), while emotional and physical closeness among women is encouraged and is perceived as a socially approved mechanism to diminish contact with men, behavior presumed to be lesbian is generally less tolerated, and greater restrictions contrast the mainstream USA culture. Greene (1994) posits that often a lesbian woman will migrate to the USA in an attempt to survive lesbophobia. However, a lesbian woman, especially if she is a recent immigrant, may develop a deeper attachment to her family and ethnic community to cope with and survive ethnocentrism, racism and internalized colonization. Greene (1994) suggests that this is "particularly problematic if the family, community and/or traditional cultural values are perceived or selectively interpreted as rejecting a lesbian sexual orientation" (p. 394).

The other face of *Marianismo* is *hembrismo*. *Hembrismo* has been reclaimed by some Latina feminists as a healthy challenge to *Marianismo*. *Nevertheless*, this concept has been often used with a negative connotation to describe women who take on some characteristics of *machismo* in order to demonstrate that they too are able to be independent, resilient and strong. One manifestation of *hembrismo is* when women prove their toughness by measuring how tolerant they are to alcohol and other drugs. In Puerto Rican folklore, the term *jodedora* is often used to describe this manifestation, as well as women who are an integral part of the illegal drug culture. *Chola* lifestyles, which may include gang, and alcohol and drug involvement (Moore, 1990), tend to be more specific to the Chicano (Mexican-American) experience. This lifestyle often promotes a reaction to *Marianismo* and a counterculture street socialization experience "which pushes the individual to adopt a *locura* mind set (thinking and acting in daring, courageous manner, and especially crazy fashion in the face of adversity) in order to manage many of the fearful and stressful situations they encounter on a daily basis" (De La Rosa et al., 1993, p. 91).

It is difficult to arrive at a complete understanding of the complex and often devastating effects that androcentric and heterocentric traditional Latino cultural values and norms have on Latina lesbian women, and how this population group is additionally impacted by USA racism, ethnocentrism and classism. Moreover, the paucity of research on this population does not adequately provide information on the complex interactions between ethnic, racial and sexual minority status and the abuse of alcohol and other drugs.

THE STUDY

The research for this article chose a sample of thirty-five (35) women. The study examined the categorized group of Chicanas (Mexican American), Cuban, Central and South American women from the West Coast, and Puerto Rican women from the East Coast. The participants were twenty-one (21) years old or older, of Latino heritage and self-identified either as lesbian, transgender or bisexual. The women self-identified either as active alcohol users or in recovery. The methodology used in the study consisted of an individual interview using ethnographies as a model. No hypothesis was drawn. The women were asked to share their stories. Only one question was posed: As a Latina and as a lesbian, what has your experience been with alcohol and other drugs?

PROCEDURE

Because of the complexity of homophobia in our society, accessing and selecting participants was done in a sensitive and respectful fashion. Announcements were placed where groups of lesbian women gather and through mailing lists of Latina lesbian organizations. Contacts were also made through the Lapis Program of the Alcoholism Center for Women, and through social workers who deliver services within the field of substance abuse. However, the primary source of outreach was through informal networks within natural support systems.

Once the women were contacted, this author informed them that their participation in the study was strictly voluntary, anonymous and confidential. Each interview lasted one hour and tapes were transcribed, and in some cases translated from Spanish to English.

RESEARCH FINDINGS

The literature review suggests that there is a paucity of research on substance use and abuse on Latina lesbians and that this population is entirely overlooked. Clearly, one major problem is a lack of standardized data collection (i.e., national surveys) in which Latina lesbians are included. Of the thirty-five (35) women interviewed, twenty-five (25) identified themselves as alcoholics and ten (10) as moderate alcohol users. Of the 35 women, twenty (20) identified themselves as polydrug users. Twenty-one (21) of the total indicated being in recovery, while twelve (12) identified themselves as active users.

The findings of McNally (cited in McKirnan & Peterson, 1989) reported that lesbian women often drink to cope with their experiences with lesbo-phobia and because of attendant drinking behavior as an integral part of a lifestyle of lesbians who frequent bars. The study presented in this article demonstrates that there is no definitive, universal patterns regarding reasons for abusing alcohol and other drugs. Barrera and Finetta's (1993) work with adolescents indicates that affiliations with peers can serve to increase or decrease substance abusing behavior. The qualitative study reported here supports this. Sixteen (16) of the women reported using alcohol and other drugs while in junior high school or high school because of cultural ex-pectations of peer groups during adolescence. For those interviewed in this study, additional risk factors were identified in regard to the norms of the culture around drinking, and the neighborhood environment.

In much of the literature on human behavior, the family and the social environment are intricately linked to the normative development of the individual (Longres, 1995; Zastrow, 1994). However, family dysfunction, along with substance abuse practices of parents, contributes largely to the use/abuse of alcohol and other drugs. In this study four (4) women reported that both father and mother abused alcohol. Of the four (4), one (1) was adopted and had no information on her biological parents. Seven (7) women reported solely their mother abusing alcohol and eleven (11) reported that their fathers were the only ones to abuse alcohol. In addition, four (4) women indicated that their father had a drinking problem, but that they did not consider them alcoholic. Two (2) women reported that their father had died due to alcohol related health problems, while one (1) woman indicated that her mother died of alcohol poisoning. Nine (9) of the 35 women reported that their parents did not use or abuse alcohol and other drugs. In the study other areas of family dysfunction emerged. Of all of the women inter-viewed, eight (8) indicated being physically abused at home by an abusive father, stepfather or mother. Sexual abuse in the home was reported among one third of those interviewed. Twelve (12) women indicated that they were sexually abused. Many of these women were sexually abused by family members including: a father, stepfather, brother-in laws or male sibling, and an uncle. This finding provides important information regarding the confluence of trauma, sociocultural factors, and social support networks. Further research is needed to determine the role of family dysfunction within the development of alcohol and other drug abusing behavior for this population.

Of the 35 participants in the study, all identified experiencing psychological distress anger and betrayal as a result of family conflict around gender expectations. The primary issue was conflict in direct relation to values of *Marianismo* and *machismo* within the family. Social relationships were interpreted by the participants as based upon oppressive manifestations of *Marianismo*. Traditional androcentric Catholic values, were also found to be major stressors and contributing factors for most of the women abusing alcohol and other drugs. Of the 35 women interviewed, only two (2) women indicated acceptance from their families when they disclosed that they were lesbians (came out of the closet). The remaining thirty-three (33) experienced lesbophobic attitudes that ranged from moderate acceptance, with continual harassment, to situations of being disowned or asked to leave the home. Some women chose to move away from the family. One woman was asked to leave her home and became homeless, joining a gang at the age of 16. For the women who left their homes, feelings of pain due to a sense of loss and continued feelings of loneliness were expressed. Several women had chosen to remain closeted and two (2) of the women indicated that they have had children because of the pressure to be heterosexual. This study showed that of the 35 women interviewed only ten (10) indicated attending lesbian bars. Most of the women stated that they drank mostly during family gatherings and in private parties with friends. Many did not participate in the bar scene because of a lack of identification with the Euro-American lesbian culture or because of fear of being out of the closet.

Apart from sexism and lesbophobia in the home, the overall environment of discrimination based upon ethnicity and race also appeared to be a risk factor which compounded the problems faced by the women who were interviewed. While the majority of the women where born and raised in the USA, many shared painful experiences with ethnocentrism, racism, classism and colonialist attitudes. Recently arrived immigrants explained that the process of biculturation or acculturation was difficult, particularly because of the pressure to assimilate and because of discrimination coming from both, Euro-Americans and other Latinos. For those going through the process of biculturation, the creation of natural support systems was more difficult since many of the women expressed the need to remain closeted because of lesbophobia. Most of the women shared how devastating ethnocentrism had been for them. This was especially true for those who at an early age were pressured to assimilate and now struggle to rediscover their roots, reclaim their heritage and language, and become politically involved. Of the 35 women interviewed fifteen (15) indicated being politically involved in their communities as Latinas. They reported being involved with the lesbian community as well.

An interesting aspect of this study is that many of the women identified a tremendous feeling of loneliness. This research shows that for some of the women this feeling grew from the loss of family kinship, their ethnic communities, and difficulties fitting or being accepted into the mainstream gay and lesbian community. Moreover, because women have been traditionally socialized to be attached and in relationship to others (Gilligan, 1982), lesbian women may find it hard to not be in a relationship. Some of the women, especially those who identified as moderate users of alcohol, indicated that they drank the most when they found themselves out of a relationship.

AIDS cases are reported as being at critically high levels and proportions for Latinos, especially Latino heterosexual women (Morales & Bok, 1997). In tandem to the issue of contracting the HIV+ virus through high risk behaviors such as sharing needles and engaging in unsafe sex, the use of alcohol and other drugs has been identified as a significant cofactor which may lower inhibitions, and impair judgement and the ability to adopt protective measures, and thus contribute to risk behavior. While there is limited research and information on the transmission of HIV+ through lesbian sex, the prevalence of HIV+ among the women interviewed was demonstrated to be low. The transmission of the HIV+ virus by sharing needles and involvement in the sex industry with male customers, or unprotected sex with men as means for payment of drugs, pose major risk factors for this population. Of the 35 women interviewed, one (1) woman identified as being HIV+. She indicated that aside from other forms of oppression due to her social group membership, her HIV+ status and the lack of support from the lesbian community were devastating to her. According to this woman, she had found more support within the gay male community than from her community of lesbian women. She also reported that she had already been in recovery for various years when she learned about her HIV+ status. Most of the women who indicated being in recovery stated that remaining in recovery was linked to a feeling that they would die otherwise.

The women shared different types of experiences regarding service delivery and treatment choices. The women who were most positive about their process of recovery spoke about agencies that had programs for Latina lesbians or that had staff that was *gay-friendly*. Fourteen (14) women identified 12 step programs as important in their recovery. Three (3) women informed that they did not feel safe to come out in 12 step programs because of fear of putting themselves at risk with homophobic members. Several women also indicated experiencing lesbophobia while in recovery homes and in other treatment facilities, which were mainly hospitals. Two (2) women indicated that they had been diagnosed with a mental or personality disorder, while no diagnosis was made on alcohol abuse. In both cases, the women were not offered appropriate alcohol abuse treatment.

DISCUSSION AND RECOMMENDATIONS

Research, Policy and Training

The findings of this study raise several implications for research, policy and training considerations. There is a need for further systematic research which would include observation of the alcohol practices and other drug-related behavior of Latina lesbians. Such research is clearly absent from national household surveys, which are instrumental for the creation of policy. Moreover, institutions working in the field of alcohol and other drugs must examine policies to include the special treatment and service needs of this population group. According to Nicoloff and Stiglitz (1987), "policy not only determines the philosophy of treatment, allocations of money, the hiring of staff, and the specific service rendered, but also who will use and benefit from the services" (p. 287).

Challenges to mainstream treatment agencies are necessary. It is evident that today many of the traditional agencies providing services to those afflicted with abusing alcohol and other drugs are monocultural Euro-American, and primarily geared toward the consumer with financial resources (i.e., medical insurance). Furthermore, while some mainstream agencies and social model programs offer services to women, they may often display heterosexist and lesbophobic behavior toward Latina lesbian women. For example, social workers delivering services in the field of alcohol and other drugs often assume that the population that they work with is heterosexual. Thus, it is the responsibility of an agency or other programs (i.e., self-help groups) to seek and provide training to staff and/or interns on competency in delivering services to Latina lesbians. Moreover, *gay-friendly* agencies, including Euro-American, gay-andro-centric agencies, need to develop or improve the quality of services since often lesbian women have reported experiencing sexism and ethnocentrism in such institutions. In addition, social work institutions must provide educational and agency internship opportunities to train students to work with this population and in the field of alcohol and other drugs. Additionally, professionals practicing in the field who stand to benefit from extension or certificate programs and fulfilling continuing education requirements comprise an important target group for specialized training.

Macro Intervention:
Community Education and Prevention

Developing an understanding about natural support networks and alternative family systems within the lesbian community while facilitating access to them is instrumental to any macro intervention. At the macro level there is a need for social work institutions to learn about and use network-centered interventions since a large part of the self-help processes that take place within the lesbian community tend to remain underground because of fear of heterosexist attitudes. Moreover, it is recommended that macro interventions such as outreach, community education and prevention programs begin by addressing strategies with lesbian youth. Lesbian adolescents are particularly vulnerable and face challenges due to issues of identity development; peer and societal pressure; powerlessness to openly and safely explore sexuality choices; and lack of information, support, and other resources. Macro intervention must also focus on the creation and facilitation of alternative socializing environments, such as sober lesbian women's activities and places to party, or a positive environment for women to meet other women. Moreover, while AA has traditionally been used as a peer-directed self help community resource, one recommendation is to expand its philosophy to be more inclusive and supportive of the special needs of Latina lesbians and challenge lesbophobia and sexism. Feminist authors support this challenge since they contend that AA's perspective of a person's need to admit to dependency and loss of self-control by giving up power is disempowering to women who have been systematically impacted and disempowered by social systems of institutional sexism, racism, etc. (Bepko, 1991). Also, to assume that a lesbian does not have to address her emotional/sexual identity because of the philosophy that alcoholism is the issue and all other realities are irrelevant is narrow in scope and negates the possibility that an individual's social group membership may be a main factor in her recovery from alcohol and other drugs.

Recovery homes also need to evaluate models of services and treatment in terms of guidelines for competency of services to Latina lesbians (i.e., linking Latina lesbians to community resources). These guidelines must be designed with a culturally competent Latino, monolingual Spanish or English component as well a bicultural component. Furthermore, these guidelines should be tested for efficiency and should guide the planning, research and testing of diverse interventions.

Micro Intervention:
The Woman and Her Family

For treatment programs, this author suggests basic intervention that is multicultural and that acknowledges, understands and celebrates lesbianism as a normal and accepting reality for women. A core understanding of the treatment needs of this population will guide and inform innovative strategies, utilizing the particular resilience of Latina lesbians and their desire to end abusing alcohol and other drugs.

Moreover, several conditions are necessary in order to deliver adequate direct services to this population. Social workers providing services with individuals and families must become culturally competent, and familiar with the strengths and challenges of a Latina lesbian participant (client). Substance abuse treatment may require including information on the role of the family regarding the woman's process of lesbian identity development and coming out process, and the role and status of the woman's partner (if partnered), as an integral member of the woman's family. Physical abuse, sexual abuse and incest must also be explored in the treatment process. This is crucial, not only regarding a therapeutic intervention on the abuse of alcohol and other drugs, but also because of the possibility of addressing related issues of intimacy and sexuality.

While not much has been written about the role of Latinas and their families in therapy (Comas-Diaz, 1994), especially relationships between daughters and mothers (Espin, 1994), it is important for family therapists to address power imbalances, *Marianismo* and heterosexism, and be sensitive to the challenge that coming out may pose for a woman and/or her family. While family dynamics may play an important role in the abuse of alcohol and other drugs, values of *Marianismo* and lesbophobia are also important factors. Family pressure to remain in the closet is a major stressor, especially when there is a preexisting context of socialization that has evolved within the cultural tradition of *familismo* and *Marianismo*. Effective treatment requires an integrative multicultural approach that takes into account all elements of social group membership, as well as cultural expectations and choices. Given that the woman's partner may either be an enabler or have substance abuse problems herself, an integrative approach also considers including a partner or significant other into the therapeutic process. Of additional importance are the therapeutic and supportive service needs that arise for lesbians who have children. Two (2) of the women interviewed in this study described a lack of support from both heterosexuals and lesbians because they were lesbian mothers.

Latina lesbian women have diverse perceptions of and experiences with the social service arena, and these affect treatment outcomes. Treatment, whether it is psychotherapy, psychoeducational group work, alternative community social models and self-help approaches, or diverse therapeutic approaches, must integrate traditional paradigms (world views) and shifting paradigms of both participant (client) and the social service provider. Moreover, such integration may potentially serve to empower both the participant (client) and the provider if a multicultural foundation–that takes into account issues of oppression and victimization, and resilience–is in place.

CONCLUSION

The literature shows that research on the alcohol practices of Latina lesbians, as well as information on services and treatment, are difficult to obtain. Latina lesbians are at risk of substance abuse because of their social group membership as women, Latinas, lesbians and often due to economic disparity. Appropriate policy and treatment recommendations must include: (1) aggressive and adequate bicultural chemical dependency services which use a multitude of treatment modalities, (2) training social work students and professionals on integrative multicultural approaches in delivering services to lesbian Latino women, (3) research and theory formulation, and (4) macro intervention. Moreover, differential preventive models of treatment and intervention with Latina lesbians must focus on the causal relationships between distress symptoms due to heterosexism and lesbophobia, ethnocentrism and racism, and the excessive use of alcohol and other drugs. Moreover, social work practitioners need to better understand the relational dynamics that exist between Latina lesbians, their families, significant others, social networks and societal forces. This understanding is a pathway leading social work practitioners who are in the field of alcohol and other drugs, to meet the needs and requirements of Latina lesbians.

REFERENCES

Amaro, H.; Whitaker, R.; Coffman, G. and Heeren, T. (1990) Acculturation and marihuana and cocaine use. *American Journal of Public Health, 80*, 54-60.
Barrera, M., Jr. and Finetta, R. (1993). Natural support systems and Hispanic substance abuse. In Mayers, Sanchez, Raymond; Kail B.L.; Watts T.D., Ed.

Hispanic Substance Abuse (pp. 115-130). Springfield, Illinois: Charles C. Thomas Publisher.

Bepko, C. (Ed.) (1991). *Feminism and addiction.* New York: The Haworth Press, Inc.

Bethell, L. (1987). *Colonial Spanish America.* Cambridge: Cambridge University Press.

Booth, M. V., Castro F. G. and Anglin, M. D. (1990). What do we know about Hispanic substance abuse? A review of the literature. In R. Glick, & J. Moore, (Eds.) *Drugs in Hispanic communities* (pp. 21-43). Rutgers University Press, New Brunswick.

Carrier, J. (1995). *De los otros: Intimacy and homosexuality among Mexican men.* New York: Colombia University Press.

De la Rosa, M. and Caris, L. H. (1993). The drug use and crime connection among Hispanics: An overview of research findings. In R. Mayers Sanchez et al. *Hispanic Substance Abuse.* Springfield, Illinois: Charles C. Thomas Publisher.

Delgado, M. and Humm-Delgado, D. (1982). Natural support systems: A source of strength in Hispanic communities. *Social Work, 27,* 83-89.

Fitzpatrick, J. (1990). Drugs and Puerto Ricans in New York City. In Glick, R. and Moore, J. (Eds.). *Drugs in Hispanic communities.* New Brunswick: Rudgers University Press.

Forth, Finegan, J. (1991). Sugar and spice and everything nice: Gender socialization and women's addiction–A review of the literature. In Bepko, C. (Ed.), *Feminism and addiction* (pp. 19-48). New York: The Haworth Press, Inc.

Gilligan, C. (1982). *In a different voice: Psychological theory and women's development.* Cambridge, Massachusetts: Harvard University Press.

Inter American Development Bank (IADB) (1995). *Women in the Americas: Bridging the gender gap.* Washington, D.C.

Mayers, Sanchez, Raymond; Kail B. L.; Watts T. D., Ed. (1993). *Hispanic Substance Abuse.* Springfield, Illinois: Charles C. Thomas Publisher.

McKirnan, T. and Peterson, P. L. (1989). Alcohol and drug use among homosexual men and women: Epidemiology and population characteristics. *Addictive Behavior,* 14(5), pp. 545-553.

Morales, A. (1984). Substance abuse and Mexican American youth: An overview. *Journal of Drug Issues, 14,* 297-311.

Morales, J. (1997). Introduction. *Journal of HIV/AIDS Prevention and Education for Adolescents and Children, 1,* 1-6.

Moore, J. (1990). Gangs, drugs and violence. In M. De la Rosa, E. Lambert & B. Gropper, (Eds.) *Drugs and violence causes, correlates, and consequences.* NIDA Research Monograph 103. pp. 160-176.

Radcliffe, S. A. & Westwood, S. (1993). Gender, racism and the politics of identity in Latin America. In S. A. Radcliffe & S. Westwood (Eds.), *VIVA: Women and popular protest in Latin America* (pp. 1-29). New York: Routledge.

SUMMARY
OF KEY PRACTICE, RESEARCH
AND POLICY IMPLICATIONS

Melvin Delgado, PhD

Abuse of alcohol and other drugs presents incredible challenges to the field of substance abuse prevention and treatment. These challenges take on greater importance when the population being addressed is of color. As highlighted in virtually all of the papers, there is tremendous work to be accomplished before cultural competence is achieved with Latinos. There is no area of the field that stands out as exemplary and worthy of replication.

As noted by all of the authors, the demographic changes occurring across the United States make Latinos much more heterogenous in composition, increasing the complexity of developing culturally competent models; these changes, as a result, necessitate development of group-specific approaches that take into account a multitude of factors, country of origin being just one.

Melvin Delgado is Professor of Social Work and Chair of Macro-Practice, School of Social Work, Boston University, 264 Bay State Road, Boston, MA 02215.

[Haworth co-indexing entry note]: "Summary of Key Practice, Research and Policy Implications." Delgado, Melvin. Co-published simultaneously in Alcoholism Treatment Quarterly (The Haworth Press, Inc.) Vol. 16, No. 1/2, 1998, pp. 193-195; and: Alcohol Use/Abuse Among Latinos: Issues and Examples of Culturally Competent Services (ed: Melvin Delgado) The Haworth Press, Inc., 1998, pp. 193-195. Single or multiple copies of this article are available for a fee from The Haworth Document Delivery Service [1-800-342-9678, 9:00 a.m. - 5:00 p.m. (EST). E-mail address: getinfo@haworth.com].

193

Nevertheless, there are several major themes that can be identified and incorporated into any culturally competent model. These themes, in turn, have currency for broad or group-specific models, and fields of practice other than substance abuse.

1. *Community Assets:* The Latino community must never be viewed as simply consisting of problems and needs. The importance of utilizing an assets paradigm goes far beyond a philosophical stance. It has implications for all phases and aspects of service delivery. Use of indigenous resources whenever possible conveys a stance, and influences how services and research are conceptualized and implemented. A shift from a deficit to an asset paradigm requires very serious thought and deliberation; it is not "business as usual" in viewing and involving the community.

2. *Biculturality:* The subject of biculturality is not restricted to staff, but is also applicable to all areas of service planning and delivery. Bicultural-ity refers to much more than language; it also encompasses procedures, instrumentation/forms, and structuring of services with a keen understand-ing of cultural values and expectations.

3. *Community Participation:* The involvement of the Latino communi-ty in the planning and delivery of services is closely associated with the use of a community asset paradigm. Involvement of the community on boards, advisory committees, task forces, and as volunteers increases the chances that a service will be relevant and utilized by those it seeks to reach.

4. *Specificity of Services:* Clarity of the "target" population is critical in planning Latino-focused ATOD services. However, clarity cannot be re-stricted to country of origin; it must also encompass a series of factors such as gender, age, acculturation, income, level of acculturation, rural-ur-ban experience, sexual orientation, religious/spiritual beliefs, educational level, and occupation. Other factors may take on greater significance depending local conditions and considerations.

5. *Staff Support:* Staff, needless to say, may have a natural ability to work across or within groups. However, this innate talent needs direction, context, and enhancement. Consequently, ATOD organizations must stress the importance of staff development approaches for both Latino and non-Latino staff. Support can take on various forms with supervision, training and consultation being the most prominent methods. Cultural competence is a dynamic process that must be addressed systematically in order for staff to be as up to date as possible.

6. *Comprehensive Services:* Cultural competence requires the availabil-ity of a comprehensive network of services with each component building upon, and supporting the other components. A missing link will seriously

undermine efforts at recovery for Latinos. Thus, the concept of cultural competence is closely interwoven with comprehensive services.

7. *Contextualizing ATOD:* Alcohol, tobacco, and other drug abuse must be viewed within a broader context of other social problems such as HIV/AIDS, school dropouts, unprotected sex, violence, crime, etc. Unfortunately, funding sources separate out social problems as if there were no relationship between these problems. A more holistic approach to ATOD will increase the likelihood that services and research are more relevant to Latinos.

8. *Qualitative and Quantitative Based Research/Evaluation:* Cultural competence is only possible when practitioners and researchers work closely with the community. Issues of alcoholism and other drug dependence are extremely complex, requiring an in-depth and broad understanding of how it impacts on individuals, families and communities. As a result, there is a tremendous need for both quantitative and qualitative research to be grounded in the Latino community experience, and for these methods to complement, rather than undermine, each other.

9. *Multiple Target Sites:* The field can no longer restrict itself to a few intervention sites which are usually home or school-based. The workplace is a very viable site for reaching out to Latinos who would not otherwise avail themselves of services. These workplace sites, however, have usually not been addressed when interventions are planned and implemented. Much groundwork must be accomplished in making these settings more amenable to prevention and early intervention initiatives. Nevertheless, the work site cannot be ignored if the Latino community is to avail itself of valuable resources in the fight against substance abuse.

CONCLUSION

Although the field of substance abuse is faced with formidable challenges in reaching Latinos, the rewards for doing so are without question just as great. This volume has provided the reader with the latest thinking on the topic of cultural competence with Latinos. The next century will provide practitioners, academics, researchers, and policy makers with an opportunity to operationalize many of the recommendations made in this volume. Failure to aggressively move forward in this arena will compound the misery associated with alcohol and other drug abuse in a population group that will continue to increase numerically.

Index

Page numbers followed by C indicate charts; page numbers followed by f indicate figures; and page numbers followed by t indicate tables.

Drug-free workplace, with Hispanic
   populations, in rural
   Arizona, 133-145
study of, 134-145
   assistance and interventions
      resulting from, 39-40
   background of, 134-135
   limitations of, 136-137
   literature review, 134
   methods, 135-136,136t
   participating communities in,
      135-136,136t
   policies resulting from,
      137-139,138c,139c
   research questions in, 134
Dungee-Anderson, D., 90-91
Dyer, L., 10

Education
   community, for AODA in Latina
      lesbians, 189-190
   community-based, beauty parlors
      in, 78
Educational level, of Hispanics, 110
Emergency room episodes,
   drug-related, among
   Hispanic drug users, 41,44t,
   45-47,46t,47f
Employee(s)
   conflict among, alcohol and drugs
      in workplace and, 140t
   turnover of, alcohol and drugs in
      workplace and, 140t
Empowerment
   in cultural competence in ATOD
      abuse, 13-14
   defined, 13-14
Environment, alcohol use among
      Latinas due to, 172
Espin, 183
Estrada, A., 60
Ethnicity
   cross cultural competency and, in
      AODA services, 89-92

as factor in alcohol abuse
   patterns, 149-150

Familism, described, 65
Familismo, described, 182
Family(ies), as factor in alcohol use
   and abuse among Latinos,
   60-62
Family intactness, defined, 61
Family pride, defined, 61
Family problems, preoccupation
   with, alcohol and drugs in
   workplace and, 140t
Feazell, 134
Felix-Ortiz, M., 9
Finetta, R., 185
Forth-Finegan, J., 181
Freeman, E.M., 11-12

Galan, F., 65
Garcia, B., 2,171
Gender, as factor in alcohol abuse
   patterns, 149-150
Gender role, changes in, alcohol use
   among Latinas due to,
   171-173
Gilbert, M.J., 57-58,60,62,67,
   111-112,150,172-173
Gordon, J.U., 8
Green, J., 65
Greene, J., 180,183
Green's crosscultural awareness
   practice, 65
Guinn, C., 60

Hardcastle, D., 93
Hashish
   death due to, by race/ethnicity of
      decedent, 46t
   emergency room episodes
      associated with, 44t
Hayes-Bautista, D., 63

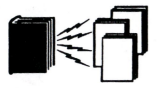

Haworth
DOCUMENT DELIVERY
SERVICE

This valuable service provides a single-article order form for any article from a Haworth journal.

- *Time Saving:* No running around from library to library to find a specific article.
- *Cost Effective:* All costs are kept down to a minimum.
- *Fast Delivery:* Choose from several options, including same-day FAX.
- *No Copyright Hassles:* You will be supplied by the original publisher.
- *Easy Payment:* Choose from several easy payment methods.

Open Accounts Welcome for . . .
- Library Interlibrary Loan Departments
- Library Network/Consortia Wishing to Provide Single-Article Services
- Indexing/Abstracting Services with Single Article Provision Services
- Document Provision Brokers and Freelance Information Service Providers

---

MAIL or *FAX* THIS ENTIRE ORDER FORM TO:

Haworth Document Delivery Service
The Haworth Press, Inc.
10 Alice Street
Binghamton, NY 13904-1580

or FAX: 1-800-895-0582
or CALL: 1-800-342-9678
9am-5pm EST

PLEASE SEND ME PHOTOCOPIES OF THE FOLLOWING SINGLE ARTICLES:
1) Journal Title: _____
   Vol/Issue/Year: _____Starting & Ending Pages:_____
Article Title:_____
_____

2) Journal Title: _____
   Vol/Issue/Year: _____Starting & Ending Pages:_____
Article Title:_____
_____

3) Journal Title: _____
   Vol/Issue/Year: _____Starting & Ending Pages:_____
Article Title:_____
_____

4) Journal Title: _____
   Vol/Issue/Year: _____Starting & Ending Pages:_____
Article Title:_____
_____

(See other side for Costs and Payment Information)

COSTS: Please figure your cost to order quality copies of an article.

1. Set-up charge per article: $8.00
   ($8.00 × number of separate articles) _____

2. Photocopying charge for each article:
   1-10 pages: $1.00 _____

   11-19 pages: $3.00 _____

   20-29 pages: $5.00 _____

   30+ pages: $2.00/10 pages _____

3. Flexicover (optional): $2.00/article _____

4. Postage & Handling: US: $1.00 for the first article/
   $.50 each additional article _____

   Federal Express: $25.00 _____

   Outside US: $2.00 for first article/
   $.50 each additional article _____

5. Same-day FAX service: $.35 per page _____

GRAND TOTAL: _____

METHOD OF PAYMENT: (please check one)

❏ Check enclosed   ❏ Please ship and bill. PO # _____
   (sorry we can ship and bill to bookstores only! All others must pre-pay)

❏ Charge to my credit card: ❏ Visa; ❏ MasterCard; ❏ Discover;
   ❏ American Express;

Account Number: _____ Expiration date: _____

Signature: ✗ _____

Name: _____ Institution: _____

Address: _____

_____

City: _____ State: _____ Zip: _____

Phone Number: _____ FAX Number: _____

MAIL or *FAX* THIS ENTIRE ORDER FORM TO:

Haworth Document Delivery Service
The Haworth Press, Inc.
10 Alice Street
Binghamton, NY 13904-1580

or FAX: 1-800-895-0582
or CALL: 1-800-342-9678
9am-5pm EST)